T0375645

# GOD SPEAKS FOR HIMSELF

*Discover the Ways of God*
*Disclosed in the Word of God*
*The Holy Bible*

Douglas Nelson

WESTBOW
PRESS®
A DIVISION OF THOMAS NELSON
& ZONDERVAN

NIV:
THE HOLY BIBLE, NEW INTERNATIONAL VERSION®, NIV® Copyright © 1973, 1978, 1984, 2011 by Biblica, Inc.® Used by permission. All rights reserved worldwide.

NIVUK:
Scripture quotations [marked NIV] taken from the Holy Bible, New International Version Anglicised Copyright © 1979, 1984, 2011 Biblica, formerly International Bible Society Used by permission of Hodder & Stoughton Publichers, an Hachette UK company All rights reserved 'NIV' is a registered trademark of Biblica UK trademark number 1448790. Reproduced by permission of Hodder and Stoughton Limited.

WestBow Press books may be ordered through booksellers or by contacting:

WestBow Press
A Division of Thomas Nelson & Zondervan
1663 Liberty Drive
Bloomington, IN 47403
www.westbowpress.com
1 (866) 928-1240

ISBN: 978-1-9736-5708-8 (sc)
ISBN: 978-1-9736-5710-1 (hc)
ISBN: 978-1-9736-5709-5 (e)

Library of Congress Control Number: 2019903133

Print information available on the last page.

WestBow Press rev. date: 4/5/2019

# DEDICATION PAGE

To the one and only true and living eternal Triune God who has disclosed *his ways* in Scripture to all who believe in him.

To my wife Bev whom I love and admire for her great faith in the Lord which she lives out daily before me by reflecting the *ways of the Lord* in all she says and does. I thank her for encouraging me to see my manuscript through to publication, and granting me the gift of time to research and set in print scriptures that speak to the *ways of God*.

To my daughter Kathy whose photographs appear throughout the book, and her husband Mike and their sons Bryan and Justin; and to our son Tim and his wife Chris and their daughters Emily and Kayley for being such a dear and precious family, and for walking in the 'ways of God'!

To Jack Diluna for editing my book to make it more readable.

To Ravi Kriss for his assistance in using his IT skills in helping me prepare to submit my computer manuscript to the publisher.

To Tom and Janis Taylor for their expression of love and generosity.

# PREFACE

# Background for Writing the Book

I t is not easy to write a book -at least a *first* book. To make my point perhaps I could ask you if you have ever written a book. If you have written one or more books you have my respect. It took me a long time to decide to write a book, and to decide what the book would be about. I pondered for a long time which topic would hold my attention long term, as well as prove meaningful to whomever might read it.

The 16ᵗʰ century scholar Erasmus helped me conclude that perhaps waiting awhile to put my research into book form has been a good thing.

> The man…who writes should choose a subject to which he is by nature suited, and in which his powers chiefly lie; all themes do not suit everyone…Next comes the importance, whatever you have chosen, of taking pains in the treatment of it, of keeping it by you for some time and often giving it further polish before it sees the light of day.
> ('The Correspondence of Erasmus' Volume 9 Letters 1252 to 1355, p. 294)

Etty Hellesum's desire as a writer should be every author's desire.

> I want every word I write to be born, truly born, none to
> be artificial, every word to be essential…Every word born
> of an inner necessity, Writing must never be anything else.
> (Etty Hillesum 'An Interrupted Life: The diaries of Etty
> Hillesum', 1941-1943)

Eventually the idea of writing on the *ways of God* emerged in my thinking and praying, coupled with several conversations with my wife seeking her wisdom. Gradually my interests focused on locating specific *ways God has revealed himself in Creation and especially in the Word of God -the Holy Bible.*

The Bible is the one book that authenticates the *ways of God*. It is the record of God making his ways known to various individuals over a period of several centuries. We can be grateful these individuals have passed on to us their learning. Altogether the scriptures give us a composite picture of God with regard to who he is and what he is like.

However, no single passage of Scripture contains everything that is to be said about **God's ways**. Job's young friend Elihu got it right when he tried to encourage Job with the words:

> Bear with me a little longer and I will show you that **there
> is more to be said in God's behalf.**"
> (Job 36:2)

According to the Psalmist there is so much more that can be said that God's glory and majesty can never be fully declared!

> Who can proclaim the mighty acts of the Lord or **fully
> declare his praise**? (Psalm 106:2)

The Bible as a whole doesn't state everything that can be said about the Lord. For example, John ends his Gospel with the words:

> Jesus did many other things as well. If every one of them
> were written down, I suppose that even **the whole world**

**would not have room for the books that would be written.** (John 21:25).

However, rejoice with Moses who wrote,

> The secret things belong to the LORD our God, **but the things revealed belong to us and to our children forever**, that we may follow all the words of this law.' (Deuteronomy 29:29).

What this means is that God is giving us essential information regarding himself, but not exhaustive information. Even after a thorough search of Scripture we are still left with a longing to know more about our Holy God. Francis Chang writes in 'Forgotten God'

> There are things about God that are mysterious and secret, things we will never know about Him. But there also are things revealed, and those belong to us (Deut. 29:29)... The point is not to completely understand God but to worship Him. Let the very fact that you cannot know Him fully lead you to praise Him (p. 29).

There is no need to look beyond the Bible when searching for the *ways of God*, because the Bible offers in one place God's progressive disclosure of *his ways* in a manner which makes himself knowable, believed, respected and loved. This corresponds with what I heard just yesterday preached from the pulpit: 'All we know about God that's true is found in the Bible!'

It became my quest to identify, compile and organize a list of the *ways of God* recorded in the Bible. When I first started, I didn't realize how daunting the task would be. Over the years I've filled three file draws with scriptures that make reference to *God's ways*. I collected and categorized so many verses that I became overwhelmed. I was tempted not to write the book thinking the task would prove impossible. I also came to believe that the definitive book on the *ways of God* had already been written -the *Bible*. What I came to see as my task, however, was to help anyone find *in* the Bible *where* the *ways of God* are mentioned.

My appreciation of **God's ways** increased as my research progressed. I saw with increasing understanding that **God's ways** reveal who he is with regard to his **unchanging character**. God doesn't simply want us to **know about him**, but that we might actually **know him** as **a Person,** and ultimately **make him known** by our life and witness. In knowing God we come to **love him** with heart, mind and soul along with the desire to worship and serve him forever. It is my delight to offer **a guide for finding your way to key verses that speak to the ways of God.** In the last book of the Old Testament God states for the record,

I the Lord do not change. (Malachi 3:6)

Nothing has ever changed regarding God or his ways. He remains the same in the New Testament as he was in the Old Testament.

> **His (unchanging) ways** are an outgrowth of an unchanging character, and in them the fixed and settled attributes of God are clearly seen. Unless the Eternal One Himself can undergo change, **His ways**, which are Himself in action, must remain forever the same. (Alistair Begg, Daily Devotional 12/12/17)

We have every reason to believe **God's ways** and **his character** will remain unchanged till the end of time. Therefore, we can be rest assured that God will operate consistently on **our** behalf in the same ways he acted toward people in biblical times. This truth gives us solid footing in an otherwise unstable world! The author of Hebrews, for example, saw no change (past, present or future) in Jesus the eternal Son of God.

> [12] **You remain the same, and your years will never end.** (Hebrews 1:12; 13:8)

The question remaining is this: **what are God's unchanging ways** whereby he expresses in the scriptures **his unchanging character**? I do not pretend to think I have located all the biblical references to the **ways of God**, but at least a significant number of God's ways which are **revealed in the Word of God.** We would do well in paying heed to Eugene Peterson's caution in his book: 'Five Smooth Stones for Ministry' where he states that there is danger in assuming we know more than we do about God.

The plain truth is that the infinite God is greater than any number of pages that can be written about *his ways*. It's my hope that the scripture references printed in this book will only whet your appetite further to discover even more of *God's ways* encoded in his Word with the objective of letting what you find increase your faith, deepen your love and increase your willing obedience to our wonderful and unchanging God. I'm confident that once the *ways of God* capture your attention you will have a sincere desire to reflect *God's ways* in your own life in all you say and do. Having been created in the image of God it's his intention that *our ways* reflect *his ways* to the praise of his glory!

My purpose is not just to 'cherry pick' verses, but to lead you *to the places in scripture* that speak to the *ways of God* so you can readily turn to the verses and do your own research. I urge you to turn these '*ways of God*' verses into a personal study by reading the verses *in context with the verses that surround them.* Consider reading the whole chapter, if not the whole book, to see as fully as possible all God intended to accomplish by revealing any one of his '*ways*' in Scripture. This deeper personal study will prove enriching as you become increasingly aware of the wonder of God's ways pointing to the majesty of his eternal unchanging character, as well as learn how he wants you to reflect his glorious ways in your daily life.

An added incentive for knowing the *ways of God* is that we might share this knowledge with the world that is desperately in need of hearing it! The 'Good News' is that God has revealed himself in *many ways* proving his *existence* and his *character* thus making himself worthy of belief, love, worship and service! Let's never forget where this Good News has not yet been proclaimed there is spiritual darkness. Was not Kierkegtaard prophetic of the times in which we now live when he wrote,

> Our age reminds one vividly of the dissolution of the Greek city-state: everything goes on as usual, and yet there is no one who believes it. The invisible spiritual bond which gives it validity no longer exists, and so the

whole age is at once comic and tragic –tragic because it is perishing; comic because it goes on.
(A Kierkegaard Anthology, p.81)

Acknowledging **God's ways** and **reflecting his ways** gives hope to a world that is otherwise perishing.

*Dear reader,*

*As for my life, this is my prayer:*

*Even when I am old and gray, do not forsake me, O God,
till I declare your power to the next generation, your might
to all who are to come.' (Psalm 71:17-18)*

*Let this be written for a future generation, that a people not
yet created may praise the Lord.
(Psalm 102:18).*

*Whenever you may be living and reading this, I just want to say hello to
you and let you know that I have prayed for you that somehow the words of
this book might prove to be a blessing and an encouragement to you.*

*I am pleased you desire to discover the **ways of God** in the inspired **Word
of God**. I know you will not be disappointed or go away unrewarded for your
time and effort. Becoming familiar with the **ways of God** is how you can
come into a fuller understanding of God's unchanging character, and thus
his worthiness of placing faith in him resulting in love for him and a desire to
worship and serve him forever. God bless you!*

# CONTENTS

CHAPTER 1

# Can We Know Anything About God?

# Is there a 'God'?

The first question doubters ask is whether or not there is a *'god'*. If there is no 'god' then, of course, it would be impossible to discover the *ways* of a 'god' who doesn't exist. When George W. Bush was running for a second term as President he appeared on a daytime television talk show. Early in the interview he was asked, "George, what do you know for sure?" Without missing a beat he replied, "**God exists!**" (Good answer ☺)

We need not be left wondering when we look up into the heavens and ask, "Is there a God, or did all of this just happen?" The jury is no longer out; the verdict is in. The research has been done and is available to everyone. It is the ***Holy Bible***. We can know what there is to know and believe about God because of the disclosure of ***his ways*** in Scripture. God himself inspired 40 authors to write about ***his ways*** over a period of 1500 years. No, God doesn't keep us guessing about his existence, or what he is like.

'***God***' is mentioned in both the first and last verses of the Bible.

> [1] In the beginning **God** created the heavens and the earth. (Genesis 1:1)

> [21] The grace of the Lord Jesus be with **God**'s people. Amen. (Revelation 22:21)

In fact, the word '***God***' appears in the NIV translation of the Bible 3,670 times, and his Name LORD appears 6687 times. The point has certainly been made by these inspired authors of Scripture: ***the LORD God exists***. It is unconscionable to conclude that the authors of Scripture wrote with pen and ink over 10,350 times about a 'god' who doesn't actually exist.

The authors of the Bible didn't set out to prove the existence of God, but to affirm his existence. Moses stated that God has thoroughly searched the heavens and come to this conclusion:

> Know and believe me and understand that I am he. **Before me no 'god' was formed, nor will there be one after me.** (Deuteronomy 3:24)

Hundreds of years after Moses's time God reported to us through the prophet Isaiah that he still stands by his conclusion.

> This is what the Lord says—the Lord Almighty: **I am the first and I am the last; apart from me there is no God**... (Isaiah 44:6, 8)

The same solid rock conclusion was reached several hundred years later in New Testament times by the Apostle Paul.

> Even if there are so-called 'gods', whether in heaven or on earth (as indeed there are many 'gods' and many 'lords'), yet for us **there is but one God**, the Father, from whom all things came and for whom we live; and there is but one Lord, Jesus Christ, through whom all things came and through whom we live. (1 Corinthians 8:5-6)

## What is This 'One God' like?

A.W. Tozar has thrown out this challenge:

> "What comes into our minds when we think about God is the most important thing about us."
> (The Knowledge of the Holy, p. 9)

The Bible has a high regard for God.

> **O LORD my God, you are very great.**
> (Psalm 104:1)

Paul has declared:

> [20] Since the **creation** of the world God's invisible qualities—his eternal power and divine nature—have been clearly seen, being understood from what has been made. (Romans 1:20)

3

You might say God has surrounded us in nature with his self-portrait! ☺

Some people are willing to concede that there must be a 'god' if the word 'god' and God's Name come up thousands of time in the Bible, but then the question becomes, ***"Is there anything that can be known about God?"***

One day a father came home and found his young daughter sitting at the dining room table drawing with her crayons. "What are you drawing?" he asked. "I'm drawing a picture of God", she said. "Honey, no one knows what God looks like." "They'll know when I get done."☺

The world has often gone astray by trying to 'put a face on God' in the visible form of ***idols*** of all shapes and sizes. The downfall of this effort is that people begin to worship their nicely shaped visible images as 'god'. But nothing could be more unlike the invisible God than a visible idol. It's impossible for something that is totally 'visible' to represent something that is totally 'invisible'. We have a desire to 'see' a visible 'god', but God is an 'invisible spirit' whom we can only see by 'faith' that the words that describe him in scripture are true. If we know nothing else, it's that visible idol 'gods' are totally useless because they are lifeless. It was said of those who worshiped idols:

> [28] They ate sacrifices offered to **lifeless gods**.
> (Psalm 106:28; Isa 46:5-7)

The truth was that they sacrificed and ate their own children (Ps 103:37-38, Jer 51:17-18; 19:5, Isa 57:5).
The prophet Jeremiah noted by contrast that Israel's living God

> [19] is not like these, for he is the Maker of all things...the LORD Almighty is his name. (Jeremiah 51:19)

Actually, the Bible unmasks idol gods as ***demons*** masquerading themselves as 'gods'. It's their deceptive way to steal for themselves worship which should be directed to God alone. As far back as Moses' time people

[17] Sacrificed to **demons, which are not God**— gods they had not known, gods that recently appeared, gods your fathers did not fear. (Deuteronomy 32:17)

By New Testament times, nothing had changed. Paul writes,

[20] The sacrifices of pagans are offered to **demons**, not to God, and I do not want you to be participants with demons. (1 Corinthians 10:20)

According to John in Revelation there will be demon worshipers till the end of time.

[20] The rest of mankind…did not repent of the work of their hands; **they did not stop worshiping demons**. (Revelation 9:20)

The *mystery of what God 'looks like'* (and is like) is solved for anyone who is willing to open the scriptures. There, for instance, we read Jesus' affirmation,

"Anyone who has seen me has seen the Father."
(John 14:9; 2 Cor 4:6)

Paul says of Jesus,

[15] "Christ is the **image of the invisible God**.
(Colossians 1:15)

The wonderful truth is that the Bible is the inspired self-disclosure of the *invisible* God who has made his *ways* known in the world –at least to humble people who are willing to believe the scriptures. Kelly Monroe Kullberg in her book 'Finding God Beyond Harvard' makes this observation as to whether or not God has or can reveal himself in a book.

If God could create a universe, it would follow that he could also manage to write and distribute a book…It is

5

full of verifiable information, useful to every person as
well as to archaeologists, historians, scientists, healers,
artists, lovers, parents and so on. (pp 138-139)

In the Bible we find several *ways* in which God simultaneously makes
himself known to his world. It's as I once heard someone say, "Only God
can attend to all things at once! He can, and he does!"

*God's 'ways'* are many and glorious. All his *ways* are perfect, complete,
and unchanging. As we'll see in detail God is '*holy*' (wholly sinless). This
is simply the *way* God is. God is also at the same time, and all the time
'*righteous*' –always doing the right thing. It is also *God's way* always to
be '*true*' to himself, to his Word and his world. God is totally '*Just*' in
all his decisions. This, however, is all tempered with the fact that God is
'*love*' –unconditional love, unfailing love, and unlimited love. Consider
also God's amazing '*grace*' (his saving grace); his tender '*mercies*'; his
'*goodness*' to a fault! From all these *ways*–hope springs eternal in the
human heart!

Tertellian wrote in the early centuries of the church,

It is fitting that we should **speak well of God** at all times,
in every circumstance.
(David Hazard, 'The Early disciples', p. 76)

To *fear the Lord* means to *speak well of God*. It does not mean simply
cringing in fear before God, although if we had our wits about us we most
certainly would be shaking in our boots if we were ever found knowingly
standing face-to-face with the living God -for he is 'God' and we are not!
God is great and we are not; he is eternal and we are not; he is holy and
we are not!

This point is made in the book of Job. We wouldn't think of wrestling
a crocodile.

[8] If you lay a hand on him, you will remember the struggle
and never do it again! (Job 41:8)

But would we be so bold as to challenge God to a wrestling match -the
God who created the crocodile? We wouldn't think of flying into the

blazing sun, but are we willing to fly in the face of the Creator of the sun and the trillions of stars throughout the universe -some of which are a million times the size of our sun which itself is a million times the size of the earth! Looking up into the starry night God asks Job to ponder this:

> [31] "Can you bind the beautiful Pleiades? Can you loose the cords of Orion?
>
> [32] Can you bring forth the constellations in their seasons or lead out the Bear with its cubs?
>
> [33] Do you know the laws of the heavens?
> (Job 38:31-33)

There are examples in Scripture of people who have sensed they have come into God's presence and they all without exception fell prostrate on their faces out of awe and reverence –in holy fear! (Deut 9:18; 1 Kg 18:39; 1 Chron 20:16, 20; 2 Chron 20:2, 4, 18; Isa 6:1-5)

Synonyms for the 'fear' of the Lord might be 'awe', 'reverence', 'respect' 'honor'. The reason our holy, righteous God wants to see a *holy fear* in us is because living this way guards us from committing *evil* and setting ourselves up for judgment.

> [6] Through the **fear of the LORD** a man **avoids evil**.
> (Proverbs 16:6 Ps 34:11-14)

Yes, to '**fear**' the Lord is the wisest thing anyone can do.

> [28] The **fear of the Lord**...is wisdom, and to **shun evil** is understanding.
> (Job 28:28; Ps 34:7, 111:10; Prov 1:7)

There are some prayers I pray every morning before I rise for the day. This is one of them:

> "I pray that the 'angel of the Lord' encamp around me and my family because we '**fear**' you God. We love, and honor,

and revere you. We entrust our very lives to you that you will deliver us today with your great strength from the Evil One, and from any destructive forces he might want to level against us whether at home or on the road."

The early Christians were noted for *fearing the Lord*.

> [31] Then the church ...grew in numbers, living in the **fear of the Lord**. (Acts 9:31)

The intellectual elites of Paul's day -the Greek philosophers- had concluded that none of the 'gods' worshipped were real so they *did not fear them* but, rather, exhibited distain and ridicule for them. They concluded the gods were merely mythological legends: toys that could be toyed with; a mere human invention to explain the phenomenon of nature. They concluded that such fables couldn't account for 'reality'. Unfortunately they could not identify what did account for reality.

When Paul was visiting Athens, he observed several imposing idols dedicated to all the then current mythological Greek 'gods'. He was surprised to come across one statue he didn't expect. It was a nondescript statue with a plaque that simply read 'To an Unknown God'. Surely it was humbling for these Greek intellects to have to plead agnostic ignorance when they prided themselves on their intelligence. Paul was determined to enlighten them.

> As I walked around and looked carefully at your objects of worship, I even found an altar with this inscription: TO AN UNKNOWN GOD. Now what you worship as something unknown I am going to proclaim to you.'" (Acts 17:22-23)

Paul went on to describe *the one true and living 'God'* of the Scriptures. After explaining the Gospel and making his appeal to their minds and their hearts, a few people became followers of Paul and believed the gospel.

The scriptures frequently point out the fact that **the one true God** is not a lifeless mythological 'god' that has taken on the shape of a statute of wood, stone or precious metal, but, rather, he alone is the '*living God*'.

> [10] **The LORD is the true God; he is the living God**, the eternal King. (Jeremiah 10:10, 12, 14-15)

This same '*living God*' of the Old Testament fills the pages of the New Testament.

> [16] We are the temple of the **living God**. As God has said: **"I will live with them** and walk among them, and I will be their God, and they will be my people."
> (2 Corinthians 6:16; 1 Tim 3:15, 1 Thess 1:9; Heb 10:31, 12:22)

Closer to our time, the spirit of atheism flared up again in the 18th and 19th centuries in the so-called 'Age of Reason' or the 'Age of Rationalism' when 'God' was again written out of existence supposedly as the result of increased human intellect.

> It was not their purpose to establish a new religion of reason, but to 'purge' Christianity of the things that seemed unreasonable (According to these thinkers) the miracles of the Bible that could not be explained by natural causes were rejected as 'fables'. Christ was robbed of His glory as a divine Savior…What remained of Christianity was a mere shadow.
> (E.E. Ryden, 'The Story of Christian Hymnody', p, 149)

Friedrich Nietzsche (1844-1900) an outspoken philosopher against morality and religion went so far as to declare that 'God is dead'. Not all that long ago someone mentioned that he saw someone wearing a tee shirt. On the front were the words *'God is dead!' signed Nietzsche*. But then as the person walked by this observer further noted that on the back of the tee shirt were the words *'Nietzsche is dead! signed 'God'*! Once when someone confronted the evangelist Billy Graham with the words

Douglas Nelson

'God is Dead' his reply was, 'This can't be true. I was just talking to him this morning!'☺

Currently, atheism has raised its voice once again in the public square predicting the total demise of Christianity within our lifetime. But proponents of atheism are ignorant of the fact that the conversion of people by the transforming faith in Jesus Christ is on the rise all around the world: in the Orient, in the Middle East, across the sub-continent of Africa and throughout South America. Recently I had the privilege of attending a church in south India that has 5 Sunday services with 5,000 attending each service! Currently it's reported that there are students in all the Ivy League colleges in America holding revival prayer meetings for the spiritual renewal of the nation. There are also many reports worldwide regarding the persecution, suffering and martyrdom of Christians who would rather lay down their lives for the Lord than renounce their faith in the existence of the living God and the Son of God who laid down his life for them!

# The Hiddenness of God

John of the Cross (1542-1591) has given us words to ponder.

> When God first breathes life into the body, it is as if the soul were a blank canvas on which nothing has been painted. From the time we are children, our souls know nothing except what we perceive by looking out through the 'windows' of our senses. So we grow to adulthood believing that what we see and know through our senses is all there *is* to know...

> For this purpose, the Holy Spirit is sent to blaze the light of truth into your soul...and it shows us the way of freedom. For as long as we see only with our bodily eyes, we will continue to live like a blind captive, fumbling around inside a prison cell in the dark of night -while all the time the door that leads to our freedom stands open...

I will show you how to escape from the 'dark night' of your imprisoned soul, to show you the way of faith that leads up into the constant light and love of God. Isn't this the cry of your heart -that God will show you an open door to himself?

Trust him to lead you out of darkness, fear, misunderstanding, and doubt. For it is the light of faith that shows you the way of perfect freedom in spirit.
(Ascent of Mount Carmel: Book 1, Chapter 3; David Hazard, 'You Set my Spirit Free', pp. 23-25)

If there is one **real 'God'** the human longing is to **know** all that can be known about **that God**. The Apostle John writes about the hope Christians have to one day in Heaven see God as he is,

"Dear friends, now we are children of God, and what we will be has not yet been made known. But we know that when he appears, we shall be like him, for **we shall see him as he is**. Everyone who has this hope in him purifies himself, just as he is pure." (1 John 3:2-3)

We learn in scripture that God does not make himself known to everyone. It is God's **way** to hide himself –from **unbelievers**.

Truly you are a God who **hides himself**, O God and Savior of Israel.
(Isaiah 45:15; Ps 18:11, 97:2, 2 Chron 6:1)

One of the most sung hymns sung by Christians contain the words:

Holy, Holy, Holy! **though the darkness hide**. Thee,
Though the eye of sinful man Thy glory may not see:
Only Thou art holy, there is none beside Thee,
Perfect in power, in love, and purity

Skeptics and unbelievers complain, "If there is a 'god' where is he? Why can't I see him? Wouldn't it be easier to believe in God if he made himself *visible*. Wouldn't that end all doubt?" The most basic 'reason' God cannot be seen is because, as Jesus says, **God is 'Spirit'.** By definition *'spirit'* is not visible.

> [24] **God is spirit**, and his worshipers must worship in spirit
> and in truth."
> (John 4:24)

We must **come to God on his terms**; God doesn't come to us on our terms! Sometimes we don't think we like his terms if at the moment we are in stress or distress, pain or suffering. This was Katherine and Jay Wolf's experience when at age 26 she suffered a brain disorder that just about claimed her life. She is still in recovery but sitting in a wheel chair with her husband standing beside her on the stage of a packed auditorium saying she heard God speak these words in her heart: "I am God and you are not. I don't make mistakes!' Her conclusion was that she and her husband Jay can hope for what they cannot understand. This of course, according to Paul, is what 'hope' is all about.

> [24] Hope that is seen is no hope at all. Who hopes for what
> he already has? (Romans 8:24)

In 'On Seeing God', Augustine writes:

> I'm sure there are many who wonder why they do not
> perceive God's presence with them, while others do....
> When God reveals himself ...it is purely an act of his
> grace.

Jesus, when on trial, refused to be defensive, refused to reveal who he really was to unbelievers -his false accusers.

> [63] Jesus remained **silent**.
> (Matthew 26:63; 12:19; 27:14; Lk 23:9; Isa 42:1-4; 53:7)

Isaiah predicted that when the Lord made his appearance on earth his features would be nondescript; he would blend in with the crowd.

> [1] He had no beauty or majesty to attract us to him, nothing
> in his appearance that we should desire him. (Isaiah 53:1)

Jesus was so non-descript to those who had turned against him that they even refused to give him the honor of calling him by his name. "***This 'fellow'...***"

> [29] We know that God spoke to Moses, but as for **this fellow**, we don't even know where he comes from. (John 9:29; Matt 12:24, 26:61, Lk 23:2)

After war victims incarcerated in a World War 2 concentration camp were set free by the liberating army, one of the soldiers saw these words inscribed on one of the walls:

> *"I believe in the sun when it doesn't shine;*
> *I believe in love even when I feel unloved*
> *I believe in God even when he is silent."*

In one of Paul's doxologies of praise to God he mentions ***God is 'invisible'***.

> [17] Now to the King eternal, immortal, **invisible,** the only God, be honor and glory for ever and ever. Amen. (1 Timothy 1:17)

***Invisible*** and ***non-existence*** are not synonyms. There are many things that exist that are not visible to the naked eye -beginning with the ***atom***. Who refuses to breathe ***invisible air*** because he thinks that if he can't 'see' air it doesn't exist. Airline pilots rely totally on invisible air while they are in flight. ***Invisible electricity*** fuels much of our civilization. Everything is crippled when a power grids goes down as happened when electricity went out for weeks across Puerto Rico following a giant hurricane.

It is true that '*seeing is believing*', but when it comes to *seeing* God, '*believing is seeing*'! Consider Thomas, a doubter, who was famous for saying

> [25] Unless I see …I will not believe.

Sure enough, when the resurrected Jesus appeared to him, he fell at his feet in worship and cried out,

> [28] "My Lord and **my God**."

However, seeing the resurrected Christ was the exception not the rule. Jesus said to Thomas,

> [29] Because you have seen me, you have believed; **blessed are those who have not seen and yet have believed.** (John 20:25, 28-29)

*That would be us who can't visibly see Jesus today.*☺ as Thomas and the disciples saw him, yet we can see the Lord with our spiritual eyes (eyes of faith). An early Christian apologist, Clement of Alexandria, writes in 'Miscellaneous Teachings'

> Faith accepts truths that cannot be 'proved'…Spiritual faith does not come about by saying, 'Show me a sign, God. Answer my prayer. Perform a miracle.' Faith begins by believing simply that **God is** –and he is above his creation…Therefore, we do not insist that God answer prayers, or bless us, in order to 'prove' he is Lord….Do not slip down into a false, earthly faith, which must rest upon answers, signs, and miracles in order to stand at all. (Quoted by David Hazard in 'You Give Me Life', pp.37-38)

*God desires not to remain hidden, but to be known.* However, he waits in every case for each individual to seek him wholeheartedly. If someone says "I looked for God and didn't find him" it's not that God is nowhere to be found; it's merely proof they haven't searched for God wholeheartedly. The good news is that God desires to disclose himself to anyone who is willing to come to God on his terms. Russia's first cosmonaut in space, Yuri Gagarin, said he looked all around him in space on April 12, 1961 and concluded that there is no God.

No half-hearted seekers please! But for anyone who does engage in a whole-hearted search, God doesn't play hard to find.

> [13] You will seek me and find me when you seek me with
> all your heart. (Jeremiah 29:13)

I once had the privilege of meeting one of the twelve men who have visited the moon. This astronaut had no problem seeing and acknowledging God's existence -even on the moon! He didn't leave his faith in the invisible God behind on the moon, instead he left a Bible on the moon where he parked his moon buggy! Astronaut Jim Irwin got it down to a sentence:

> It is more important to know that God walked on earth
> than that man walked on the moon!

Who doesn't know that there are things in our world that are *invisible and yet exist*. We are ourselves *invisible* spiritual beings living in visible physical bodies. What we say and do in our physical bodies is how we *make our invisible spirits 'visible'*.

*How does God make his 'invisible Spirit visible*? Certainly not on demand. When an unbeliever demands that God 'Jump', God does not reply, 'How High?' God does not cooperate with unbelievers who demand *proof* of his existence before they are willing to believe. Jesus didn't come down from the cross to meet the demand of those who said this was the only condition whereby they would believe.

> [42] "He saved others," they said, "but he can't save himself!
> He's the King of Israel! Let him **come down now from
> the cross**, and **we will believe in him**.

> [43] He trusts in God. Let God rescue him now if he wants
> him, for he said, 'I am the Son of God.'"
> (Matthew 27:42-43)

The Son of God stayed on the cross to save the very people who hung him there!

Once, when I was directing a Christian Coffee House ministry, a young teen sat down with me late on a Friday evening and challenged God to 'show himself' to him. He said, pointing to a bare light bulb shining down on a spool table and its nail keg chairs, "If God makes this light bulb go out I'll believe there is a 'god'." Needless to say, the bulb didn't go out -until shortly after he exited the coffee house and I was still sitting at the table! The bulb flickered off and then on again. God chooses his *time* for revealing himself. God is not *unable* to meet the demand to be seen by unbelievers; he's *unwilling*! God sets the conditions.

## God is a Living Person

It's important to know that the God we seek is not an *impersonal force of nature*, but is a *spiritual being* who is a *living Person*; an *intelligent living being*. When God first disclosed himself to Moses he revealed himself as a 'Person'.

Many things are attributed to God as a *Person*. Repeatedly in scripture appear the words *'God is'*... then *one thing after another is attributed to the living God.* Here are a few examples that speak to the fact that *God is a Person.*

> [9] The LORD your **God is gracious and compassionate.** (2 Chronicles 30:9)

> [7] **God is the King of all the earth.** (Psalm 47:7)

> [4] **God is my help**; the Lord is the one who sustains me. (Psalm 54:4)

> [9] The LORD our **God is holy.** (Psalm 99:9)

> [9] **God is merciful and forgiving** (Daniel 9:9)

[14] **God is righteous in everything he does**
(Daniel 9:14)

[33] **God is truthful**. (John 3:33)

[13] **God is faithful.**(1 Corinthians 10:13)

[6] **God is just**(2 Thessalonians 1:6)

[8] **God is love**. (1 John 4:8)

# God wants to be known by His Ways

The good news is that *God wants to be known through his ways*! The truth is that God does *not* want to remain hidden from anyone. It is God's desire to for us to *know about him*! Yes, but God doesn't just want us to *know about him*, he wants us to *know him* as a *Person*! The fact that God is not a blind, lifeless force in the universe, but an *intelligent person of character* gives us *hope* that we can not only *know about* God, but, if God is willing (and he is), we can actually *know* God as a living personal being, and enter into an interpersonal relationship with him -albeit under his terms and conditions. Moses knew that knowing God's 'ways' was how he could come to *know* God.

> [13] If you are pleased with me, teach me **your ways** so
> I may **know you** and continue to find favor with you.
> (Exodus 33:13)

Ultimately, to *make God known and knowable* to the world should be our goal in life. God longs for us to know him, as well as make him known, but the question is this: Do we want to know about God, as well as know God and make him knowable? May we find ourselves with the same longing as the Psalmists did when they wrote:

> [25] Whom have I in heaven but you? And **earth has nothing
> I desire besides you**. (Psalm 73:25; 84:2)

The ultimate proof that God is a '*knowable Person*' is *Jesus Christ the 'Son of God'*. He has revealed himself to the world as *God personified.*

> [14] **The Word became flesh** and made his dwelling among us. We have seen his glory, the glory of the One and Only, who came from the Father, full of grace and truth. (John 1:14)

Paul states in no uncertain terms who Jesus really is.

> [15] He is **the image of the invisible God.** (Colossians 1:15)

> [9] In Christ all the fullness of the **Deity lives in bodily form**. (Colossians 2:9)

The Author of Hebrews states it well.

> [3] **The Son is the radiance of God's glory and the exact representation of his being.** (Hebrews 1:3)

The question in the minds of some may be '*How can we know that Jesus is 'God' become 'visible'?* The answer lies in his *resurrection after he died.* Resurrection from the dead is something no one can fake. Jesus didn't merely have a 'near death experience' -he actually died. He predicted that he would in three days conquer death forever by coming back alive. He did what he said he would do, and he is now resurrected from the dead and is alive forevermore. He is immortal, and thus imperishable.

On three occasions in my life I lived near a cemetery. I would quip, "If I ever saw anyone get up from a grave I would run over to him and ask him, "How did you do this? Is there any hope for me?" This was what the disciples of Jesus actually did experience, and we have their eye witness accounts till this day!

Did the resurrection really take place *historically*? *What year is it on the calendar?* The calendar year represents the number of years since Jesus' life, death and resurrection. Surely the history of the world is not dated back to a legend that never happened! Paul began his Romans letter focusing on the truth that ***Christ's historic resurrection*** from the dead ***validates*** once and for all that ***he truly is the eternal Son of God***! He was

> [4] **declared with power to be the Son of God by his resurrection from the dead: Jesus Christ our Lord.** (Romans 1:4)

Paul is an example of someone who not only wanted to ***know about God***, he ***wanted to know God*** by knowing Jesus Christ ***God's Son.***

> [10] **I want to know Christ** and the power of his resurrection and the fellowship of sharing in his sufferings, becoming like him in his death, (Philippians 3:10)

Jesus prayed to his Heavenly Father later on the evening of his betrayal,

> [3] This is eternal life: that they may **know you, the only true God, and Jesus Christ**, whom you have sent. (John 17:3)

'***Knowing God***' comes by way of ***faith***...that is, by giving God the benefit of the doubt that he actually exists, and ***exists in all the ways*** the Scripture says he exists. ***God wants to be known,*** and is grieved over anyone who does not want to know him.

> [34] How often I have longed to gather your children together, as a hen gathers her chicks under her wings, but **you were not willing**! (Luke 13:34)

According to the Psalmist this is what this 'unwillingness' looks like:

> [4] In his pride the wicked does not seek him; **in all his thoughts there is no room for God.** (Psalm 10:4, 7, 10-11)

God does not expect us to know everything about him, but God does expect us to know what he has disclosed about himself -which is enough to acknowledge his existence and his true greatness, and humbly bow before him in worship as well as love him heart and soul.

Describing ***God's awesome greatness*** is one of the repeated truths of Scripture. In ***The Message*** Eugene Peterson powerfully states that God exceeds all our expectations!

> [33] Have you ever come on anything quite like this...? We'll never figure it out.
>
> [34] Is there anyone around who can explain God? Anyone smart enough to tell him what to do?
>
> [35] Anyone who has done him such a huge favor that God has to ask his advice?
>
> [36] Everything comes from him; everything happens through him; everything ends up in him. Always glory! Always praise! **Yes. Yes. Yes.**
> (Romans 11:33-36)

This was what David had been saying all along.

> [2] How **awesome is the LORD** Most High, the great King over all the earth!
> (Psalm 47:2; 40:5, 72:18, 86:10, 145:3, 17; 147:5)

If anyone ever was tempted to write God out of existence it was Job. In the span of one day he lost his family, his livelihood, his health, and his friends. However, he clung to his belief that he hadn't lost God, nor the awareness of God's ongoing greatness even in the midst of suffering.

> [23] **The Almighty is beyond our reach** and exalted in power. (Job 37:23)
>
> [4] **His wisdom is profound, his power is vast...**

[10] He performs **wonders that cannot be fathomed, miracles that cannot be counted.**
(Job 9:4, 10; 11:7, 25:2, 33:12, 36:22-23, 26, 37:5)

As we can see, Job was a man who suffered but still believed in God and was well qualified to teach on the *ways of God.*,

[1] "I will **teach** you about the power of God; the **ways** of the **Almighty** I will not conceal.
(Job 27:11)

## God is the Teacher of His Ways

Ultimately God himself is the *teacher* of *his glorious ways.* David prayed,

[11] **Teach me your way**, O LORD, and I will walk in your truth; give me an undivided heart, that I may fear your name. (Psalm 86:11)

This is so important to me that I have attempted to draw attention to this need to be taught the ways of God on the cover of this book.

### *Show me your ways, O LORD Psalm 25:4*

How does God respond to such a prayer?

[8] Good and upright is the LORD; therefore he **instructs sinners in his ways.**

[9] He guides the humble in what is right and **teaches them his way.**
(Psalm 25:8-9; Isa 48:17; 54:13; Mic 4:2)

To be sure, God hasn't told us everything about any of his *ways*. To do so would be more than we could process with our finite minds. Jerry Bridges cautions us to take into consideration that,

> **God's ways**, being the **ways of infinite wisdom**, simply cannot be comprehended by our finite minds....we must come to the place where we truly believe that God's **ways** are simply as Isaiah writes: **beyond us.**
> ('The Pursuit of Holiness', p.125)

Here are Isaiah's words:

> [28] Do you not know? Have you not heard? The LORD is the everlasting God, the Creator of the ends of the earth. He will not grow tired or weary, and **his understanding no one can fathom.** (Isaiah 40:28)

Paul was as equally overwhelmed as the Old Testament authors regarding God's infinite greatness. Paul wrote:

> [33] Oh, the depth of the riches of the wisdom and knowledge of God! **How unsearchable his judgments, and his paths beyond tracing out!** (Romans 11:33)

Paul, however, prayed everyone might be able to grasp as much understanding about God as possible.

> [17] I pray that you, being rooted and established in love,
>
> [18] may have power, together with all the saints, to grasp **how wide and long and high and deep is the love of Christ,**
>
> [19] and to know this love that **surpasses knowledge**—that you may be filled to the measure of all the fullness of God. (Ephesians 3:17-19; Col 2:2-3; 2 Cor 2:6-7, 9-16)

Although we cannot know everything about God, he has revealed in Scripture some of his ways. Wayne Grudem writes,

> If we are to know God at all, it is necessary that he reveal himself to us....All that Scripture tells us about God is true (Systematic Theology, p. 151, 149)

God gives us permission to *boast* of one thing!

> [24] Let him who boasts **boast** about this: that he understands and **knows me,** that I am the LORD, who exercises kindness, justice and righteousness on earth, for in these I delight," declares the LORD. (Jeremiah 9:24)

The good news is that the day will come when it will be as Jeremiah predicted

> [34] **They will all know me, from the least of them to the greatest**," declares the LORD. "For I will forgive their wickedness and will remember their sins no more." (Jeremiah 31:34; Isa 11:9)

## God Reveals Himself to Those who Humble Themselves Before Him

> [6] Though the LORD is on high, **he looks upon the lowly**, but the proud he knows from afar. (Psalm 138:6)

> [15] This is what the high and lofty One says— he who lives forever, whose name is holy: "I live in a high and holy place, but also with him who is *contrite and lowly* in spirit, to revive the spirit of the lowly and to revive the heart of the contrite. (Isaiah 57:15)

It's the *lowly* and the *contrite* who are the most likely to read the Bible when it's put into their hands, or listen to someone whom God sends into their lives to share the gospel of salvation. By contrast, it is unlikely that the **proud** and **arrogant** are ever willing to hold the Bible in their hands or give the right time of day to anyone who attempts to lead them to a saving faith in Jesus Christ. It's the **lowly** and **contrite** who are willing to do what God desires, namely to love him heart and soul.

By contrast, to say God 'is the high and lofty One' is to speak of his **sovereignty.**

# God is Sovereign over All Creation

22 "How great you are, O **Sovereign** LORD! **There is no one like you**, and **there is no God but you**, as we have heard with our own ears. (2 Samuel 7:22; Ps 71:16)

As such, time and again in Scripture we note that it was **the Lord's way** to act **sovereignly over his creation**. When Jesus **calmed the stormy lake instantly into a mirror milk pond** his disciples were flabbergasted!

[41] They were terrified and asked each other, "Who is this? **Even the wind and the waves obey him!**"
(Mark 4:41; Jude 1:4)

**God Through His Word has Made His Sovereign Ways Known on Earth.**

Franklin Graham in his book 'Through My Father's Eyes' noted the many times in his father's messages he said, 'The Bible says…' and then would quote a scripture verse to make his point regarding God and his ways. Franklin writes:

My father encouraged people to explore the Bible's authenticity. To do that, we must go to the Source -what God says about Himself in the Bible. Without understanding this basic truth, we have no foundation. What does God say about Himself? (p. 43)

God discloses *his ways* through his inspired *Word -the Holy Scriptures.*

> [19] He has **revealed his word** to Jacob, his laws and decrees to Israel.
>
> [20] He has done this for **no other nation**; they do not know his laws. Praise the LORD.
> (Psalm 147:19-20; Am 3:7, Rom 3:1-2, Heb 1:1)

Is it any wonder that the authors of the inspired Word of God considered their inspired words more valuable than gold?

> [72] The law from your mouth is more precious to me than thousands of pieces of **silver** and **gold**.
> (Psalm 119:72; 19:1)

Whether we turn to the Old Testament or the New Testament we see the *same ways of God* staring us in the face *unchanged.* This is worth something; it's worth a lot!

> [6] "I the Lord do not change." (Malachi 3:6; Heb 13:8)

John Stott writes,

> "God is always himself and never inconsistent…God is God; he never deviates one iota, not even one tiny hair's breath, from being entirely himself."
> (The Cross of Christ, p. 128)

# God Through his Son has made his Ways Known on Earth

Irenaeus writing 'Against the Heresies' in the end of the second century noted that

There is no way we could have learned the **ways of God** unless our Teacher, the Word, had been made man. For no one else could have shown us what the Father is like, or how He wants us to live -no one except the Word of the Father. He alone knows the mind of God and understands the wisdom of **His ways.**

Jesus has said,

⁶ "I am **the way...** (John 14:6)

What we learn from Scripture is that the visible Son of God reflected perfectly his Heavenly Father -the invisible God! It is in the Bible, for instance, that we read Jesus' bold statement,

Anyone who has seen me has seen the Father. (John 14:9)

We say, '*Like father; like son*' No truer words were ever said when applied to Jesus. He says he is just like his Heavenly Father right down to the 'crossing of the 't's and the dotting of the 'i's!...

I did not speak of my own accord, but the Father who sent me commanded me **what to say** and **how to say it**...So **whatever I say is just what the Father has told me to say.**" (John 12:49-50)

So, for example, Jesus has said,

³⁰ I and the Father are one." (John 10:30)

'One' in essence; 'one' in heart and mind; 'one' in every way! This is why Scripture identifies *Jesus* as being the very '*image of God*'.

¹⁵ He is the **image of the invisible God.** (Colossians 1:15; 2 Cor 4:4-6)

In the ancient Letter to Diognetus (author unknown) we read:

"**God came to us as the Son of Man**, in gentleness and humility. Indeed, He is the king of all creation —and yet **He came as a Savior.**"

Jesus' greatest disclosure was that *he had come from his Father in Heaven to bring salvation to all who believe* -and at such a great price!

> ² [He] endured the cross, scorning its shame, and sat down at the right hand of the throne of God. (Hebrews 12:2)

## God through his Holy Spirit has Made His Ways Known on Earth

God further discloses himself through his *Holy Spirit*.

> ²⁶ The Counselor, the **Holy Spirit**, whom the Father will send in my name, **will teach you** all things and **will remind you of everything I have said to you.** (John 14:26; 16:12-13)

> ²¹ For prophecy never had its origin in the will of man, but **men spoke from God** as they were carried along **by the Holy Spirit.** (2 Peter 1:2)

The result is the Holy Spirit inspired Scriptures that reveal God's ways!

## God Through His Church has Made His Ways Known on Earth

God, having created us in his image, enables us to reflect his ways in all we say and do to display his glory for all to see! Christians (the 'Body of Christ') by our words and deeds, *reflect the ways of God* on earth in that *God lives in us* and calls us *his Temple* –his dwelling place on earth.

[19] Do you not know that **your body is a temple of the Holy Spirit**, who is in you, whom you have received from God? You are not your own;

[20] you were bought at a price. Therefore **honor God with your body.** (1 Corinthians 6:19-20; 12:27)

[23] **Christ is the head of the church, his body**, of which he is the Savior. (Ephesians 5:23)

*When anyone looks at the Church they are seeing Christ in action* on earth in *his Body* -of which *he is the Head.* As such, anyone can know God exists simply by observing the *visibly transformed lives* of those who believe in Christ. The *evidence of the Spirit of God living in believing Christians* is palpable, because they are exuding

the **fruit of God's Holy Spirit** (which) is love, joy, peace, patience, kindness, goodness, faithfulness, gentleness and self-control. (Galatians 5:22)

# All God's Ways are Operational Simultaneously

Although it's possible for us to think about only __one__ of *God's ways* at a time, it's important to remember that __all God's ways__ are __simultaneously__ operational __all the time__. Indeed, it may seem to us that one or more of his 'ways' conflict with each other when juxtaposed one over against another, such as God's justice calling for punishment vs his love, mercy and grace calling forth forgiveness and reconciliation. With God all things are possible. Thus with God it is actually the case that *all his ways are in operation at the same time* without any one of his ways conflicting with another, or one 'way' cancelling out another 'way'.

A.W. Tozar addresses this truth in his book 'The Knowledge of the Holy'

There is nothing in God's justice which forbids the exercise of his mercy...God is never at cross-purposes with

himself. No attribute of God is in conflict with another…
God's compassion flows out of his goodness and goodness
without justice is not goodness. God spares us because he
is good, but he could not be good if he were not just. When
God punishes the wicked…it is just because it is consistent
with their deserts, and when he spares the wicked it is
just because it is compatible with his goodness; so God
does what becomes him as the supremely good God…The
problem of how God can be just and still justify the unjust
is found in the Christian doctrine of redemption. It is that
through the work of Christ in atonement, justice is not
violated but satisfied when God spares a sinner.
(p. 94)

Wayne Grudum adds this insight.

Although some of God's attributes may seem to be
emphasized more than others, it is important to realize
that God is unified in all his attributes (ways). He is not
more of one attribute than another. He is not divided into
parts, and he is not one attribute at one point in history
and another attribute at another time. He is fully and
completely every attribute at every time.
('Christian Beliefs', p. 36)

Derek Rishmawy writes in Christianity Today (July/August 2017,
p. 24)

With God it is not a matter of love or justice…but of one
God in his fullness acting in perfect consistency with all
that he is…We see God's mercy is righteous, his love is
holy, his power is good, his wisdom is gracious, and his
glory is unchanging. This is the beauty and comfort of
God's singular nature.

For instance,

[13] **Mercy** triumphs over **judgment**! (James 2:13)

We may prefer one of God's ways over another, such as his love or his grace or his mercy rather than his holding the line for justice -especially when we have treated someone unjustly. Glyn Evans writes in 'Daily With the King',

> One of the tests of my spiritual health is: How well do I accept God's **ways**? It is one thing to accept God's **Word,** but it is quite another thing to accept his **ways.** That is because His **ways** strike me directly and, sometimes, contrarily. Yet, however I like or dislike **God's ways**, 'the **ways of the Lord are right**' (Hosea 14:9)…God's love does not change the content of His ways. They may still be bitter or heavy, but love guarantees me that however rough those ways may be, they are leading me to something better, something glorious in the days to come." (September 19)

## What are the Ways of God Disclosed in the Word of God?

The question remaining is this: ***What are the actual ways of God recorded in Scripture***? My desire is simply to locate and bring together ***biblical*** references that point to specific ***ways of God***, and how we can reflect his ways by godly living. I will devote each chapter to one of ***God's ways.***

This book represents only a ***partial list*** of the ways of God, but it is beginning. Hopefully, not only will you delight in the ***ways of God*** mentioned in this book, but you will also delight from your own ongoing effort to discover even more of God's wonderful unchanging ***ways*** encoded in Scripture, and the dynamic impact God intends for all his ***ways*** to make upon your life.

In the chapters ahead let's let one scripture lead us to another scripture and another and another so that we can get as complete a picture as possible of God's revealed ways.

The question remaining is this: what should we do with this information? Remember, God's desire is **not merely** that we **know about him** but rather, that we come to **desire to know God intimately**, and let him **be known** by **reflecting his ways** in and through our lives by all we say and do.

## God Wants us to Walk in the Light of His Ways

[12] O Israel, what does the LORD your God ask of you but to fear the LORD your God, to **walk in all his ways**, to love him, to serve the LORD your God with all your heart and with all your soul. (Deuteronomy 10:12; 11:22; 26:17, 19, 28:9, 30:16; Josh 22:5)

Georg Neumark (1641) sums everything up beautifully in a majestic hymn.

'If Thou But Suffer God to Guide Thee'

Sing, pray, and **keep his ways unswerving**, offer your service faithfully, and trust his word; though undeserving, you'll find his promise true to be. God never will forsake in need the soul that trusts in him indeed.

**Are we devoted to the ways of the Lord** even in the midst of trials and testing? May we so live that **God's ways** will be known on earth by anyone observing our lives under any circumstance.

[1] May God be gracious to us and bless us and make his face shine upon us,

[2] that **your ways** may be known on earth, your salvation among all nations. (Psalm 67:1-2)

Here is a list of the 'ways of God' that will be highlighted in the rest of this book.

### *Holy*

[13] Your **ways**, O God, are **holy**. What god is so great as our God? (Psalm 77:13)

### *Righteous*

The LORD is **righteous** in all **his ways** and faithful in all he does. (Psalm 119:111)

### *True*

Great and marvelous are your deeds, Lord God Almighty. Just and **true** are your **ways**, King of the nations. (Revelation 15:3)

### *Just*

He is the Rock, his works are perfect, and all his **ways** are **just**. A faithful God who does no wrong, upright and **just** is he. (Deuteronomy 32:4)

### *Loving*

All the **ways** of the LORD are **loving** and faithful toward those who keep the demands of his covenant. (Psalm 25:10)

### *Gracious*

[1] May God be **gracious** to us and bless us and make his face shine upon us, Selah

² that your **ways** may be known on earth, your salvation among all nations. (Psalm 67:1-2)

## *Merciful*

¹² **I am merciful**,' declares the LORD.
(Jeremiah 3:12)

## *Good*

No one is **good**—except God alone. (Mark 10:18)

We need to be alert when the Lord points out his *ways* for us to follow.

¹⁶ This is what the LORD says: "Stand at the crossroads and look; ask for the ancient paths, ask where **the good way** is, and **walk in it, and you will find rest for your souls**. (Jeremiah 6:16)

²¹ Whether you turn to the right or to the left, your ears will hear a voice behind you, saying, "**This is the way**; walk in it."
(Isaiah 30:21; 1 Kg 8:58, Ps 81:13-14; 119:59)

Are we prepared to *'Let God Speak for Himself'*? We can by focusing on *the ways of God which he has revealed in the Word of God – the Holy Bible.* It becomes our joy, in turn to *reflect his ways in our lives* for his glory and our joy!

**Soli Deo Gloria - To God be the Glory!**

CHAPTER 2

# The Ways of God in Nature Confirmed in the Word of God

# God Created the Heavens and the Earth

I n the very first verse of the Bible the connection is made between God and creation.

> [1] In the beginning **God created the heavens and the earth**. (Genesis 1:1)

This was the first point Paul made when speaking to people who didn't know for sure which 'god' was the Creator, or even if there was a Creator.

> [15] We are bringing you good news, telling you to turn from these worthless things [idols] to the living **God**, who **made heaven and earth** and sea and everything in them. (Acts 14:15)

In the end of the Bible God is highlighted one last time as the ***Creator of everything***. John records in Revelation that God is still till now being praised in Heaven as the Creator.

> You are worthy, our Lord and God, to receive glory and honor and power, for you **created all things**, and **by your will they were created** and have their being."
> (Revelation 4:11)

**God of Wonders**

**Lord of all creation**
Of the water, earth and sky
The Heavens are Your Tabernacle
Glory to the Lord on high

God of wonders, beyond our galaxy
You are holy, holy
The universe declares Your majesty
You are holy, holy
　　　　　-Marc Byrd, Steve J. Hindalong

One day God asked these questions of Job:

> [4]**Where** were you when I laid the earth's foundation? Tell me, if you understand. **Who** marked off its dimensions? Surely you know! **Who** stretched a measuring line across it? On **what** were its footings set, or who laid its cornerstone— while the morning stars sang together and all the angels shouted for joy? (Job 38:4)

Paul Tripp reminds us that we ought to have a humble estimation of ourselves.

> 'In the beginning God'... Those words are meant to change the way we think about yourself, life, God, and everything else. God was on site before you were. The earth and everything in it is an expression of his design and his purpose. Because he is the Creator of all things, all things belong to him. God created you. That means you belong to him. We did not make ourselves.
> (New Morning Mercies, February 27)

However old creation is, God is older still. God existed before creation. He is the Creator, the Origin, the Source, the Fountain, the Author, the First Cause of everything. Simply put: God is always *prior!*

> [2]**Before** the mountains were born or you brought forth the earth and the world, from **everlasting to everlasting** you are God. (Psalm 90:2; 93:1-2; Hak 3:6)

When did time begin? No one knows for sure, but in Scripture we learn that God existed before time began

> [9]**Grace** was given us in Christ Jesus **before the beginning of time.** (2 Timothy 1:9; Tit 1:2)

Then the beginning began! The 'clock' began clicking!

[1] **In the beginning** God **created** the heavens and the earth. (Genesis 1:1)

**Creation** is an often repeated topic in Scripture.

[24] I am the LORD, who has **made all things, who alone stretched out the heavens,** who **spread out the earth** by myself. (Isaiah 44:24)

[2] Has not **my hand made all these things,** and so **they came into being**? declares the LORD.
(Isaiah 66:2; 48:12-13; 66:2; Ps 33:6, 9, 89:11, 121:1-2, 146:5-6, Jer 33:2, Ac 4:24, Ro 11:36)

[3] By faith we understand that the universe was formed at God's command, so that what is seen was not made out of what was visible. (Hebrews 11:3)

Yes, it's by faith we believe. But is it all that hard to believe? We are at this very moment surrounded by a very visible creation, and we ourselves are a part of it. If there was nothing anywhere, then, yes, doubt the existence of God. If there was nothing here we wouldn't be here asking this question. *But we **are** 'here'*! It's as someone has said, 'It takes more faith to be an atheist than to believe there is a God who created everything.'

As such, *God* is the first topic in the Bible beginning with the fourth word, and *creation* is the second topic -the fifth word in! They cannot be unimportant topics!

[1] In the beginning **God created** the heavens and the earth. (Genesis 1:1; Ps 96:5; 102:25-27; Isa 40:21-22, 28; 42:5; 45:18)

## Scriptures Teach that Nature is a Way God Makes Himself Known

There is more to nature than nature. Nature is not an end in itself. There is a divine purpose behind Nature. *'Nature'* is the <u>way</u> the *invisible* God has chosen to *visibly* express himself by what he has created. Ron Rhodes in his 'The Big Book of Bible Answers' responds to the question 'Has God given a witness of himself in the universe around us?'

> We know...from Scriptures that God is **invisible spirit** (John 4:24). But his existence is nevertheless reflected in what he has made -the Creation. The **creation**, which is **visible**, reveals the existence of the **Creator,** who is **invisible.** (p. 189)

*'Invisible'* does not mean *'non-existent'*. There are many aspects of creation that are *not visible* to the naked eye, but their existence is not doubted. There's the lowly *atom -invisible* to the naked eye, but we know the atom is the building block of *everything we see in creation*. From cover to cover the Bible asserts that *'nature'* is one of the *ways* the *invisible God expresses himself visibly*: his existence, his intelligence; his sovereignty!

## The Invisible God has Made Himself Known in Creation

> [10] In the beginning, O Lord, **you laid the foundations of the earth,** and **the heavens are the work of your hands.** (Hebrews 1:10)

> [6] By the **word of the LORD** were the heavens made, their starry host by the breath of his mouth. (Psalm 33:6, 148:3-6; Gen 1:3; Col 1:16-17)

Paul has affirmed that the Son of God:

¹⁵ is the image of the **invisible God**, the firstborn over all creation.

¹⁶ For **by him all things were created**: things in heaven and on earth, visible and invisible, whether thrones or powers or rulers or authorities; all things were created by him and for him. (Colossians 1:15-17)

⁶ By the **word of the LORD** were the heavens made, their starry host by the breath of his mouth.
(Psalm 33:6, 148:3-6; Gen 1:3; Col 1:16-17)

# By Faith We Observe the Triune God in Nature

It is not hard to come to the conclusion that God is greater than everything he has created. God is greater in the same way the builder of a house is greater than the house he has built.

³ The builder of a house has greater honor than the house itself.

⁴ For every house is built by someone, but **God is the builder of everything**. (Hebrews 3:4-5)

It's just that God doesn't hang a sign on rose bush that reads: 'Compliments of God'. He has given us the ability to put 2 and 2 together and conclude that God the Creator is behind such beauty.

Actually, God isn't all that invisible in nature. To be sure, he is not 'nature' as pantheists conclude. God created a rock but the rock is not 'god'; God created a tree but the tree is not 'god'. What does hold true is that there is a *rock* and a *tree*; therefore, there must be a Creator of the rock and the tree. God has left an indelible imprint upon all creation. In 'The North Face of God' Ken Gire says it's as

C. S. Lewis explains, **God is in his creation in much the same way that Shakespeare is in his plays.** The playwright cannot be found in any one scene, one character, or one line of dialogue. Yet, at the same time, he is everywhere –in every scene, every character, every line of dialogue...' Where is God? We wonder. We look around us, and he is nowhere to be found. And then, when we look with the right eyes, we see traces of him everywhere. (p. 122)

*Eyes of faith* is what the resurrected Lord Jesus wants for us. Thomas saw him and believed but Jesus, though speaking face-to-face with Thomas, was thinking of *us* who do not have the privilege of seeing as Thomas saw.

> [29] Jesus told him, "Because you have seen me, you have believed; **blessed are those who have not seen and yet have believed.**" (John 20:29)

Years later Peter wrote to the new generation of Christians who had not seen Jesus in the flesh as had been his privilege.

> [8] Though **you have not seen him**, you love him; and even though you do not see him now, you believe in him and are filled with an inexpressible and glorious joy.
> (1 Peter 1:8)

Looking at it another way, there's a sense in which God has indeed left his *signature* on what he's created, like artists who sign their artwork. Study art and eventually you'll be able to recognize a 'Rembrandt' even if you cannot find his signature on the canvass. There's a sense in which the painting itself is his signature. Why? Because all Rembrandt paintings express his unchanging painting techniques. His own personality shows up in all his artwork as well. The same is the case for other paintings whether the work of Rubens or Thomas Kinkade. Paul Brand has made this observation:

> A great artist may use a variety of media for expression, but common themes of style, content, and approach will run through all the works. It should not surprise us, then,

that the Supreme Artist [God] has left His signature in
many different forms. ('In His Image', p. 10)

So the question is this: Does the *'signature' of the Triune God*
(God the Father, God the Son, God the Holy Spirit -three persons; yet
inseparably one essence) show up anywhere in his art masterpiece we call
'Creation? This was the subject of Nathan Wood's book 'The Secret of the
Universe'. He looked closely and observed the signature of the triune God
again and again *in nature*.

Here are just a few of many examples of things in nature that are
distinctly *three and yet inseparably one at the same time.*

Reality: space, matter, time
Time: past, present, future
Three dimensions: height, length, depth
The atom: electron, proton, neutron
The 3 primary colors: red, yellow and blue

In each case, 'three' and yet inextricably 'one'! ☺ Just because we can't
explain how it is that God is **triune**, it doesn't mean that it cannot be true. It
only means that it's beyond our ability to understand. A.W. Tozar in his book
'The Knowledge of the Holy' reminds us that

God is not like anything or anybody. (p. 14)

The Triune God's signature in creation is but a whisper at best, but it
is at least it's a 'whisper'. It's *God's way in nature* (his invisible presence in
creation) whereby he intends to stimulate everyone's curiosity and prompt
them to search for him with all their hearts.

[20] Since the creation of the world **God's invisible
qualities—his eternal power and divine nature—have
been clearly seen,** being understood from what has been
made, so that men are without excuse. (Romans 1:20)

God's promise to those who search for him wholeheartedly is this:

[13] You will seek me and find me **when** you seek me with all your heart. (Jeremiah 29:13)

John Stott has noted that the Triune God

who in himself is invisible and unknowable, has made himself both visible and knowable through what he has made.
('The Message of Romans', p. 73)

*'Creation'* is the self-disclosure of the *invisible* God.

Scripture says God reveals basic truth about himself in nature. His...invisible attributes, such as his wisdom, power and beauty are on constant display in what he's created. (John MacArthur, 'The Truth War')

# In Nature God Expresses Himself as Omnipotent, Omnipresent, Omniscient, Perfect

### Omnipotent:

**God the Father is Omnipotent** (all powerful; almighty; sovereign over everything)

[1] The **earth is the LORD's, and everything in it**, the world, and all who live in it.
(Psalm 24:1; 89:11; 93:4; Dt 10:14; 1 Cor 10:26)

Not only everything in the world, but *he has also laid claim to every star in the universe!* That is no small number considering that the total number of stars may rival the number of grains of sand bordering the world's oceans.

[25] "To whom will you compare me? Or who is my equal?" says the Holy One.

<sup>26</sup> Lift your eyes and look to the heavens: Who created all these? **He who brings out the starry host one by one, and calls them each by name.** Because of his great power and mighty strength, **not one of them is missing.** (Isaiah 40:25-26)

The heavens gave Franz Joseph Hayden (1732-1809) the inspiration to compose his oratorio ***The Creation*** which has a majestic anthem '***The Heavens are Telling***'.

'In all the lands resounds the word,
Never unperceived, ever understood.
**The Heavens are telling the glory of God**,
The wonder of his work displays the firmament.'

<sup>1</sup> The heavens **declare** the glory of God; the skies **proclaim** the work of his hands. (Psalm 19:1, 145:10)

Thomas Chisholm hymn 'Great is Thy Faithfulness' written in 1923 is a fine example of one of many hymns praising God for his great creation.

Summer and winter and springtime and harvest,
Sun, moon and stars in their courses above
Join with all nature in manifold witness
To Thy great faithfulness, mercy and love.

Great is Thy faithfulness!
Morning by morning new mercies I see.
All I have needed Thy hand hath provided,
Great is Thy faithfulness, Lord, unto me!
(Thomas Chisholm, 1866-1960)

*Douglas Nelson*

# God the Son is Omnipotent

[17] He is before all things, and **in him all things hold together.** (Colossians 1:17)

Daniel saw in a vision when the Son of Man

[14] was given authority, glory and **sovereign power.** All peoples, nations and men of every language worshiped him. His dominion is an everlasting dominion that will not pass away, and his kingdom is one that will never be destroyed. (Daniel 7:14)

At the close of Jesus' ministry on earth he

[3] knew that the Father had put **all things under his power**, and that he had come from God and was returning to God. (John 13:3)

Following Christ's resurrection, Paul affirms that

[10] At the name of Jesus **every knee should bow**, in heaven and on earth and under the earth,

[11] and every tongue confess that Jesus Christ is **Lord**, to the glory of God the Father. (Philippians 2:10-11)

Paul has disclosed that in the future we will reign with him in power.

[12] If we endure, we will also **reign with him.**
(2 Timothy 2:12; Ac 1:8; 1 Cor 6:2-3)

## The Holy Spirit Possesses Omnipotent Power

Witness the Holy Spirit's 'power', for example, in the resurrection of Jesus from the dead.

> [3] Regarding his Son, who as to his human nature was a descendant of David,
>
> [4] and who through the **Spirit of holiness** was declared with **power to be the Son of God by his resurrection from the dead**: Jesus Christ our Lord. (Romans 1:3-4)

## God is Omnipresent (God is everywhere)

> [4] Does he not **see my ways** and **count my every step?** (Job 31:4)
>
> [13] From heaven the LORD **looks down** and **sees all mankind;**
>
> [14] from his dwelling place he **watches all who live on earth…**
> (Psalm 33:13-14, 18; 113:5-7; 121:3-8; 139:7-12; Prov 15:3; Jer 16:17, 23:23-24)
>
> [13] **Nothing in all creation is hidden from God's sight.** Everything is uncovered and laid bare before the eyes of him to whom we must give account. (Hebrews 4:13)

It is as Job has said,

> [24] He views the ends of the earth and **sees everything** under the heavens. (Job 28:24)

Many people are familiar with the saying that came out of Washington, 'You can run, but you can't hide.' This is especially true when the saying is applied to sinful people who are trying to hide from the God who sees all.

> [8] You have set our iniquities before you, our secret sins in the light of your presence. (Psalm 90:8)

## Jesus is Omnipresent

Jesus disclosed his omnipresence to his disciples. While he was physically present with his disciples he was at the same time fully aware of what was going on elsewhere. He gave these instructions to his disciples:

> [30] "Go to the village ahead of you, and as you enter it, you will find a colt tied there, which no one has ever ridden. Untie it and bring it here.
>
> [31] If anyone asks you, 'Why are you untying it?' tell him, 'The Lord needs it.'"
>
> [32] Those who were sent ahead went and **found it just as he had told them**. (Luke 19:30-32)

Jesus' awareness of what was going on everywhere surfaced again later that week when he gave his disciples instructions regarding where to find a room to prepare for the Passover.

> [10] "As you enter the city, a man carrying a jar of water will meet you. Follow him to the house that he enters,
>
> [11] and say to the owner of the house, 'The Teacher asks: Where is the guest room, where I may eat the Passover with my disciples?'...
>
> [13] **They left and found things just as Jesus had told them.** So they prepared the Passover. (Luke 22:10-11, 13)

# The Holy Spirit is Omnipresent

The Spirit of God is everywhere at work in our lives.

> [7] Where can I go from your Spirit? Where can I flee from your presence?

> [9] If I rise on the wings of the dawn, if I settle on the far side of the sea,

> [10] even there your hand will guide me, your right hand will hold me fast. (Psalm 139:7, 9-10)

This truth was a comfort to my wife and me when we moved to the 'far side of the sea' which for us was the South Seas. We used to quip, "This is not 'the ends of the earth' -but you can see it from here". ☺ Indeed, we have sensed the presence of the Spirit of God all around the globe wherever we have travelled.

# God is Omniscient (has all knowledge)

> [2] You know when I sit and when I rise; you perceive my thoughts from afar.

> [3] You discern my going out and my lying down; you are familiar with all my ways.

> [4] Before a word is on my tongue you know it completely, O LORD. (Psalm 139:2-4)

For instance, God knows our needs.

> [31] Do not worry, saying, 'What shall we eat?' or 'What shall we drink?' or 'What shall we wear?'...

[32] **Your heavenly Father knows** that you need them.
(Matthew 6:31-32)

The fact of the matter is that God knows everything about everything. There is nothing that he does not know. David Jeremiah shared in a message on the omniscience of God,

> God knows everything that is actual and all that is potential. God knows what lies beyond the galaxies and beyond the grave!

God has gone on record that there is nothing he does not know.

> [10] I make known the end from the beginning, from ancient times, what is still to come. I say: My purpose will stand, and I will do all that I please. (Isaiah 46:10)

> Nothing can take the Almighty by surprise or happen contrary to what He has foreseen." (Alistair Begg, Truth for Life, Daily Devotional, 12/12/17)

David prayed to God,

> [2] You know when I sit and when I rise; you perceive my thoughts from afar.

> [3] You discern my going out and my lying down; **you are familiar with all my ways**.

> [4] Before a word is on my tongue **you know it completely**, O LORD. (Psalm 139:2-4)

Paul was overwhelmed by his awareness of the profundity of God's wisdom and knowledge!

33 Oh, **the depth of the riches of the wisdom and knowledge of God**! How unsearchable his judgments, and his paths beyond tracing out! (Romans 11:33)

# Jesus is Omniscient

Hear Jesus' words to his disciples in the Upper Room when he informed them one of them would betray him that very evening.

18 'He who shares my bread has lifted up his heel against me.'

19 **"I am telling you now before it happens, so that when it does happen you will believe that I am He.** (John 13:18-19)

It is comforting to know that the Lord knows the end from the beginning. Nothing ever takes Jesus by surprise. This truth gives peace of mind!

25 He did not need man's testimony about man, for **he knew** what was in a man. (John 2:25)

4 **Knowing their thoughts**, Jesus said, "Why do you entertain evil thoughts in your hearts? (Matthew 9:4)

8 Jesus **knew what they were thinking**. (Luke 6:8)

64 **Jesus had known from the beginning** which of them did not believe and who would betray him. (John 6:64)

Paul's words are informative and at the same time comforting. 19 God's solid foundation stands firm, sealed with this inscription:

"The Lord **knows** those who are his," (2 Timothy 2:19)

# The Holy Spirit is Omniscient

The Scripture discloses how incredibly great are God's thoughts regarding his Creation, and his thoughts of us in particular.

> [10] The Spirit searches all things, even the deep things of God...

> [11] No one knows the thoughts of God except the Spirit of God. (1 Corinthians 2:10-11)

> [8] "My thoughts are not your thoughts, neither are your ways my ways," declares the LORD.

> [9] "As the heavens are higher than the earth, so are my ways higher than your ways and my thoughts than your thoughts. (Isaiah 55:8-9)

> [27] He who searches our hearts knows **the mind of the Spirit**, because the Spirit intercedes for the saints in accordance with God's will. (Romans 8:27)

# God Makes his Ways Known in Nature

It is **God's way** to make himself known to anyone who is willing to believe in him. Even **before** a person has access **to the Word of God,** he gives verifiable proof of his existence in nature. For example, God daily displays his **kindness** in nature. Paul has said of **God's kindness** displayed in nature,

> [17] He has not left himself without testimony: He has **shown kindness** by giving you rain from heaven and crops in their seasons; he provides you with plenty of food and fills your hearts with joy." (Acts 14:17)

God shows us kindnesses all the time. Even when issues come up and things don't seem to be going well, I try to remember God's ongoing kindnesses in my life. In spite of what I'm facing I still have the blessing of eyesight. I can still hear and taste and smell and touch. I still have food on the table and a roof over my head, a spouse whom I love by my side, and a family I care for. And this is just the beginning.

## It Is God's Way in nature to Reflect His Unchanging Character by the Unchanging Laws of Nature

Natural Law is one way God chooses to express his 'unchanging' character. We cannot change any 'natural law' God has set in place in nature. We know that following the laws of nature work to our advantage; whereas, trying to skirt around the laws of nature always work to our disadvantage. In the case of 2+2=4, there is one correct answer and an infinite number of wrong answers. The right answer always works to our advantage; whereas, none of the wrong answers ever work out. We have made it as far as the moon with right answers. If we had relied on wrong answers getting us to the moon, the Apollo moon rocket ship never would have lifted off the launch pad. These unchanging laws speak of an unchanging divine intelligence that put the laws of nature in place.

## God our Creator is the Intelligent Designer

Complicated design throughout creation is God's way of expressing his intelligence! Nature is very complex. God's *way* in creation is *intelligent design.* Even though the Authors of Scripture didn't have access to telescopes or microscopes or science labs, they understood the complexity of creation.

> [24] How many are your works, O LORD! In **wisdom** [**intelligent design**] you made them all; the earth is full of your creatures.
> (Psalm 104:24; 136:5; Prov 3:19; Jer 51:15)

⁵ Many, O LORD my God, are the **wonders you have done**. The things you planned for us no one can recount to you; were I to speak and tell of them, they would be too many to declare. (Psalm 40:5)

⁵ You hem me in—behind and before; you have laid your hand upon me.

⁶ Such knowledge is too wonderful for me, too lofty for me to attain…

¹⁴ I praise you because I am fearfully and wonderfully made; your works are wonderful, I know that full well. (Psalm 139:5-6, 14)

God has created so much! Our sun is but one star of the hundreds of millions of stars in our Galaxy, and, in turn, our Galaxy is but one of hundreds of millions of Galaxies. The Psalmist amazes us with the statistic that God has a unique name for every star in the universe.

⁴ He determines the number of the stars and **calls them each by name**! (Psalm 147:4)

If we focus just on our own world the vastness of what we can observe on earth is mindboggling. To the best of our understanding no two things are identical. Every snowflake has a different pattern; every set of fingerprints is unique, as is everyone's DNA. Identical twins are not really 'identical' but each is unique.

⁹ He performs **wonders that cannot be fathomed**, miracles that cannot be counted. (Job 5:9)

What we are learning about creation is growing exponentially, but it's still the case that most of what there is to know is still unknown because creation is simply too complex and too vast -ranging from subatomic particles beyond the reach of even the most powerful electron microscopes to the Hubble telescope focusing its gaze on the countless galaxies that are millions of not billions of light years away.

Yes, God is greater than all he has made to an infinite degree. Solomon prayed to God when he dedicated his newly constructed temple:

> 27 The heavens, even the highest heaven, cannot contain you. How much less this temple I have built! (1 Kings 8:27)

A clear night sky is ablaze with thousands of sparkling stars visible to the naked eye. Calculating the immense size of the known universe is no small task considering the number of stars. It's estimated that in our Milky Way galaxy alone there are a billion stars, and perhaps an equal number of stars in each of the estimated 170 billion galaxies in the visible universe! Astronomers who man the world's largest telescopes estimate there are upwards of a trillion trillion or more stars in our rapidly expanding universe.

The Psalmist speaks of the *expanding* universe

> 2 He **stretches out the heavens** like a tent
> (Psalm 104:2)

Isaiah's words are awe inspiring.

> 22 He sits enthroned above the **circle of the earth**, and its people are like grasshoppers. He **stretches out the heavens** like a canopy. (Isaiah 40:22-26)

Job further notes what God *stretches the earth over nothing*!

> 7 He spreads out the northern [skies] over empty space; he **suspends the earth over nothing**. (Job 26:7)

Is it any wonder Job concludes:

> 14 These are but the outer fringe of his works; how faint the whisper we hear of him! (Job 26:14)

Ann Marrow Lindbergh wrote in her journal how she was once out walking with her young son Jon and he was asking who made the world. When she explained that God made it he said that that was what he thought because it was too big for any man to make. The good news is that creation is not so vast that God can't keep up with everything, or that he's lost us between the cracks. God is more than able to keep up with the whole universe, including us right down to the number of hairs on everyone's heads!

Note how observant God is.

> ⁷ Indeed, the very hairs of your head are all numbered.
> Don't be afraid; you are worth more than many sparrows.
> (Luke 12:7)

One of the joys my wife and I have is stocking a birdfeeder with seed and watching birds fly to the feeder all day every day. In a small way we're part of the fulfillment of Psalm 145:6 in that God through us is feeding many birds of a feather -of many 'feathers' in fact- as they gather as one at the feeder to eat.

Do you know how many '*living things*' there are in the world? Beyond number, I'm sure, but God tracts with them all.

> ¹⁶ You open your hand and satisfy the desires of **every living thing.** (Psalm 145:16)

> ¹¹ I know **every** bird in the mountains, and the creatures of the field are mine. (Psalm 50:11)

The more that 'nature' is studied with telescopes and microscopes and all kinds of scientific instruments of increasing sensitivity, the more apparent it becomes as to the profound complexity of creation. It's as someone has said, "One cell in the human body is more complex than New York City!" Consider the complexity found in our DNA chain.

The authors of Scripture took a humble position with reference to what they knew compared to what they didn't know or understand about the world they lived in.

¹ My heart is **not proud**, O LORD, my eyes are **not haughty**; I do not concern myself with great matters or things too wonderful for me.

² But I have stilled and quieted my soul; like a weaned child with its mother, like a weaned child is my soul within me. (Psalm 131:1-2)

From what we observe in nature we are uniquely made. Consider the **uniqueness of Man in the image of God** when compared with any other creature on earth. There are 'worlds within worlds', e.g. ants nesting, birds flocking; bees swarming; deer mating. Man is vastly more complex than any other creature on earth. All share the same earth with mankind in that we all live and breathe and eat and drink and move about, but when all is said and done, Man alone has been created in the **image of God** and is thus the pinnacle of God's complex creation. Consider that compared with any of us,

A frog has never flown a plane.
A cat has never built a home.
No dog has ever graduated from Harvard.
A monkey has never written a book.
A cow has never jumped over the moon☺
No animal on its own has ever worn clothes.

Once when touring historic Sturbridge Village in Massachusetts, my wife and I joined several tourists in a wagon ride pulled by large Clydesdale horses. One lady remarked, "Aren't these horses smart to pull this wagon?" I quipped, "If they *were* smart they wouldn't pull the wagon at all." ☺

⁹ Do not be like the horse or the mule, which have **no understanding** but must be controlled by bit and bridle or they will not come to you. (Psalm 32:9)

Horse lovers may debate this and talk about 'horse sense', but I remain convinced that human 'common sense' trumps 'horse sense' every time. ☺

Animals are not human, even though we want to assign some animals with humanlike characteristics. With a little imagination consider...

A *playful* kitten
A *curios* cat
A *funny* monkey
A *wise* old owl
An *eager* beaver
A *sly* fox
A *cunning* snake
A *raging* bull

When all is said and done animals are not human even though many people talk to their pets as though they were human.

## God's Glorious Revelation in Creation Has Been Darkened by Man's Sin

The fact of the matter is that God created the world with the possibility of it becoming a *fallen world*; therefore, when it did fall it did not take him by surprise. God knew that if he created man with freedom to choose to obey or disobey him; choose to tell the truth or lie; choose to love or not to love -his perfect 'Paradise' would no longer remain perfect. But he *also* knew that its 'fall' would ultimately redound to his *glory* by the way he had always intended to restore it permanently to its pristine beauty and perfection.

The insertion of the 'tree of the knowledge of good and evil' was how God offered man *freedom of choice*. Man had to have a real opportunity to *choose what is right* and enjoy its consequences, and the opportunity to *choose wrong* (with fair warning) and suffer its consequences.

Everyone to the man has chosen to sin, so until now we have lived in a sin-cursed world. *God is not 'evil'* nor is he the *cause* of evil in our world, but he has by granting us free will, *allowed* evil to visit our world. God however, responds tit-for-tat to man's every act of evil by offering forgiveness for the repentant, but judgment for the unrepentant.

God freely admitted to Moses at the burning bush that *the world was no longer perfect* as it once was.

> [11]Who makes man deaf or mute? Who gives him sight or makes him blind? Is it not I, the LORD? (Exodus 4:11)

It was never mandatory that God give any of us sight or hearing or any of our five senses we've come to take for granted. Actually, God has no moral imperative to grant us an inherent right to see or hear or feel or taste or smell. God is free to design us anyway he might choose. It is only by his grace that we are able to have and enjoy the use of our five senses!

In fact, God was under no compunction to create us at all. So, we need to praise the Lord that we are '**here**' at all no matter what physical, mental, emotional or spiritual state we may be in at the moment -or at any moment.

What can be said is that *God has good reason* for what he allows or disallows in our life for any length of time. Consider, for example, the day Jesus and his disciples came across a man born blind.

> [1] As he went along, he saw a man **blind from birth**.
>
> [2] His disciples asked him, "Rabbi, who sinned, this man or his parents, that he was born blind?"
>
> [3] "Neither this man nor his parents sinned," said Jesus, **"but this happened so that the work of God might be displayed in his life.** (John 9:1-3)
>
> [7] "Go," he told him, "wash in the Pool of Siloam" (this word means Sent). So the man went and washed, and **came home seeing.** (John 9:7)

We need to be careful, however, in concluding that if God healed one person he is duty bound to heal everyone the same way. God has a unique story line for each one of us. God may heal us -whatever our situation- but he is not compelled to treat us all alike. God may heal us but not in the same way he heals someone else. He may heal us, but not before he has something he wants to accomplish for his glory in our lives (or the lives of onlookers) before ending the affliction.

I praise the Lord for his presence in my various 'afflictions' over the years, and how in his time (not mine) and in his way he sustained and quieted me with his love until he chose for the affliction to end. I hold out for you that if you give the Lord time and space with your affliction you will not be disappointed by how he resolves your situation in the process of time.

I remember once sitting down and writing out all the times I could remember Lord intervening in my life in one way or another to spare me from accident, or heal me from illness. To my amazement when I was done I had 3 pages filled with reasons to praise the Lord for his goodness to me.

Even when the Lord does not relieve us of an affliction -whether physical, mental, emotional, or all of the above- we can still be assured he nevertheless has something good in mind that he intends to bring to pass by means of the affliction. I think of Joni Tada who has been confined to a wheel chair for over 50 years, yet she has said that if given a choice she would rather be in the chair with the Lord in her life than to be free to run and jump -without the Lord in her life. Sitting in her chair she ministers love and grace and hope to multitudes of people through her public speaking events, her radio ministry, her music, her many books, her paintings, and her provision of hundreds of wheel chairs for people around the world who could not otherwise afford them.

The Lord does not abandon us in affliction. His 'way' is to be closer to us than ever before as we depend on his grace to offset our weakness with his all-sufficient strength.

> [9] He (the Lord) said to me, "My grace is sufficient for you, for my power is made perfect in weakness." Therefore I will boast all the more gladly about my weaknesses, so that Christ's power may rest on me.

> [10] That is why, for Christ's sake, **I delight in weaknesses**, in insults, in hardships, in persecutions, in difficulties. For **when I am weak, then I am strong.**
> (2 Corinthians 12:9-10)

The question is '*why*'? Why did God put a tree with forbidden fruit in the garden? It all comes down to this: we learn from Scripture that it was *God's way* of making *love* possible. *Love is possible only where there is '*free will*' -the freedom *to love* or *not love*.* When God asked Adam and Eve not to eat from the tree it gave them a chance to express love for God by refraining from doing what he asked them not to do.

If we had not been created with the freedom to love, we would have been nothing more than a pre-programed robot, or a creature of mindless instinct at best. We would not be the 'image of God' who chooses to love. Why did God make 'love' foundational in creation? Because 'love' is foundational to God!

*God is love.* 'LOVE is what God is to the core of his being!

> [8] Whoever does not love does not know God, because **God is love**. (1 John 4:8; 4:16)

It is a highly distressing thought that God actually has no compelling reason to love us in our wretched sinful state, but the good news is that *God can and does love us unconditionally, unfailingly and without limit!* ☺

The question is this: Do we love God. Jesus stated it simply:

> [15] "**If** you love me, **you will** obey what I command. (John 14:15)

Therefore, to obey the Lord by faith is the only way we can express love for him. But it is not hard to love him who first loved us by allowing his Son to lay down his life for us.

## God's Glory is Restored to Us by Jesus Christ

The most familiar verse in the Bible is John 3:16

> [16] God **so loved** the world that he gave his one and only Son, that whoever believes in him shall not perish but have eternal life. (John 3:16)

Every time I stay in a hotel I pull a Gideon Bible out of the desk drawer, open it up to John 3:16. I lay it open on the table with the hope that someone might come across it and focus their eyes on John 3:16. I pray they will not only read it but begin to believe God loves them, and wants to save them from everything they ever said or did that they wish they had never said or done. I met a man once who was saved from committing suicide by happening to thumb through the pages of a hotel Bible and opening to a passage that spoke to his situation.

Once when touring in San Juan Capistrano, California my wife and I toured the old Mission San Juan Capistrano. Among the centuries-old artifacts was an old Bible lying open on a table. True to form, I turned the page to John 3:16. I noticed right away that it was the most worn page in the Bible, a page that had been turned to countless times over the years! Evidently, not only do thousands of swallows return to this mission every March 19 from their 6,000 mile migration flight, but thousands of Christians also land at this quaint mission every year, and open the old Bible to John 3:16! ☺

Someone has researched the sounds of nature and concluded that *all* the sounds of nature are in a *minor key* -perhaps due to the fact that God placed a curse on his fallen world the very day he exited Adam and Eve (and all of us) from Eden that perfect place where there was fullness of joy in God's presence. Our hope is in the promise we'll be permitted re-entry through the gates of Paradise -as was the case of the repentant thief on the cross next to Jesus! He prayed:

> [42] "Jesus, remember me when you come into your kingdom."

> [43] Jesus answered him, "I tell you the truth, **today you will be with me in paradise**." (Luke 23:42-43)

Nature's return to 'Paradise' is ultimately what this world is coming to! Paul describes the future *lifting of the curse* when Jesus returns to earth from heaven.

²¹ The **creation itself will be liberated** from its bondage to decay and brought into the glorious freedom of the children of God. (Romans 8:21)

Can you hear the excitement and childish wonder in Paul's words?

⁹ "No eye has seen, no ear has heard, no mind has conceived what God has prepared for those who love him". (1 Corinthians 2:9)

Peter gives us an additional glimpse into the new world that is coming.

¹³ In keeping with his promise we are looking forward to a **new heaven and a new earth, the home of righteousness**. (2 Peter 3:13)

Jesus prayed to this end in the Garden of Gethsemane.

²⁴ "Father, I want those you have given me to be with me where I am, and to see my glory, the glory you have given me because you loved me before the creation of the world. (John 17:24)

John pulls back the curtain and gives us a sneak peek into this 'future' the Lord will one day bring to pass.

⁴ He will wipe every tear from their eyes. There will be no more death or mourning or crying or pain, for the old order of things has passed away."

⁵ He who was seated on the throne said, "**I am making everything new**!" Then he said, "Write this down, for these words are trustworthy and true."
(Revelation 21:4-5; Isa 11:6-9)

We express longing for this to come to pass whenever we pray these words found in the end of the Bible: 'Come Lord Jesus!' (Rev 21:20)

*Douglas Nelson*

# God is not Bound to the Laws of Nature

We are limited to the laws of nature, but God is not limited to the laws he has established in nature. This is only to say that God is greater than nature -to an infinite degree. Mary heard these words from an angel when she as a virgin was to give birth to the Son of God.

> [37] Nothing is **impossible** with God." (Luke 1:37)

Jesus was living proof God is well able to do the impossible. Here are his own words:

> [27] What is **impossible** with men is **possible** with God. (Luke 18:27)

We are limited to the Laws of Nature, but God is not limited to them. If someone falls out of a tree he will get hurt -whether he is a believer in God or an atheist. The unchanging Laws of Nature apply equally to everyone. However, if God wants to step outside the laws of nature to perform a 'miracle' he can and he does. Otherwise God would have been unable to divide the Red Sea for the escaping Hebrew slaves, shut the lions' mouths for Daniel, feed 5000 men with only a few fish and loaves of bread, instantly calm a raging sea, or rise from the dead.

Mary herself witnessed God doing the 'impossible' -doing something outside the Laws of Nature. As a virgin she was enabled by God to give birth of the eternal Son of God. A virgin birth never happens. Mary did not do the impossible, but God accomplished the impossible in her. Thirty-three years later Mary once again witnessed the 'impossible' -the resurrection of her son from the dead validating him as the Son of God -the Savior of the world!

More often than not, however, God works within the laws of nature to accomplish his plans. When being tempted by the devil, Jesus did not turn stones into bread to feed his hunger; he did not jump off the roof of the Temple to defy the laws of gravity.

Are we willing to leave the decision with God when he deems it necessary to perform a miracle to accomplish his purposes -even when we cannot understand why a 'miracle' happens '*here*' but not '*there*'? This is information locked up in the counsels of God.

In Acts 12, for instance, James and Peter were both in the same prison. *James was taken out of prison and executed* by the sword, whereas *Peter was miraculously set free by an angel* (Acts 12:1-2, 7).

Delivered or not delivered…that was the decision Shadrach, Meshach and Abednego were willing to leave in God's hands as they faced being thrown into a blazing furnace unless they renounced their faith in God.

> [17] If we are thrown into the blazing furnace, **the God we serve is able to save us** from it, and he will rescue us from your hand, O king.
>
> [18] But **even if he does not**, we want you to know, O king, that **we will not serve your gods** or worship the image of gold you have set up." (Daniel 3:17-18)

This was one of those rare times when God stepped outside the boundaries of natural law to rescue these young men of faith.

> [27] They saw that the fire had not harmed their bodies, nor was a hair of their heads singed; their robes were not scorched, and there was no smell of fire on them. (Daniel 3:27)

# God's Power Over Nature is Incomparable

It is *God's way* to speak to us through the forces of nature in our world. He has our attention in the midst of any cataclysmic event whether earthquake or flood, fire, famine or erupting volcano. God may employ the mighty forces of nature to get the attention of wicked people who need to repent. C.S. Lewis writes in his book 'The Problem of Pain',

> God whispers to us in our pleasures, speaks in our conscience, but shouts in our pain: it is His megaphone to rouse a deaf world. (p.93)

The Psalmist concluded that 'pain' was God's teacher for building character.

> [67] Before I was afflicted I went astray, but **now I obey your word.** (Psalm 119:67, 71, 75)

As it has been said, "There are no atheists in foxholes!" If God never had their attention before, he has it in the midst of calamity when life itself is hanging in the balance.

God can use the same forces of nature to release innocent people from the evil clutches of anyone seeking to do them harm.

> [6] In my distress...I cried to my God for help...

> [7] The earth trembled and quaked...

> [9] He parted the heavens and came down...

> [16] He reached down from on high...
> he drew me out of deep waters...

> [17] He rescued me from my powerful enemy.
> (Psalm 18:6-7, 9, 13, 16-17)

For Paul and Silas, their means of divine escape from the forces of evil was not a category 5 storm, but an earthquake.

> [26] Suddenly there was such a violent earthquake that the foundations of the prison were shaken. At once all the prison doors flew open, and everybody's chains came loose. (Acts 16:26)

# God honors Anyone Willing to Suffer at the Hands of Sinners

In his Sermon on the Mount Jesus said with compassion,

> [10] Blessed are those who are persecuted because of righteousness, for **theirs is the kingdom of heaven.** (Matthew 5:10)

Jesus reminded his followers.

> [20] Remember the words I spoke to you: 'No servant is greater than his master.' **If they persecuted me, they will persecute you also.** (John 15:20; 14:27, 16:33)

Peter reflected on his sufferings, and wrote that we should not be surprised if we find ourselves suffering at the hands of unbelievers.

> [12] Dear friends, **do not be surprised** at the painful trial you are suffering, as though something strange were happening to you.

> [13] But **rejoice** that **you participate in the sufferings of Christ**, so that you may be overjoyed when his glory is revealed. (1 Peter 4:12-13)

Paul has set the pace for us. He learned to *take suffering in stride* letting nothing stop him from continuing in his loving service for the Lord!

> [11] We are brutally treated, we are homeless...

> [12] When we are cursed, we bless;
> When we are persecuted, we endure it.
> (1 Corinthians 4:11-12)

> [8] We are hard pressed on every side, but not crushed;
> perplexed, but not in despair;

⁹persecuted, but not abandoned;
struck down, but not destroyed.
(2 Corinthians 4:7-9)

Paul considered what he had suffered for the Lord was his 'badge of honor'.

¹⁷Let no one cause me trouble, for I bear on my body the marks of Jesus. (Galatians 6:17; Phil 1:20-21; 3:10)

# How Are we to Respond to the Ways of God we Discover in Creation?

The Psalmist was more than willing to *sing* the praises of the Creator!

⁴You make me glad by your deeds, O LORD; **I sing for joy at the works of your hands**.

⁵How great are your works, O LORD, how profound your thoughts! (Psalm 92:4-5)

One of the best known and beloved hymns is in praise of our triune Creator God!

Holy, holy, holy
Lord, God Almighty
**All Thy works shall praise Thy name**
in earth and sky and sea
Holy, holy, holy
Merciful and mighty
God in three persons blessed Trinity.
    -Reginald Heber (1783-1826)

If you can't sing, are you willing to *ponder?*

Great are the works of the LORD; they are pondered by
all who delight in them (Psalm 111:2)

In design, in size, in number, in excellence all the works of the Lord are
great. 'Even the little things of God are great.' (Spurgeon, 'The Treasury
of David')

God can capture our attention through nature's magnificent beauty.
I recall one summer's eve at sunset standing with my wife and a group of
vacationers on the top of Cadillac Mountain in Maine's Arcadia National
Park watching a stunning sunset. At the moment the sun dipped below
the horizon all of us standing there felt we had enjoyed a 'mountain top
experience'. We spontaneously gave God a loud and long standing ovation!
Our hearts ached with joy!☺ The gorgeous sunset left us all with a deep
yearning for more -more of God's beauty; more of God!

This longing is like "a scent of a flower we have not found;
the echo of a tune we have not heard; news from a far
country we have never yet visited.
(Phillip Yancy, 'Open Windows', p. 148)

Augustine (354-430) writing in his **Confessions** kept this balance
between the Creator and his creation. He acknowledged all the things God
created that he loved. However, he wanted to go on record that he loved
even more the Creator himself knowing that he is infinitely greater than
everything he has made!

What do I love, when I love Thee? Not beauty of bodies,
not the fair harmony of time, not the brightness of the
light, so gladsome to our eyes, nor sweet melodies of varied
songs, nor the fragrant smell of flowers, and ointments,
and spices, not manna and honey, not limbs acceptable to
embracement of flesh. None of these I love, when I love
my God; and yet I love a kind of light, and melody, and
fragrance, and meat, and embracement when I love my
God, the light, melody, fragrance, meat, embracement
of my inner man: where there shines unto my soul what

space cannot contain, and there sounds what time bears not away, and there smell what breathing disperses not, and there taste what eating diminishes not...This is it which I love when I love my God.

Stuart McAllister the regional director at Ravi Zacharias International Ministries writes in 'A Slice of Infinity' (July 24, 2014)

> In today's world, **many are sincerely inspired by nature**. They love long walks, visits to the country, and absorbing the beauties of the world around. They often make nature an end in itself. They celebrate its magnificence, but are left to see it all as a random outcome of chance and necessity. Some Christians, through neglect, do much the same thing...Take a few moments today to look at the birds, contemplate the trees, enjoy a walk, and smell the flowers. Perhaps you may just experience a glimmer of God's glory, too.

But we must not stop with 'nature' in our search to know about God and his ways. Elihu throws out this challenge:

> [2] Bear with me a little longer and I will show you that there is more to be said in God's behalf. (Job 36:2)

Yes, *there is more that can be said about God and his ways* but *the 'voice'* is not coming from nature. We must go beyond the study of nature. It *is God's voice coming from the scriptures* that we must hear! God has thus spoken in the pages of scripture in such a way that we can not only learn all we need to know *about God's ways*, but also we can come to *know him* personally. C.S. Lewis implores us to search for God's ways in Scripture.

> We must leave the hills and woods and go back to our studies, to church, to our Bibles, to our knees, otherwise, the love of nature is beginning to turn into a nature religion...Nature cannot satisfy the desires she arouses nor

answer theological questions....[We must not demand] of nature more than it is designed [by God] to give or you may end up worshipping nature.
(The Four Loves, pp. 24-25)

We have a self-disclosure of the ***ways of God*** in God's own understandable words -the Word of God, the Holy Bible! Accepting what God has said about himself we can not only ***know about God***, but way beyond this we can also ***know God*** personally, trust God completely, love God fervently, serve God willingly, and worship God unendingly.

God through Jeremiah has given hope to all who are truly searching for God with all their heart.

> [7] **I will give them a heart to know me**, that I am the LORD. (Jeremiah 24:7; 29:13)

Here is a surprise! What we discover when we bless God by our faith in him, our love for him, our service to him and our worship of him, we end up being blessed by God. He willingly lets himself be known by us not only by observing him generally in nature, but specifically through his Holy Word! Let's begin to observe **ways** the 'Maker of Heaven and Earth' has also revealed himself to us in the Holy Scriptures.

**Glory be to God for the revelation of his ways in nature** ☺

CHAPTER 3

# The Way of God is Holiness

## God's Way is Holiness

G od alone is holy. This is the conclusion of all the saints in Heaven who have lived on earth from the beginning of time. Their prayer is this:

> [3] Great and marvelous are your deeds, Lord God Almighty. Just and true are your ways, King of the ages.
>
> [4] Who will not fear you, O Lord, and bring glory to your name? For **you alone are holy**. All nations will come and worship before you, for your righteous acts have been revealed. (Revelation 15:3-4)

John Stott observes that to say

> **'God is holy'** is foundational to biblical religion... Christianity is concerned with **God's holiness** before all else." (John Stott, 'The Cross of Christ', p. 102, 131)

## All God's Ways are Holy

> [13] **Your ways, O God, are holy**. What God is so great as our God? (Psalm 77:13)

Scripture discloses that *holiness* is at the root of everything that is true about God and his character. Because he is *holy* we can also count on *all God's ways* being *holy* and righteous, *holy* and true, *holy* and just, *holy* and loving, *holy* and gracious, *holy* and merciful, *holy* and good. *Holiness* is foundational to everything that's true about God.

A.W. Tozar in his book 'The Knowledge of the Holy' writes,

> **Holy** is the **way** God is. To be **holy** he does not conform to a standard. He is that 'standard'. (p. 112)

# What is Meant When We Say that God is Holy?

We cannot grasp the true meaning of the **divine holiness** by thinking of someone or something very pure and then raising the concept to the highest degree we are capable of. **God's holiness** is not simply the best we know infinitely bettered. **We know nothing like the divine holiness.** It stands apart, unique, unapproachable, **incomprehensible** and **unattainable**. The natural man is blind to it. He may fear God's power and admire his wisdom, but his **holiness** he cannot even imagine.
(A.W. Tozar, 'Knowledge of the Holy', p. 111)

John Stott has noted that it's *the cross of Christ* that helps us realize that *God's holiness* is infinite!

The cross is the only place where the loving, forgiving, merciful God is revealed in such a way that we perceive that **his holiness** and **his love** are **equally infinite.**
(John Stott, 'The Cross of Christ', p. 470)

Theologian Rudolf Otto has written a book on the *holiness of God* titled 'The Idea of the Holy'. He identifies the *holiness of God* as the *mysterium tremendum* -a tremendous mystery. Otto speaks of *the Holy God* as being filled

with something which has no place in the natural world of ordinary experience.
(Otto, p. 15)

This was Otto's way of saying God is 'wholly other'. God has gone on record:

[9] "As the heavens are higher than the earth, so are **my ways higher than your ways and my thoughts than your thoughts.** (Isaiah 55:9; 57:15)

We would do well to live with the understanding that there is more to reality than our fallen, sinful world. The **uncreated holy God** exists. In the end of his book 'The Knowledge of the Holy' A.W.Tozar highly recommends we take into consideration throughout every day

> God's utter **holiness** extols continually the greatness of
> His dignity and power. (Ibid, p. 124)

Our awareness of **God's holiness** should make us feel *'awful'* -not a fearful, terrifying, dreadful 'awful', but rather *full of awe* -over awed by the holiness of our *Holy God*!

In Job we find *holiness* contrasted with two *antonyms.*

> [15] If God places no trust in his **holy** ones, if even the heavens are not pure in his eyes,
>
> [16] how much less man, who is **vile** and **corrupt**, who drinks up evil like water! (Job 15:15-16)

*Holiness* is the antithesis of all that is *vile* and *corrupt*. Webster's classic 1828 Dictionary defines the word *'holy'* this way:

**HOLY**, *adjective*

> Whole, entire or perfect, in a moral sense. Hence, pure in heart, temper or dispositions; free from sin and sinful affections. Applied to the Supreme Being, *holy* signifies perfectly pure, immaculate and complete in moral character...We call a man *holy* when his heart is conformed in some degree to the image of God, and his life is regulated by the divine precepts.

As for God himself, he is wholly against ever doing anything wrong, and he is at the same time wholly for doing what is right!

Moses reinforced this truth on the hearts and minds of the people whom he had just led through a divided Red Sea with a high wall of water on either side of their escape route from Egypt. He stood on the far bank of the Red Sea and prayed to God before all the people:

> [11] "Who among the gods is like you, O LORD? Who is like you— **majestic in holiness, awesome in glory**, working wonders? (Exodus 15:11)

The majestic **holiness** of God thundered onto the scene the day Israel was standing at the base of Mt. Sinai -the 'Mountain of God'- and heard the audible voice of God. To say the least, they were shaken in their boots.

> [21] The sight was so terrifying that Moses said, "I am trembling with fear."
> (Hebrews 12:21)

They were so shaken in their boots that they pled they would never hear his voice again.

> [23] When you heard the voice out of the darkness, while the mountain was ablaze with fire, all the leading men of your tribes and your elders came to me.
>
> [24] And you said, "The LORD our God has shown us his glory and his majesty, and we have heard his voice from the fire. Today we have seen that a man can live even if God speaks with him.
>
> [25] But now, why should we die? This great fire will consume us, and **we will die if we hear the voice of the LORD our God any longer.**
>
> [26] For what mortal man has ever heard the voice of the living God speaking out of fire, as we have, and survived? (Deuteronomy 5:23-26)

Hundreds of years later Isaiah had this instruction for Israel.

¹³ The LORD Almighty is the one you are to **regard as holy**, he is the one you are to **fear**, he is the one you are to dread. (Isaiah 8:13)

## God was known as the 'Holy One of Israel'

Over 25 times scripture identifies the one true and living God as the *'Holy One of Israel'*. King David sat on Israel's throne but he willingly gave place to God the true King of Israel, the 'Holy One' of Israel.

³ You are enthroned **as the Holy One**; you are the praise of Israel. (Psalm 22:3; 71:22)

The prophet Isaiah praised the *Holy one of Israel*.

⁶ Shout aloud and sing for joy, people of Zion, for great is the **Holy One of Israel** among you."
(Isaiah 12:6, 17:7, 29:19, 41:14, 47:4, 54:5)

## What Does it Mean that God is 'Holy'?

Andrew Murray has written:

What now is this '**holiness of God**'? It is the highest and most glorious and most all-embracing of all the attributes of God. '**Holiness**' **is the most profound word in the Bible.**
('The Prayer Life' (p. 74)

Consider the word 'perfect'. It seems to be that we have an innate desire for 'perfection'. I recall when I was young hearing over and over again the soap commercial that boasted that the soap being advertised was 99 and 44/100 % pure! More recently I've been submitted to commercials for a mouthwash that supposedly kills 99.9% of germs in the mouth. Because of concern for 'truth in advertising' no one claims 100%.

Unfortunately, where we are not concerned about 100% perfection is with regard to moral purity. No one can boast of 'sinless perfection'. No one seemingly wants to, lest they be labeled as a 'goody-two-shoes'. But God is 'Perfect'! God is not in any way sinful, wicked, immoral, vile or corrupt. He never has been and he never will be. Throughout human history God has made himself known as *perfectly Holy.*

> [14] He is the Rock, his works are **perfect**, and **all his ways are just.** A faithful God who does no wrong, upright and just is he.
> (Deuteronomy 32:4; 2 Sam 22:31; Isa 25:1)

# God is Sinless

The prophet Habakkuk acknowledged God's holy purity.

> [13] Your eyes are **too pure to look on evil;** you cannot tolerate wrong.
> (Habakkuk 1:13)

God is totally *sinless.*

God has never even once been tempted to sin and never will be tempted. James made this abundantly clear when he wrote,

> [13] When tempted, no one should say, "God is tempting me." For **God cannot be tempted by evil,** nor does he tempt anyone; (James 1:13)

In contrast to the *Holy God* the 'righteous deeds' of the holiest person on earth are as 'filthy rags'!

> [6] All our **righteous acts** are like **filthy rags.**
> (Isaiah 64:6)

# Jesus the Son of God is Holy!

One day Simon Peter became acutely aware of the Lord's holiness contrasted with his own sinfulness. This happened when Jesus filled his boat with fish giving Peter an indication of who he really was.

> [8] When Simon Peter saw this, he fell at Jesus' knees and said, **"Go away from me, Lord; I am a sinful man!"** (Luke 5:8)

Peter fell at Jesus' feet perhaps thinking of Job's words:

> [17] 'Can a mortal be more righteous than God? Can a man be more pure than his Maker? (Job 4:17)

Later on Peter wrote with reference to Jesus the 'Son of God',

> [22] **"He committed no sin**, and no deceit was found in his mouth." (1 Peter 2:22)

It's as Paul noted by contrast,

> [23] All have sinned and fall short of the glory of God. (Romans 3:23)

The good news, however, is that God's Holy Son Jesus does not turn away from any 'sinful' man or woman.

> [32] I have not come to call the righteous, but sinners to repentance." (Luke 5:32)

> [10] The Son of Man came **to seek and to save what was lost**." (Luke 19:10)

The sinless, holy purity of the Son of God is our only hope!

> [5] You know that he appeared so that he might take away our sins. And **in him is no sin**. (1 John 3:5)

*Douglas Nelson*

# The Holy God does not Lie

Holiness and lying do not mix. Fran Schaeffer has written:

> The **holiness** of the God who exists demands that there
> be **no compromise in the area of truth**.
> ('Joshua and the Flow of History', p.175)

John believed the words of Jesus

> [7] are the words of him who is **holy and true**. (Revelation 3:7)

These were the very words John heard in Heaven describing God.

> [10] They called out in a loud voice, "How long, Sovereign
> Lord, **holy and true**, until you judge the inhabitants of
> the earth and avenge our blood?"
> (Revelation 6:10)

With our hand resting on a Bible we may swear by God in a court of law that we will "tell the truth, the whole truth and nothing but the truth"; whereas God *swears by his own holiness he will not lie*. The truth of the matter is that the God of all Truth will not and cannot lie!

> [18] It is **impossible for God to lie**. (Hebrews 6:18)

# God's Holiness Provides a Solid Foundation for Life

Hannah had been barren for many years. One time when she was praying she knew in her spirit that the Lord had heard her prayer for a child. She prayed:

> [2] "There is no one **holy** like the LORD; there is no one
> besides you; there is no Rock like our God.
> (1 Samuel 2:2)

Hannah's rock-solid hope in a Holy God was his promise to her that she would give birth a son. She believed her holy God was telling her the truth even though her situation seemed hopeless! That son was Samuel.

## The Triune God is Holy

When we think of God as *triune,* we must think that God the Father, the Son and the Holy Spirit are equally *holy.*

## -God the Father is 'Holy'

When Jesus taught his disciples what to pray, he told them always to begin by praying

> [9] **Our Father** in heaven, **hallowed be your name.** (Matthew 6:9)

Jesus affirmed the *holiness of God his Father* when praying protection over his disciples.

> [11] **Holy Father,** protect them by the power of your name— the name you gave me—so that they may be one as we are one. (John 17:11)

## -God the Son is 'Holy'

Jesus is the **holy** Son of God'. Mary was the first to hear this truth from an angel sent to her from God.

> [35] The angel answered, "The Holy Spirit will come upon you, and the power of the Most High will overshadow you. So the **holy one** to be born will be called **the Son of God.** (Luke 1:35)

The first Christians addressed Jesus as *Holy*.

> [69] We believe and know that you are the **Holy One of God**." (John 6:69)

It is the desire of Christians to be holy like the Lord

> Oh! to be like Thee, oh! to be like Thee,
> Blessed Redeemer, **pure** as Thou art;
> Come in Thy sweetness, come in Thy fullness;
> Stamp Thine own image deep on my heart.
>
> **Oh! to be like Thee, lowly in spirit,**
> ***Holy* and harmless, patient and brave**
> -Thomas Chisholm 1866-1960

Jesus was the *sinless* Son of God who asked his assailants,

> Can any of you prove me guilty of sin? (John 8:46)

No one could! The thief on the cross next to Jesus said of him:

> [41] We are punished justly, for we are getting what our deeds deserve. But this man has **done nothing wrong**." (Luke 23:41)

David prophesied Jesus as the Holy One who would rise from the dead.

> [27] You will not abandon me to the grave, nor will you let your **Holy One** see decay. (Acts 2:27)

Peter quoted this prophecy on the Day of Pentecost when in the public square addressing the very men who had crucified Jesus. His summary observation of the resurrected Lord Jesus Christ was that he was *holy*. He said to those who had orchestrated his crucifixion:

[14] You disowned **the Holy and Righteous One** and asked that a murderer be released to you. (Acts 3:14)

It is because of Jesus' **holiness** that the world has a 'Savior'. Only a person who is without sin qualifies to pay sin's penalty for sinners. Jesus was without sin and, joy of all joys, he was willing to take our place on the cross and die to set us free of the guilt and consequences of our sins.

[21] God made **him who had no sin** to be sin for us, so that in him we might become the righteousness of God. (2 Corinthians 5:21; Heb 4:15; 7:26; 1 Jn 3:5)

# -The Spirit of God is God's 'Holy' Spirit

Even in Old Testament times David knew the Spirit of God to be the *Holy* Spirit. In his prayer of confession he acknowledged God's Spirit as '*Holy*'.

[11] Do not cast me from your presence or take your **Holy Spirit** from me. (Psalm 51:11)

People in Isaiah's day questioned whether or not the Holy Spirit was among them as he had been among their ancestors when they came out of Egypt centuries before.

[11] Then his people recalled the days of old, the days of Moses and his people— where is he who brought them through the sea, with the shepherd of his flock? Where is he who **set his Holy Spirit among them.** (Isaiah 63:11)

Beginning with the first chapter of Matthew in the New Testament the *Holy* Spirit was on the scene.

[18] This is how the birth of Jesus Christ came about: His mother Mary was pledged to be married to Joseph, but

before they came together, she was found to be with child through the **Holy Spirit**. (Matthew 1:18)

Luke records that John the Baptist was filled with the *Holy Spirit* from birth. The angel said to Zechariah,

> [15] He will be great in the sight of the Lord. He is never to take wine or other fermented drink, and he will be **filled with the Holy Spirit** even from birth. (Luke 1:15)

## The Holy Spirit is our spiritual lifeline

At the beginning of Jesus' public ministry John the Baptist announced that the purpose of the Son of God coming into the world was to make it possible for the *Holy Spirit* to take up permanent residence in the lives of those who believe in him.

> [8] I baptize you with water, but he will baptize [immerse] you with the **Holy Spirit**." (Mark 1:8)

> Spiritually, I cannot survive the alien atmosphere of earth without live contact through **the Spirit**...The astronauts walked in the cold, forbidding atmosphere of the moon only by carrying with them resources from another world that would keep them alive. I need just that kind of **reliance on the Spirit of God**. (Paul Brand, 'In His Image', p. 218)

We can rely on the **Holy Spirit** knowing he lives within the hearts of Christians. As the result of **spiritual rebirth** which is the gift of our salvation, Paul makes this point:

> [19] Do you not know that **your body** is a temple of the **Holy Spirit**, who is **in you**, whom you have received from God? You are not your own. (1 Corinthians 6:19)

This is what Paul means by saying the *Spirit of Christ* is <u>in</u> you.

> [9] You…are controlled not by the sinful nature but by the Spirit, if the **Spirit of God** lives in you. And if anyone does not have the **Spirit of Christ**, he does not belong to Christ…
>
> [11] And if **the Spirit of him who raised Jesus from the dead** is living <u>in you</u>, he who raised Christ from the dead will also give life to your mortal bodies through his Spirit, who lives in you. (Romans 8:9, 11)

During my last year of seminary training I was privileged to be a student pastor during a time when a church was searching for a new senior pastor. I recall one Sunday after speaking on this scripture a teenager asked me *how it is possible for the Spirit of Christ to live inside anyone*. It was the first time I was ever asked this question. I was honest in saying that I didn't know how Christ could do this, but I affirmed that it was possible to believe he is able and willing to live within anyone who believes in him even if it's not known how he is able to do so. I don't know if I satisfied this young lady's sincere question that day, but I hope that by now she has opened her heart's door and has for a lifetime known the joy of the sweet presence of Christ's Spirit.

Paul was referring to God's indwelling *Holy Spirit* when he wrote Timothy -a young believer:

> [14] Guard the good deposit that was entrusted to you—guard it with the help of the **Holy Spirit** who **lives in us**. (2 Timothy 1:14)

The indwelling presence of the **Holy Spirit** is the **power** behind the Church's effective gospel witness around the world.

> [8] You will receive **power** when the **Holy** Spirit comes on you; and you will be my witnesses in Jerusalem, and in all Judea and Samaria, and to the ends of the earth." (Acts 1:8)

The presence of the powerful Spirit of the Lord in Paul's life was what convinced the Thessalonians of the truth of the Gospel.

> ⁵ Our gospel came to you not simply with words, but also with **power**, with the **Holy Spirit** and with deep conviction. (1 Thessalonians 1:5)

In many countries where once there was only a handful of Christians, today there are literally millions of Christians in response to the *power of the Holy Spirit* to spiritually transform lives! One of those countries is Myanmar (formerly called Burma). The first American missionaries to arrive there in the early 1800s were Adoniram and Ann Judson. It was over seven years before they knew the joy of seeing anyone come to faith in Christ. Now, two hundred years later it's estimated that there are more than four and a half million Christians in Myanmar -the work of God's powerful Holy spirit (Operation World, 2010, p. 610)

# God's name is Holy

God is not only called 'holy', but his very name is 'Holy'

> ⁹ **Holy and awesome** is his **name**. (Psalm 111:9)

If ever two words belong together it's *holy* and *awesome*. God is zealous when it comes to protecting his awesome, holy name.

> ³ Let them praise your great and **awesome name**— he is **holy**...(Psalm 99:3)

God is so concerned about his *holy name* being upheld that he's carved it in stone as one of his *Ten Commandments.*

> ⁷ You shall **not misuse the name of the LORD your God**, for the LORD will not hold anyone guiltless who misuses his name. (Exodus 20:7; Lev 22:32)

All who put their trust in the Lord have cause to rejoice because they are trusting in *God's holy name.* God backs his promises to us with his own *good name.*

> [21] In him our hearts rejoice, for **we trust in his holy name.** (Psalm 33:21)

Mary is an example of someone who trusted in God's holy Name!

> [49] **The Mighty One** has done **great things for me— holy is his name.** (Luke 1:49)

Can you hear in her voice profound *gratitude and joy?*

> [4] **Sing to the LORD,** you saints of his; **praise his holy name.** (Psalm 30:4; 97:12; 105:3; 145:21)

Do you, like David, feel like singing words of praise to *God's holy name* right now?

> Blessed be the name,
> Blessed be the name.
> Blessed be the name of the Lord.
>
> Blessed be the name,
> Blessed be the name.
> Blessed be the name of the Lord. –Charles Wesley (1707-1788)

# Holy, Holy, Holy

One day Isaiah had a heavenly vision while worshipping in the Temple. He saw the awesome Holy God on his Holy Throne.

> [1] **I saw the Lord seated on a throne,** high and exalted, and the train of his robe filled the temple.

[2] Above him were seraphs, each with six wings: With two wings they covered their faces, with two they covered their feet, and with two they were flying.

[3] And they were calling to one another: "**Holy, holy, holy is the LORD Almighty**; the whole earth is full of his glory."

[4] At the sound of their voices the doorposts and thresholds shook and the temple was filled with smoke. (Isaiah 6:1-4)

How did Isaiah respond to what he saw

[5] "Woe to me!" I cried. "I am ruined! For I am a man of unclean lips, and I live among a people of unclean lips, and my eyes have seen the King, the LORD Almighty." (Isaiah 6:5)

The 19th century poet Karl von Gerok longed to experience what Isaiah experienced. Maybe we can have the same longing.

> *Holy, holy, holy*, blessed Lord, All the choirs of heaven now adore Thee O that I might join that great white host, Casting down their golden crowns before Thee.
> -E.E. Ryden,
> (The Story of Christian Hymnody, p, 157)

Eight hundred years after Isaiah's time John had a vision of heaven, and heard voices singing God's praises. Nothing had changed!

[8] Each of the four living creatures had six wings and was covered with eyes all around, even under his wings. Day and night they never stop saying: "**Holy, Holy, Holy** is the Lord God Almighty, who was, and is, and is to come." (Revelation 4:8)

It's not that the angels have been stuck on the first stanza of this hymn affirming the holiness of God. For them there is no second stanza. The *holiness* of God has left them eternally awestruck knowing there is absolutely nothing that surpasses the *holiness* of God. Tertullian, an early Christian writer, noted that

> the angels who stand nearest the throne of God cry out day and night in endless awe as they search the wonders of God's being. '*Holy, Holy, Holy*' is the cry of unending delight and amazement.
> (Quoted by David Hazard in 'You Give Me New Life', p. 76)

God's *holiness* is the only '*way of God*' that is mentioned in triplicate: *Holy, Holy, Holy*. The Authors of scripture never fuse together 'love, love, love; grace, grace, grace, mercy, mercy, mercy, etc. Why '*Holy, Holy, Holy*'? There is no definitive explanation in scripture, but I would like to think it might be a reference to the *Trinity*: God the *Holy* Father, the *Holy* Son of God, and the *Holy* Spirit. *Holiness* -perfect, pure, sinless- has forever been foundational to the very nature and character of the Father, Son and Holy Spirit!

I once heard the testimony of an Eastern European Christian who had been arrested when exiting a Middle Eastern airport and incarcerated for over a year -confined in a tiny cell with several prisoners who mistreated him horribly. He said that one verse of Scripture sustained him through it all, Revelation 4:8. He surmised that if the angels for endless years have never tired of praising God's holiness, he determined to join his voice with theirs, and never tire of calling out "*Holy, Holy, Holy is the Lord God Almighty, who was, and is, and is to come.*"

The Psalmist never lost sight of the fact that God is forever '*holy*' and worthy of worship.

⁹ Exalt the LORD our God and **worship at his holy mountain**, for the LORD our **God is holy.**
(Psalm 99:9)

# Holy ground (earth)

Do we need to wait till heaven to worship our *holy* God, or can we do so here and now on earth? Moses learned that wherever on earth the Lord reveals himself is *holy ground*. He was instructed at the 'burning bush' to remove his sandals as a mark of respect of God's holy presence.

> [5] "Do not come any closer," God said. "Take off your sandals, for the place where you are standing is **holy ground**." (Exodus 3:5)

The ground was made holy by God's presence. Forty years later, Joshua was given the same instruction.

> [15] The commander of the LORD's army replied, "Take off your sandals, for **the place where you are standing is holy**." And Joshua did so. (Joshua 5:15)

David came to understand that God had chosen Jerusalem to be his holy dwelling place on earth.

> [25] David... said, "The LORD, the God of Israel, has granted rest to his people and has come to **dwell in Jerusalem forever**. (1 Chronicles 23:25; Ps 68:16)

> [20] **The LORD is in his holy temple**; let all the earth **be silent** before him." (Habakkuk 2:20)

My wife and I have had the privilege of visiting the Temple Mount in Jerusalem where the Temple once stood. (It was there that God resided in the Temple's *Holy of Holies*.) We were told we could not walk on the Temple Mount wearing shoes. We gladly removed them as instructed by our Islamic guide. But I think there's more to the story. The Temple is long gone, but I think the spot where the *Holy of Holies* once stood is still *holy ground*. How appropriate it was for us to remove our shoes conscious that God was still very much present at that *holy* spot!

If *Heaven is the 'Throne of God'*, surely the Temple on Mount Zion is *God's 'Footstool'*!

> [5] Exalt the LORD our God and **worship** *at his* **footstool**; he is **holy.** (Psalm 99:5)

The Temple mount, however, is not God's only dwelling place on earth today. Anywhere we bow before God in prayer we are in his presence.

> [7] The LORD our **God is near** us whenever we pray to him. (Deuteronomy 4:7)

The question is how we should present ourselves when coming into the presence of a *Holy* God? Not bared feet, but stunned silence! John Piper notes in his book 'Desiring God',

> "Perhaps the first response of the heart at seeing the majestic **holiness** of God is **stunned silence**." (p. 68)

Song writer Bart Millard muses what being in the Lord's presence in heaven will be like.

> What will my heart feel
> Will I dance for you Jesus
> Or in awe of You be still
> Will I stand in your presence
> Or to my knees will I fall
> Will I sing hallelujah
> Will I be able to speak at all
> I can only imagine.

*Quiet Humility* is the only appropriate response when approaching the *Holy God*.

> [10] "**Be still**, and know that I am God; I will be exalted among the nations, I will be exalted in the earth." (Psalm 46:10)

*Douglas Nelson*

# Fear Our Holy God

[10] "The **fear of the LORD is the beginning of wisdom**,
and knowledge of the Holy One is understanding.
(Proverbs 9:10)

Several times in Scripture we are exhorted to maintain a holy fear of
the Lord, as being the wisest thing we can do. To *fear* God is to *honor*,
and *revere* and *esteem* God. In a word, it is to *delight in worshiping* our
*holy* God heart and soul because he is worthy!

[8] Let all the earth **fear** the LORD; let all the people of the
world **revere** him. (Psalm 33:8)

How can we express the 'fear of the Lord'? By *meditating on his
holiness* until the very thought grips us with a '*holy fear*' that takes our
breath away. *God's holiness* is so awesome, so overwhelming, so majestic,
so stunning that it should drive us to our knees. When we acknowledge
*God's holiness on earth* we are simply confirming what is already being
acknowledged in Heaven.

When we sing the hymn '**Holy, Holy, Holy**' we're joining voices
with the angles and all the saints in heaven. In fact, how about taking a
break from reading, and focus on God's holiness by singing in your heart
or out loud this great hymn of the church written by Reginald Heber!
(1783-1836)

**Holy, Holy, Holy**! Lord God Almighty!
Early in the morning our song shall rise to Thee.
Holy, Holy, Holy! Merciful and Mighty!
God in Three Persons, blessed Trinity!

**Holy, Holy, Holy**! all the saints adore Thee,
Casting down their golden crowns around the glassy sea;
Cherubim and Seraphim falling down before Thee,
Which wert, and art, and evermore shalt be.

**Holy, Holy, Holy**! though the darkness hide Thee,
Though the eye of sinful man Thy glory may not see:
Only Thou art holy, there is none beside Thee,
Perfect in power, in love, and purity.

**Holy, Holy, Holy**! Lord God Almighty
All Thy works shall praise thy name in earth and sky
and sea;
Holy, Holy, Holy! Merciful and Mighty
God in Three Persons, blessed Trinity!

## God's Word is Holy

We reverently call the Scriptures 'the *Holy* Bible' because it is the *great and glorious and true Word of God!*

[21] It pleased the LORD for the sake of his righteousness to make **his law great and glorious**. (Isaiah 42:21)

It was David's firm conviction that *God's Word* was exalted because it is *flawless* -reflecting *God's holy way* which is *perfect*.

[30] As for God, **his way** is **perfect**; the **word of the LORD** is **flawless**. (Psalm 18:30)

Of all the nations of the world, Israel had the unique privilege of being the conduit for the very words of the holy God to be spoken to the whole world.

[8] What other nation is so great as to have such **righteous decrees and laws** as this body of laws I am setting before you today? (Deuteronomy 4:8)

Peter affirmed that the Authors of Scripture knew what they wrote was inspired by God's Holy Spirit.

²¹ Prophecy never had its origin in the will of man, but men spoke from God as they were carried along by the **Holy Spirit**. (2 Peter 1:21)

It was Paul's understanding that what he spoke were not his words but were actually the holy inspired Words of God. He reminded the Thessalonians,

¹³ When you received the **word of God**, which you heard from us, you accepted it not as the **word of men**, but as it actually is, the **word of God**, which is at work in you who believe. (1 Thessalonians 2:13)

## Truth is the standard for God's Holy words

Recall Jesus' commitment to Truth!

³⁷ For this reason I was born, and for this **I came into the world, to testify to the truth**. Everyone on the side of **truth** listens to me. (John 18:37)

¹⁷ Sanctify them by the truth; **your word is truth**. (John 17:17)

Paul affirmed to the Corinthian Christians (and to us who believe) that

²⁰ No matter how many **promises** God has made, **they are "Yes" in Christ**. (2 Corinthians 1:20)

This is the way it has always been.

¹⁴⁰ Your **promises** have been thoroughly tested, and your servant loves them.

[148] My eyes stay open through the watches of the night,
that I may meditate on your **promises**.
(Psalm 119:149, 148)

The young missionary Harriet Newell wrote in her journal while aboard a sailing ship in the early 1800s heading from Boston to India to become a missionary,

*Sooner will the universe sink into nothing,*
*than God fail of performing his promises.*

My wife and I can relate to Harriet's words. Over the years we've travelled to India 14 times to teach the Holy Scriptures to church leaders in marriage and family conferences. We made these long trips convinced that what we had to share with them was the true Word of God. It would have been a waste of time and energy to teach what is not true. But the Word of God is true, and this has made all the difference in the form of spiritually transformed lives.

# The Command to be holy

*God is holy*, and he wants those who believe in him to *reflect his holiness* in their everyday lives.

[26] **You are to be holy** to me because I, the LORD, am holy, and I have set you apart from the nations to be my own. (Leviticus 20: 26)

[9] God has saved us and **called us to a holy life—not because of anything we have done** but because of his own purpose and grace.
(2 Timothy 1:9; 1 Pe 1:15; 2 Pe 3:11)

# Define Holiness as Separation

In biblical times God called out Israel from the rest of the world and separated this one nation unto himself. Shortly after the exodus from Egypt God confirmed the distinctive separation he was making between the descendants of Abraham who lived by faith from the rest of mankind. The distinction was '*holiness*'. God instructed Moses to declare to the Israelites,

> [6] You will be for me a kingdom of priests and a **holy nation**.
> (Exodus 19:6; 22:31; Lev 20:24, 26; Deut 7:6; 26:17, 19)

The word '*separation*' defines the word *holy* as well as any word does. It represents a willingness to follow in Jesus' footsteps who 'separated' himself from sinners. The Author of Hebrews was referring to Jesus when he wrote,

> [26] Such a high priest meets our need—one who is **holy**, blameless, pure, **set apart from sinners**, exalted above the heavens. (Hebrews 7:26; Ps 4:3)

True believers *desire to separate themselves from sin,* because God has put this desire and ability in them. We cannot make ourselves holy, but we can invite the Lord to make us holy through his Holy Spirit's presence and power within us. So any 'holiness' seen in our lives is not our doing but the Lord's doing. *Holiness*, then, is all about *God separating us* from anything and everything that is sinful, impure or evil in thought, word or deed, and enabling us to live holy lives powered by his Holy Spirit within us.

# Being Made Holy is an Ongoing Process

> [14] By one sacrifice he has **made perfect** forever those who are **being made holy** (Hebrews 10:14)

It's good to know that becoming holy and being holy is not the result of self-effort; it's all the work of God's indwelling *Holy* Spirit whom we invite to take over our lives!

> ⁸ I am the LORD, **who makes you holy.**
> (Leviticus 20:8)

Although God sees us as '*Perfect*' in his sight from the moment of salvation as we stand before him clothed in Christ's imputed righteousness; *becoming holy* (spiritually mature) by contrast is *a process* that is ongoing. We are once and for all *made Perfect* from the moment of salvation, nevertheless we are still in the daily *process of being made holy*. In and of ourselves we are neither 'perfect' nor 'holy'. It's all the work of God in our lives. He has *made us 'perfect'* –perfectly acceptable (clothed as we are in Christ's 'righteousness'), while at the same time continuing *in the daily process of being made 'holy'.*

Our *position* in Christ is that he has made us *perfect* once and for all by means of his shed blood resulting in the forgiveness of all our sins, the cancelling of being punished for our sins, and the granting of the gift of eternal life.

By contrast, we become *progressively more holy* moment-by-moment, *by giving place to the presence and the strength of the indwelling Holy Spirit.* This is all about the life-long process of becoming *spiritually mature* resulting in more, and greater and longer lasting victories over ongoing temptations to sin. Praise the Lord!

> ¹⁴ By one sacrifice he has **made perfect (positional)** forever those who are **being made holy (progressive).**
> (Hebrews 10:14)

It's God's Spirit within us as believers who gives us *the desire* and *the ability to live a holy life.*

> ¹³ It is God who works in you to will and to act according to his good purpose.
> (Philippians 2:13; 2 Cor 7:1)

It must be possible to 'be holy' in that God does not ask us to do what is impossible. The Holy Spirit living within us makes it possible.

> [15]Just as he who called you is holy, so **be holy** in all you do. (1 Peter 1:15)

It was with great concern that David pleaded with God after his adulterous affair with Bathsheba not to take his ***Holy Spirit*** from him. He knew it was only God's Spirit within him that could give him once again a 'pure heart' and return the 'joy' of his salvation. This alone would sustain him.

> [10] Create in me **a pure heart**, O God, and renew a **steadfast spirit** within me.

> [11] Do not cast me from your presence or take your **Holy Spirit** from me.

> [12] **Restore to me the joy of your salvation** and grant me a willing spirit, to sustain me. (Psalm 51:10-12)

God offers us this same Holy Spirit, who is able to transform our lives from being sinful to becoming increasingly holy, pleasing and blameless in God's sight! What we once were is not what the Lord wants to enable us to become. God himself does the transforming by the work of the Holy Spirit in us. It is in the strength of the Holy Spirit we find ourselves increasingly being able to say yes to what is right and no to what is wrong.

# What Does Being Holy Look Like

> [3] Among you there must not be even a hint of sexual immorality, or of any kind of impurity, or of greed, because these are improper for God's **holy** people. (Ephesians 5:3)

Holy means being '**blameless**', that is, without reproach.

Job was a good and godly man, "blameless and upright" (Job 1:1), meaning that he was beyond reproach. No one could make a charge against him in any area of his life. (Timothy Keller, Walking With God Through Pain and Suffering, p. 271)

We are *blameless* in God's sight due to his cleansing us from all sin and clothing us in his own righteousness.

> [4] He chose us in him before the creation of the world to be **holy and blameless** in his sight. In love (Ephesians 1:4)

> [37] Consider the **blameless**, observe the upright; there is a future for the man of peace. (Psalm 37:37)

> [11] The LORD God is a sun and shield; the LORD bestows favor and honor; no good thing does he withhold from those whose walk is **blameless**. (Psalm 84:11)

It's God's intention that we lead **blameless** lives.

> [7] The righteous man leads a **blameless** life; blessed are his children after him. (Proverbs 20:7)

> [14] Do everything without complaining or arguing,

> [15] so that you may become **blameless** and pure, children of God without fault in a crooked and depraved generation, in which you **shine like stars in the universe.** (Philippians 2:14-15)

Noah led a **blameless** life in his generation.

> [9] Noah was a righteous man, **blameless** among the people of his time, and he walked with God. (Genesis 6:9)

The Lord wants **blameless** people living on earth till the day of his return.

> ⁷ You do not lack any spiritual gift as you eagerly wait for our Lord Jesus Christ to be revealed.
>
> ⁸ He will keep you strong to the end, so that you will be **blameless on the day of our Lord Jesus Christ.**
> (1 Corinthians 1:7-8)
>
> ⁹ This is my prayer: that your love may abound more and more in knowledge and depth of insight,
>
> ¹⁰ so that you may be able to discern what is best and may be pure and **blameless until the day of Christ.**
> (Philippians 1:9-10)

# How to be holy

From the day of your repentance and conversion to Jesus as your Savior what changes is that from now on you have the permanent presence of the Holy Spirit in you which is God's gift to you.

> ³⁸ Peter replied, "Repent and be baptized, every one of you, in the name of Jesus Christ for the forgiveness of your sins. And you will receive the **gift of the Holy Spirit.**
> (Acts 2:38)

Then, begin discovering 'spiritual gifts' that accompany the Holy Spirit's presence within you, and accessing them by inviting the Holy Spirit to produce in you the fruit of his presence, namely, love, joy, peace, patience, kindness, goodness, faithfulness, gentleness and self-control. This is how the Lord *'makes anyone holy'*.

# How God Deals with Anyone Who Despises His Holiness

Sin is an affront to *God's holiness*. God will not let our sinful words and actions go unaddressed, because he is *jealous to guard his holiness*. He does not just stand by, and let his *holy name* be defamed. Here, for example, was what Isaiah faced head on as he recorded in the very first chapter of his prophecy the condition of a nation of people who *despised God's holiness*.

> [4] Ah, sinful nation, a people loaded with guilt, a brood of evildoers, children given to corruption! They have forsaken the LORD; **they have spurned the Holy One of Israel** and turned their backs on him. (Isaiah 1:4)

Hosea, Isaiah's contemporary, made the same grim report.

> [12] Ephraim has surrounded me with lies, the house of Israel with deceit. And Judah is unruly against God, even against the faithful Holy One. (Hosea 11:12)

They had spurned their holy God. Really? There was something terribly wrong with that picture. No one should spurn the holy God, but, rather, humbly bow before him. Something needed to change and it wasn't God. They needed to change. They needed to stop showing contempt for God, and start showing contempt for their own sins by confessing and forsaking them They needed to do an about face by expressing a willingness to worship their *holy God*, and reflect his *holiness* in their lives.

How did they get to such a deplorable condition that they actually spurned God? Once they had been faithful to the Lord, and to each other, but everything had changed; everything had gone from bad to worse.

> [21] See how **the faithful city has become a harlot**! She once was full of justice; righteousness used to dwell in her— **but now murderers**! (Isaiah 1:21)

Gradually they began to decline a slippery slope by increasingly mistreating one another. Then they crossed a line, and gave way to all forms of outright wickedness -resorting even to murdering anyone who stood in their way.

God was *not negligent* in dealing with their sinful disobedience because he is both *holy and just!*

> [16] The LORD Almighty will be **exalted by his justice,** and **the holy God** will show himself **holy by his righteousness.** (Isaiah 5:16)

Because God is **holy** he is duty bound to exercise his justice by disciplining unholy people who defile his Name.

## God Desires for Us to Radiate His Holiness

Let's accept the challenge set forth in Hebrews.

> [4] Make every effort to live in peace with all men and to **be holy;** without holiness no one will see the Lord. (Hebrews 12:14)

It's only when we are living *holy lives* that anyone can 'see the Lord' in us! And, yes, the watching world needs to see that the only thing that can explain our words, our attitudes, our actions is that we truly are under the control of the *Holy Spirit of God.* More than we realize, people define 'God' by what they observe in those who claim to be 'godly'. No one will conclude *God is holy* unless they *see the holiness of God radiating out of Christian lives.* However, we must never forget to let the world know that *it is God who makes us holy and not ourselves.*

> [23] The nations will know that I am the LORD, declares the Sovereign LORD, when **I show myself holy through you before their eyes.** (Ezekiel 36:23)

# God Makes Us in the Process of Time into His Holy Saints

Tim Keller states it well with regard to the process of *being made holy*.

> In reality, we know that there are some deep things in our hearts that will thwart us from becoming the true selves we should be. The **process of sanctification**, of growth into the likeness of Christ...is the **process of becoming the true self God created us to be**. (Preaching, p. 139)

It's critical to note that holiness is not something we achieve through self-effort. We do not make ourselves 'saints' by self-effort. We are 'saints' as the result of being *made holy by the work of the Holy Spirit* in our lives.

> [8]I am the LORD, who **makes you holy**.
> (Leviticus 20:8; Heb 2:11)

With the *Holy Spirit of God* within them enabling them to do what pleases the Lord, Christians do what God asks of them *not because* they have to, *but because* they want to (and can in the power of the Holy Spirit) as an expression of their love for the Lord!

Jesus makes it so simple that he gets living a holy life down to one sentence. Here it is: it's the *'Golden Rule'* coming from his lips.

> [31] **Do to others as you would have them do to you**.
> (Luke 6:31; Matt 25:40)

For those who need more specifics as to what *living a 'holy life'* looks like, Paul provides the following:

> [31] **Get rid of all bitterness, rage** and **anger, brawling** and **slander, along with every form of malice.**

> [32] **Be kind** and **compassionate** to one another, **forgiving each other**, just as in Christ God forgave you.
> (Ephesians 4:31-32, 25-32; 1 Thess 4:3-4, 7-8)

These moral constraints are rejected by selfish, lawless people who want to live free from any moral restraint. Let us not allow anything deter us from living a **holy life** which expresses selfless love for others by what we say and do for the glory of God.

David summed it up this way:

> [3] **As for the saints** who are in the land, **they are the glorious ones** in whom is all my delight.
> (Psalm 16:3)

# Worship the Lord in the 'Splendor of His Holiness'

> [2] Ascribe to the LORD the **glory** due his name; worship the LORD in the **splendor of his holiness.**
> (Psalm 29:2, 8:1; 96:9; 1 Chron 16:29)

God is 'holy' and the splendor of his holiness will last forever as is noted by the voices around God's Throne in Heaven which cry out ceaselessly, 'Holy, Holy, Holy is the Lord God Almighty!'.

The good news for us is that being in Christ Jesus *our holiness* will *also continue on forever* in Heaven. Note that one of the last things mentioned in Scripture is that *we will remain holy.*

> **Let him who is holy continue to be holy."**
> (Revelation 22:11)

In the last book of the Bible John foresaw a day in the distant future when all redeemed humanity will be gathered around God's Heavenly Throne. He heard everyone singing these words:

> [4] "Who will not fear you, O Lord, and bring **glory to your name**? For **you alone are holy."** (Revelation 15:3-4)

**To our Holy God be the Glory!**

CHAPTER 4

# The Way of God is Righteousness

Scripture affirms from beginning to end that *God is righteous* and *he is righteous in all his many ways.* The words *righteous* and *righteousness* appear a total of 125 times in the Psalter's 150 Psalms. It is fitting that in the last Psalm attributed to David he concluded that

> [17] The LORD is **righteous** in **all his ways** and loving toward all he has made. (Psalm 145:17)

About 250 years later the prophet Isaiah found himself living among a people who had abandoned *justice* and *righteousness* -the very things God looks for in people whom he has created in his image to *reflect his own justice and righteousness.*

> [7] The LORD Almighty...looked for **justice**, but saw bloodshed; for **righteousness**, but heard cries of distress. (Isaiah 5:7)

Isaiah was increasingly aware of the fact that although people in his day were abandoning righteousness for unrighteousness, God had not ceased being holy and righteous.

> [16] The LORD Almighty...**the holy God** will show himself **holy** by his **righteousness**. (Isaiah 5:16)

Beginning in Genesis and throughout the Bible God can be observed expressing his *righteousness.* For example, when God confided with Abraham that he was about to destroy the wicked city of Sodom, Abraham voiced his concern.

> [25] Far be it from you to do such a thing—to kill the **righteous** with the wicked, treating the **righteous** and the wicked alike. Far be it from you! Will not the Judge of all the earth do **right**?" (Genesis 18:25)

The prophet Zephaniah, for example, noted that although the world (like Sodom) is sinful, God remains totally *righteous.* To make his point the prophet contrasted the *wicked city* of Jerusalem with the *righteousness of God.*

¹ Woe to the **city of oppressors**, rebellious and defiled…

⁵ **The LORD within her is righteous**; he does no wrong. Morning by morning he dispenses his justice, and every new day he does not fail, yet the unrighteous know no shame. (Zephaniah 3:1, 5)

# Definition of 'Righteousness'

To understand what is meant by saying God is *righteous* it is necessary to define the word. Simply put, what is *'righteous' is what is completely right*. C.S. Lewis writes,

It has sometimes been asked whether God commands certain things because they are **right**, or whether certain things are **right** because God commands them. Because God is **prior** to everything; he is the **first cause** of everything -even when it comes to defining what is 'right' and 'wrong'. It seems God had already determined in himself that 'right' and 'wrong' in creation would reflect his own eternal commitment to himself to do only what he would call 'right'. Therefore 'right' **is whatever God does**; wrong is whatever he has never done, never will do. ('The Problem of Pain', p.100)

What does '*the way of God is righteous*' mean?

"God's righteousness means that **God always acts in accordance with what is right** and is himself the final standard of what is right…If indeed God is the final standard of righteousness, then there can be no standard outside of God by which we measure righteousness…He himself is the final standard."
(Wayne Grudem, 'Systematic Theology', pp. 203-204)

Moses, the first of the biblical authors, was profoundly aware of *God's righteous ways*. He came to the conviction that God would prove himself *righteous* even though Israel was at the time enslaved to unrighteous and cruel Egyptian taskmasters. Pharaoh was unrighteous in the way he abused his Hebrew slaves, but in the midst of the ten plagues he summoned Moses to the palace and confessed to him.

> 27 "This time I have sinned," he said to them. **"The LORD is in the right**, and I and my people are in the wrong." (Exodus 9:27)

God through Isaiah the prophet brought this indictment against backslidden Israel. They didn't want to be 'righteous' so they set about redefining 'right' and 'wrong' by calling good 'evil' and evil 'good'. Isaiah gave this caution:

> 20 Woe to those who call evil good and good evil, who put darkness for light and light for darkness, who put bitter for sweet and sweet for bitter. (Isaiah 5:20; 29:16)

This is the vain attempt of the *unrighteous* to redesign reality after their liking by calling what God calls 'good' 'evil' and what God calls 'evil' 'good'. God is not beholding to us to make reality whatever we want it to be. We must conform to reality as our righteous God has created it to be.

## God is Righteous in all His Ways

David and the Psalmists were more than willing to focus everyone's attention on *God's righteousness*.

> 13 **Righteousness** goes before him and prepares **the way** for his steps.
> (Psalm 85:13; Psalm 119:137; 11:7, 31:1, 40:10, 71:16, 85:13)

*Isaiah* had the assurance that God would always stretch forth his *righteous right hand* to help him.

> ¹⁰ Do not fear, for I am with you; do not be dismayed, for I am your God. I will strengthen you and help you; I will uphold you with my **righteous** right hand. (Isaiah 41:10)

> ²¹ There is no God apart from me, **a righteous God** and a Savior; there is none but me. (Isaiah 45:21)

God is referred to in Scripture as '*The Righteous One*'

> ¹⁶ From the ends of the earth we hear singing: "Glory to the **Righteous One**. (Isaiah 24:16; Prov 21:12)

*Paul* focused on the *durability* of God's *righteousness*.

> ⁹ As it is written: 'He has scattered abroad his gifts to the poor; his **righteousness endures forever**.'
> (2 Corinthians 9:9)

We live in a fallen sinful world, and there are times when things seem so out of control we are tempted to *doubt God's righteousness endures at all, much less forever*. The authors of Scripture encourage us to see the 'big picture' and know that on every occasion God will unfailingly validate his righteousness before all is said and done, From now till the end of time our task is to wait on the Lord giving him time and space to validate his righteousness even in seemingly impossible situations.

*Micah* lived at a time when Israel was spiritually apostate and ripe for judgment, but he held out for God's *righteousness* to win the day.

> ⁹ Because I have sinned against him, I will bear the LORD's wrath, until he pleads my case and establishes my right. He will bring me out into the light; **I will see his righteousness**. (Micah 7:9)

*Douglas Nelson*

# God Delights in Righteousness

> [5] The LORD **loves righteousness** and justice.
> (Psalm 33:5)

Korah bundled *righteousness* together with *love, faithfulness and peace.*

> [10] Love and faithfulness meet together; **righteousness** and peace kiss each other.

> [11] Faithfulness springs forth from the earth, and **righteousness** looks down from heaven...

> [13] **Righteousness** goes before him and prepares the way for his steps. (Psalm 85:10-11,13)

Yes, may our Good Shepherd

> [3] lead us in paths of **righteousness** for his name's sake.'
> (Psalm 23:3)

The prophet Hosea agrees:

> [9] The **ways** of the LORD **are right**; the **righteous walk in them,** but the rebellious stumble in them. (Hosea 14:9)

God's own *righteousness* is extensive, as Samuel noted at the end of a long life of service to his righteous God.

> [7] 'Now then, stand here, because I am going to confront you with evidence before the LORD as to **all** the **righteous acts performed by the LORD** for you and your fathers.'
> (1 Samuel 12:7)

David (whom Samuel had mentored) believed he was praying to a *righteous God*; therefore, he was confident God would always come to his aid and sustain him in his difficulties.

> [1] Answer me when I call to you, O **my righteous God.** Give me relief from my distress; be merciful to me and hear my prayer. (Psalm 4:1, 7:9)

The magnitude of God's ***unchanging righteousness*** gave David an ***increased incentive to pray,***

> [5] You answer us with **awesome deeds of righteousness,** O God our Savior, the hope of all the ends of the earth and of the farthest seas. (Psalm 65:5, 36:6, 71:19)

# Righteousness is Enduring

'*Everlasting*' is another way of looking at **God's righteousness.**

> [142] Your **righteousness is everlasting** and your law is true.

> [160] All your words are true; all your **righteous laws** are **eternal.** (Psalm 119: 142, 160)

If there is anything we want to last forever it is '*righteousness*' and it is our '*salvation*'

> [6] My **salvation** will last forever, my **righteousness** will never fail...

> [8] my **righteousness** will last forever, my **salvation** through all generations. (Isaiah 5:6, 8, 51:6)

'Righteousness' will be the last act in human history, and according to Peter it is going to last forever.

¹³ We are looking forward to a new heaven and a new earth, the **home of righteousness.**
(2 Peter 3:13)

The ancient Psalmist knew even in his day that his only hope was that God's righteousness alone would preserve his life.

⁴⁰ **Preserve** my life **in your righteousness.**
(Psalm 119:40)

# God's Righteousness is Revealed in Jesus Christ

In only a matter of days after Christ's death and resurrection Peter stood in the Temple courtyard and addressed those who had called for Jesus' crucifixion.

¹⁴ You disowned the Holy and **Righteous One** and asked that a murderer be released to you.'
(Acts 3:14)

Stephen, in his very last words just moments before being stoned to death, reaffirmed his conviction that Jesus was the *Righteous One.*

⁵² Was there ever a prophet your fathers did not persecute? They even killed those who predicted the coming of the **Righteous One**. And now you have betrayed and murdered him. (Acts 7:52)

Surely no one would willingly lay down his life for an *unrighteous* man. Stephen was willing to lay down his life for Jesus 'the *Righteous One*'!

*Saul of Tarsus* was stopped him in his tracks on the road to Damascus by the *'Righteous One'*. Years later when on trial he reviewed that moment before those assembled in the court room. He repeated the words he had heard from the lips of Ananias on the day of his conversion.

¹⁴ He said: 'The God of our fathers has chosen you to know his will and to see the **Righteous One** and to hear words from his mouth.'(Acts 22:14)

The good news we learn from *John* is that *we also* have access to the *Righteous One* –even if we have sinned.

¹ My dear children, I write this to you so that you will not sin. But if anybody does sin, we have one who speaks to the Father in our defense—Jesus Christ, the **Righteous One**.

² He is the atoning sacrifice for our sins, and not only for ours but also for the sins of the whole world. (1 John 2:1-2)

**Christ's righteousness** is plainly seen by all in heaven.

⁴ Who will not fear you, O Lord, and bring glory to your name? For you alone are holy. All nations will come and worship before you, for **your righteous acts** have been revealed." (Revelation 15:4)

John Sellers in one of his praise songs pens the words:
'You are crowned with many crowns, and rule all things in **righteousness...** You rule in power and reign in glory! You are the Lord of heaven and earth! You are the Lord of all!'

# The Imputed Righteousness of the Son of God

The Son of God is willing to *credit us with his own righteousness* thus making us acceptable to God with none of our sins ever being held against us. *'Impute'* may not be a familiar word to you in that this word doesn't normally come up in daily conversation. The dictionary definition of 'impute' is

'to ascribe, assign, attribute goodness [righteousness] to a person as coming from another.'

Douglas Nelson

(New World Dictionary; Webster's Dictionary 1828)

*Paul* understood *imputed righteousness* and spelled it out plainly.

> [21] **A righteousness <u>from</u> God, apart from law,** has been made known...

> [22] This **righteousness <u>from</u> God comes through faith in Jesus Christ** to all who believe. (Romans 3:21-22)

Paul gave an illustration of what this looks like when God is doing the imputing.

> [3] What does the Scripture say? "Abraham believed God, and it **was credited to him as righteousness."**

> [4] Now when a man works, his wages are not credited to him as a gift, but as an obligation.

> [5] However, to the man who does not work but trusts God who justifies the wicked, his **faith is credited as righteousness.** (Romans 4:3-5)

James echoed Paul's words.

> [23] The scripture was fulfilled that says, "Abraham **believed God,** and **it was credited to him as righteousness,"** and he was called God's friend. (James 2:23)

*God imputed righteousness* to Abraham *in response to his faith*. His 'faith' was all about believing God justified him without requiring him to work to earn righteousness.

The result of *righteousness imputed to <u>our</u> account* is sins forgiven and never counted against us at the Last Judgment

> [7] Blessed are they whose transgressions are forgiven, whose sins are covered.

[8] Blessed is the man whose sin the Lord will **never** count against him. (Romans 4:7-8)

Paul noted that this is the *result of God's Grace.*

[21] I do not set aside **the grace of God, for if righteousness could be gained through the law, Christ died for nothing!"** (Galatians 2:21)

What Paul meant by this is that if we can gain entrance into heaven on the basis of our good works it would have been insane for God to put his Son through the excruciating suffering of the cross and the agony of death on behalf of sinners.

[21] God made him who had no sin to be sin for us, **so that in him we might become the righteousness of God.** (2 Corinthians 5:21)

[30] You are in Christ Jesus, who has become for us wisdom from God—that is**, our righteousness**, holiness and redemption. (1 Corinthians 1:30)

[26] You are all sons of God through faith in Christ Jesus,

[27] for all of you who were baptized into Christ have **clothed yourselves with Christ.** (Galatians 3:26-27)

By this Paul means 'clothed in *Christ's* righteousness'.

This was all predicted by Jeremiah who anticipated the coming of the Messiah whom he called 'A *righteous* Branch'.

[5] "The days are coming," declares the LORD, "when I will raise up to David **a righteous Branch**, a King who will reign wisely and do what is just and **right** in the land.

⁶ In his days Judah will be saved and Israel will live in safety. This is the name by which he will be called: **The LORD Our Righteousness.**
(Jeremiah 23:5-6)

He took our sin in His own body and died our death so we could live His life; **He took our sin so we could take His righteousness.**
(O.S. Hawkins, 'The Believer's Code', p. 114)

God declares righteous those who have faith in Jesus... There can be no doubt that those whom God declares righteous are righteous...**Here is solved the apparent paradox of a righteous God declaring sinners righteous.**
(Baker Bible Dictionary, p. 462)

⁴ Christ is the end of the law so that there may be **righteousness for everyone who believes.**
(Romans 10:4)

When *Adam and Eve* sinned they attempted to cover their sinful shame with an inadequate covering of fig leaves. God gave them a *covering* of animal skins. Thus God began to teach mankind that

²² Without the shedding of blood there is no forgiveness.
(Hebrews 9:22)

For God to cover Adam and Eve with animal skins meant the death of the animals. We all need a covering for our sin and shame that meets God's approval. The 'Lamb skin' that covers our sinful nakedness to God is the righteousness of the slain Lamb of God.

²⁹ John saw Jesus coming toward him and said, "Look, the Lamb of God, who takes away the sin of the world!
(John 1:29)

Jesus is known in Heaven as the 'slain Lamb of God'.

⁶ Then I saw a Lamb, looking as if it had been slain, standing in the center of the throne. (Revelation 5:6)

People living as far back in history as **Job** understood the concept of *imputed* righteousness.

¹⁴ *I put on righteousness* as my clothing; justice was my robe and my turban. (Job 29:14)

*Abraham* understood God's *imputed substitutionary righteousness* when God asked him to sacrifice his son, but then provided a lamb for him in his son's place.

¹³ Abraham looked up and there in a thicket **he saw a ram** caught by its horns. He went over and took the ram and **sacrificed it as a burnt offering instead of his son.** (Genesis 22:13)

The *Psalmist* understood *imputed righteousness* as a covering for sin, as symbolized in the clothing of Israel's priests who represented God before the people.

⁹ May your priests be **clothed with righteousness**; may your saints sing for joy." (Psalm 132:9)

*Isaiah* understood *imputed righteousness* when he said of God:

¹⁰ I delight greatly in the LORD; my soul rejoices in my God. For **he has clothed me with garments of salvation** and **arrayed me in a robe of righteousness**, as a bridegroom adorns his head like a priest, and as a bride adorns herself with her jewels. (Isaiah 61:10)

Perhaps Paul was thinking of this 'robe of righteousness' when he described our spiritual armor protecting the heart.

[14] Stand firm then, with the belt of truth buckled around your waist, with the **breastplate of righteousness** in place. (Ephesians 6:14)

*Jeremiah* understood *imputed righteousness.*

[6] In his days Judah will be saved and Israel will live in safety. This is the name by which he will be called: **The LORD Our Righteousness.** (Jeremiah 23:6)

*Hosea* understood *imputed righteousness.*

[12] It is time to seek the LORD, until he comes and showers **righteousness on you.** (Hosea 10:12)

*The righteousness that is acceptable to God* does not come from our obeying his Law perfectly, but from placing saving faith in his Son the Lord Jesus Christ, and what he did to make saving faith possible. He did for us what we could never do for ourselves. He died *for* us, and *as* us, in our place to pay the full penalty for sin. We all have sinned and fallen short of the glory of God, but, joy of all joys, we are justified freely by God's grace through the redemption Christ provided by becoming the adequate sacrifice for our sins!

[1] There is now no condemnation for those who are in Christ Jesus. (Romans 8:1)

[21] God made him (Christ) who had no sin to be sin for us, so that in him we might **become the righteousness of God.** (2 Corinthians 5:21)

Edward Mote (1797-1874) wrote a hymn that is still being sung to this day.

My **hope** is built on nothing less
Than **Jesus' blood and righteousness**;
I dare not trust the sweetest frame,

But wholly lean on Jesus' name.
On Christ, the solid Rock, I stand;
All other ground is sinking sand.

The *righteousness of God* rather than our own self-righteousness is the 'righteousness' the Lord says we should be seeking when he said,

> [33] Seek first his kingdom and **his** righteousness. (Matthew 6:33)

John Stott suggests that

> "The righteousness of God might be defined as God's righteous way of 'righteousing' our **un**righteousness. It is the righteous status which he bestows on sinners whom he justifies." (The Cross of Christ, p. 210)

As such, Paul was delighted to be

> [9] found in him [Christ], **not having a righteousness of my own** that comes from the law, but that which is **through faith in Christ**—the **righteousness that comes from God** and is **by faith**. (Philippians 3:9)

From now on our whole demeanor is to be *Christ-like righteousness.*

> [22] You were taught, with regard to your former way of life, to **put off your old self**, which is being corrupted by its deceitful desires;
>
> [23] to be made new in the attitude of your minds;
>
> [24] and to **put on the new self**, created to be **like God** in **true righteousness** and holiness. (Ephesians 4:22-24)

Paul affirmed to the Philippian Christians that due to Christ's *imputed righteousness* they would be considered as

.

[10] **pure** and **blameless** until the day of Christ,

[11] filled with the **fruit of righteousness** that **comes through Jesus Christ**—to the glory and praise of God. (Philippians 1:10-11)

Paul exhorted Timothy to pursue *righteousness.*

"Pursue **righteousness** [along with] godliness, faith, love, endurance and gentleness. "
(1 Timothy 6:11; 2 Tim 2:22)

Why *pursue righteousness?* Because there is nothing more God wants for us than that *we be considered righteous as he is righteous.* God's innate righteousness overshadows all that he is and overshadows all his ways. God, in turn, longs that we whom he has created 'in his own image' allow *his imputed righteousness* to shine out through us.

In 1739 Count Nikolaus L. Von Zinzendorf (1703-1791) on a sea voyage from Saint Thomas, West Indies wrote this remarkable hymn regarding being dressed in Christ's righteousness and what this looks like.

**Jesus, Thy blood and righteousness**
<u>My</u> **beauty are, <u>my</u> glorious dress;**
'Midst flaming worlds, in these arrayed,
With joy shall I lift up my head...

This **spotless robe** the same appears,
When ruined nature sinks in years;
No age can change its glorious hue,
The **robe of Christ** is ever new...

O let the dead now hear Thy voice;
Now bid Thy banished ones rejoice;
**Their beauty this, their glorious dress,**
**Jesus, Thy blood and righteousness.**

# The Word of God is Righteous

After speaking to the breathtaking glory of the heavens, David spoke of the equal *glory of God's Word.*

> [9] The ordinances [words] of the LORD are sure and **altogether righteous**.
>
> [10] They are more precious than gold, than much pure gold; they are sweeter than honey, than honey from the comb. (Psalm 19:9-10)

One of the first congregational hymns I recall singing as a young child focused on the beauty and *the wonder of God's righteous Word.* The hymn is 'Thy Word is like a garden Lord' written by Edwin Hodder (1863)

> Thy Word is like a garden, Lord, with flowers bright and fair; and everyone who seeks may pluck a lovely cluster there.
> Thy Word is like a deep, deep mine; and jewels rich and rare are hidden in its mighty depths for every searcher there.
> [6] The words of the LORD are flawless, like silver refined in a furnace of clay, purified seven times. (Psalm 12:6)

# God's Laws are Righteous

*All God's laws* which he has enacted upon mankind *are righteous.* They're great and glorious.

> [21] "It pleased the LORD for the sake of his **righteousness** to make **his law great and glorious**." (Isaiah 42:21)

After having spent 40 years in the wilderness with Israel God asked them,

[8] What other nation is so great as to have such **righteous decrees and laws** as this body of laws I am setting before you today? (Deuteronomy 4:8)

[9] The ordinances of the LORD are sure and **altogether righteous**. (Psalm 19:9)

The *righteousness of God's holy Law -the Word of God-* is the Psalmist's repeated focus throughout his great 119th Psalm in praise of God's Word.

[75] 'I know, O LORD, that **your laws are righteous**.

[138] The statutes you have laid down are **righteous**; they are fully trustworthy.'

[172] 'May my tongue sing of your word, for all your **commands are righteous**.
(Psalm 119:172, 7, 62, 106, 123, 137, 142; 160, 164)

There are many reasons for believing and obeying the *true* and *righteous Law of God*. One important reason is that doing so is a testimony to the whole world that *God's unchanging, righteous laws are the pathway to wisdom and understanding.*

[6] Observe (my laws and decrees) carefully, for this will show your **wisdom** and **understanding** to **the nations**, who will hear about all these decrees and say, "Surely this great nation is a wise and understanding people."...

[8] And what other nation is so great as to have such **righteous** decrees and laws as **this body of laws** I am setting before you today? (Deuteronomy 4:6, 8)

Paul affirmed that the Law of God is **righteous.**

¹² The *law* is holy, and the commandment is holy, **righteous** and good. (Romans 7:12)

*Keeping God's righteous Law is 'righteousness'.* Moses included himself when he spoke these words the day the whole nation of Israel had assembled before him in the desert wilderness.

²⁵ **If we are careful to obey all this law** before the LORD our God, as he has commanded us, **that will be our righteousness.** (Deuteronomy 6:25)

Hypothetically, Paul is in agreement.

¹³ It is not those who hear the law who are righteous in God's sight, but it is **those who obey the law** who will be declared **righteous.** (Romans 2:13)

There is just one catch. *No one obeys the Law perfectly* in thought, word and deed 24/7 over a lifetime -which is the criteria for being declared 'righteous' by the Law. With God it's all or nothing! If a person breaks the Law only once in a lifetime, it is all over, because this has set him up to be judged by the Law as a lawbreaker to be condemned.

James puts it into this formula:

¹⁰ Whoever **keeps the whole law** and **yet** stumbles at just <u>one</u> point is guilty of breaking **all** of it. (James 2:10)

This might not sound fair, but with God the passing score is 100 and he doesn't mark on a curve. This may sound severe, but we must remember that it is God who is calling the shots. It's severe, but being 99.9% perfect is not 'perfect'; only 100% is 'perfect. If God requires 100% and he does, we all need a 'Savior'; even the best of us, for who can say he's never slipped up even once in a lifetime? If someone wants to meet up with God at the Last Judgment and be judged on the basis of 'good works' God is willing, but it won't go well. The reason is that if the passing score is 100 no one has collateral to work with to offset whenever he or she has sinned and fallen short of the passing score of 100.

No one keeps the Law perfectly. We are all fallen creatures born in sin -inherited from Adam and Eve's Original Sin. So the Law which was designed to be our friend showing us how to live a perfect life before God, exposes us as not having lived a 100% perfect life. The Law has instead become our 'judge, jury and hangman.'

Here's the scenario.

> ⁶ God "will give to each person according to what he has done."

> ⁷ To those who by persistence in doing good seek glory, honor and immortality, he will give eternal life.
> (Romans 2:6-7)

But things will not go well for those who go this route.

> ¹⁰ As it is written: "There is no one righteous, not even one...

> ¹² All have turned away, they have together become worthless; there is no one who does good, not even one."
> (Romans 3:10, 12, 23; Ecc 7:20)

Paul says that when we sin we should know better. We have no excuse.
> ³² Although they know God's **righteous** decree that **those who do such things deserve death,** they not only continue to do these very things but also approve of those who practice them. (Romans 1:32, 2:12)

If ever there was a *righteous man* it was the godly prophet **Isaiah**, and yet even he, when he found himself in the Temple in the presence of a Holy God, admitted he was a sinful man and lived in the midst of sinful people.

> ⁵ "Woe to me!" I cried. "I am ruined! For I am a man of unclean lips, and I live among a people of unclean lips, and my eyes have seen the King, the LORD Almighty."
> (Isaiah 6:5; 59:9)

If ever there was a godly, *righteous* man it was **Daniel**, and yet even he, when praying to the Lord, admitted he was still a sinful man and lived in the midst of sinful people.

> ⁷ "Lord, **you are righteous**, but this day **we are covered with shame**. (Daniel 9:7)

If ever there was a godly, *righteous* man it was **Ezra**, and yet even when he was praying to the Lord he admitted he was still a sinful man, and lived in the midst of sinful people.

> ⁶O my God, I am too ashamed and disgraced to lift up my face to you, my God, because our sins are higher than our heads and our guilt has reached to the heavens. (Ezra 9:6)

If ever there was a *righteous* woman it was Mary, the mother of our Lord, but even she acknowledged the need for a 'Savior'. She prayed,

> ⁴⁷ My spirit rejoices in **God my Savior**, (Luke 1:47)

If ever there was a *righteous* man it was **John** the 'beloved disciple', yet he included himself when he wrote with indelible ink,

> ⁸ If *we* claim to be without sin, *we* deceive ourselves and the truth is not in *us*.
>
> ⁹ If *we* confess our sins, he is faithful and just and will forgive *us* our sins and purify *us* from all unrighteousness. (1 John 1:8-9)

If ever there was a *righteous* man it was **Paul**, yet listen to what he was compelled to admit regarding his past.

> ¹⁵ Christ Jesus came into the world to save sinners—of whom I am the worst. (1 Timothy 1:15)

The Psalmist put his commitment to follow God's righteous laws in the form of an oath.

> [106] **I have taken an oath** and confirmed it, that I will follow your **righteous** laws. (Psalm 119:106)

Oh that we would make the same faith pledge to the Lord to willingly comply with his righteous laws. God wants us to reflect his righteousness by Spirit-empowered compliance to his righteous laws as an act of faith. Years ago my wife and I made a pledge to the Lord that we would spend time reading God's Word every day, and be willing by faith to do what he instructs us in his Word to do in his strength to express his righteousness. We have never had second thoughts about having made that vow. It has made all the difference in our lives!

# God Wants Us to be Righteous

> [9] The LORD...loves those who pursue **righteousness**. (Proverbs 15:9; Ps 146:8)

The Lord is more than willing to teach us his righteous ways.

> [9] He **guides the humble in what is right** and **teaches** them **his way**. (Psalm 25:9; Hos 14:9)

What does following in the '*right' ways* of the Lord' look like? We have an answer in David's words.

> [2] He [who] whose walk is blameless and who **does what is righteous**.
> [He is the person who]
> speaks the truth from his heart
>
> [3] and has no slander on his tongue, who does his neighbor no wrong and casts no slur on his fellowman,

⁴ who despises a vile man but honors those who fear the LORD, who keeps his oath even when it hurts,

⁵ who lends his money without usury and does not accept a bribe against the innocent. (Psalm 15:2-5)

We live righteously when we are *just* in all our transactions.

²⁴ Let **justice** roll on like a river, **righteousness** like a never-failing stream!
(Amos 5:24; Lev 19:15; Prov 21:3; Am 5:15)

Does living righteously work to our advantage? God made this promise to Solomon, David's son:

³⁸ If you do whatever I command you and **walk in my ways** and **do what is right** in my eyes by keeping my statutes and commands, as David my servant did, **I will be with you.** (1 Kings 11:38)

There is nothing more comforting than to know **God is with us.** The question is not so much 'is God with us' as it is 'are we with him'? The Lord wants us to *travel with him* on *paths of righteousness.* David wanted the Lord to lead him in *paths of righteousness.*

³ He guides me in **paths of righteousness** for his name's sake. (Psalm 23:3; 5:8)

David made it clear that he was not asking God to lead him in a path of *self*-righteousness, but the path that is *God's righteousness!*

Solomon, in his early years, determined to follow in the footsteps of 'righteous' men. He wrote of his desire to do so in the form of proverbs.

²⁰ Walk in the ways of good men and keep to the paths of the **righteous.** (Proverbs 2:20; 15:9, 21:2; Hos 14:9)

Paul encouraged Timothy repeatedly to pursue righteousness.

<sup>11</sup> You, man of God, flee from all this, and ***pursue righteousness***, godliness, faith, love, endurance and gentleness. (1 Timothy 6:11; 2 Tim 2:22)

# God Wants us to Live Righteously, but not Boastfully.

The Lord through Jeremiah gives us permission to boast not about our own self-righteousness, but boast about ***God's righteousness***

<sup>23</sup> 'This is what the LORD says: "Let not the wise man boast of his wisdom or the strong man boast of his strength or the rich man boast of his riches, <sup>24</sup> but let him who boasts boast about this: that he understands and knows me, that I am the LORD, who exercises kindness, justice and **righteousness** on earth, for in these I delight," declares the LORD.' (Jeremiah 9:23-24)

Based on this conviction Jeremiah 'boasted' of the Lord and not of himself:

<sup>1</sup> You are **always righteous**, O LORD.
(Jeremiah 12:1)

And remember, Jeremiah made this confession in 'the worst of times' -when his nation was on the verge of being dismantled by Babylon -the reigning world power.

# Righteousness vs Spiritual Battle

At the beginning of his ministry, in the Sermon on the Mount Jesus taught his disciples to pray to God the Father,

<sup>13</sup> Lead us not into temptation, but deliver us from **the evil one.** (Matthew 6:13)

At the close of his public ministry, on the eve of his Passion, he prayed to his Heavenly Father for his disciples,

> [15] My prayer is not that you take them out of the world but that you protect them from **the evil one.** (John 17:15)

John lets us know how pervasive and extensive is the work of the *evil one.*

> [19] We know that we are children of God, and that **the whole world is under the control of the evil one.** (1 John 5:19)

Paul lets us know in no uncertain terms that we are engaged in spiritual battle with the *evil one.*

> [11] Put on the full armor of God so that you can take your **stand against the devil's schemes.** (Ephesians 6:11)

> [3] The Lord is faithful, and he will strengthen and protect you from the *evil one.* (2 Thessalonians 3:3)

One of the pieces of armor the Lord equips us with to fight defensively against the *evil one* is *righteousness.*

> [14] Stand firm then, with the belt of truth buckled around your waist, with **the breastplate of righteousness** in place. (Ephesians 6:14)

Paul has informed us that we have at our disposal

> [7] **weapons of righteousness** in the right hand and in the left. (2 Corinthians 6:7)

Isaiah graphically portrayed the Lord as fighting the spiritual battle to rescue us from the Evil One.

¹⁴ Justice is driven back, and **righteousness** stands at a distance; truth has stumbled in the streets, honesty cannot enter.

¹⁵ Truth is nowhere to be found, and whoever shuns evil becomes a prey. The LORD looked and was displeased that there was no justice.

¹⁶ He saw that there was no one, he was appalled that there was no one to intervene; so his own arm worked salvation for him, and **his own righteousness** sustained him.

¹⁷ **He put on righteousness as his breastplate**, and the helmet of salvation on his head; he put on the garments of vengeance and wrapped himself in zeal as in a cloak. (Isaiah 59:14-17)

This is the kind of **righteous** God we need and have –to the praise of his glory! ☺

# Self-righteousness

God is *righteous*, and will not tolerate in the kingdom of heaven anything (anyone) that is the opposite of himself, namely, *self-righteous*. Jesus said bluntly in the Sermon on the Mount:

²⁰ I tell you that unless your righteousness surpasses the righteousness [**self-righteousness**] of the Pharisees and the teachers of the law, you will certainly not enter the kingdom of heaven. (Matthew 5:20; 23:27-28)

*Self-righteousness* from God's point of view smells to high heaven.

⁶ All of us have become like one who is unclean, and **all our righteous acts are like filthy rags**. (Isaiah 64:6)

*How does a person become 'self-righteous'* and thus odious to God? John of the Cross (1542-1591) writes in 'Living Flame of Love' (Stanza 3), The self-righteous are those who

> want to achieve the sense of righteousness that comes -a false sense, really- when you think you have gotten the better of sin. Then you wrongly think that you no longer have the need to cast yourself on the mercy of God each day...These souls are greatly harmed, even as they think they are becoming so good.
> (David Hazard, You Set My Spirit Free, pp. 94-95)

A self-righteous person is one who justifies his every thought and action and always concludes, 'I never did anything wrong.' I recall one night in my life when I couldn't fall asleep the whole night, because I was so distraught over two people who had treated me very abusively, but when confronted with their hurtful words they responded smugly: "We never did anything wrong."

> [2] **All a man's ways seem right to him**, but the LORD weighs the heart. (Proverbs 21:2)

Suppose a man wrote a book and titled it 'Righteousness and How I Achieved It'. I doubt such a crass self-righteous book would ever make it onto the NY Times Bestsellers List. In a parable, Jesus gave a graphic contrast between a *boastful 'self-righteous'* man and a *humble 'sinner'*.

> [10] "Two men went up to the temple to pray, one a Pharisee and the other a tax collector.

> [11] The Pharisee stood up and **prayed about himself**: 'God, I thank you that I am not like other men—robbers, evildoers, adulterers—or even like this tax collector.

> [12] I fast twice a week and give a tenth of all I get.'

[13] "But the tax collector stood at a distance. He would not even look up to heaven, but beat his breast and said, **'God, have mercy on me, a sinner.'**

[14] "I tell you that this man, rather than the other, went home justified before God. For everyone who exalts himself will be humbled, and he who humbles himself will be exalted." (Luke 18:10-14)

There is a worship song that moves my spirit with these simple words,

Lord have *mercy*; Christ have *mercy*; Lord have *mercy* on me.

Lord have *mercy*; Christ have *mercy*; Lord have *mercy* on me.

How does a person become 'self-righteous' and thus odious to God? Paul has answered the question by observing self-righteous people and how they got that way.

[3] Since they did not know the righteousness that comes from God and sought to establish their own, **they did not submit to God's righteousness.** (Romans 10:3)

Paul gave himself as an example. Before his conversion to Christ his 'righteousness' by his own admission was only empty 'self-righteousness'.

[4] If anyone else thinks he has reasons to put confidence in the flesh, I have more...

[6] as for zeal, persecuting the church; as for **legalistic righteousness**, faultless.

[7] But whatever was to my profit I now consider loss for the sake of Christ...

[8] I consider them rubbish, that I may gain Christ

[9] and be found in him, **not having a righteousness of my own** that comes from the law, but that which is through faith in Christ—the **righteousness that comes from God** and is by faith. (Philippians 3:4, 6-9)

The Son of God's mission was to save the *'self-righteous'* because there are none *'righteous'*.

Job asked a compelling question.

[2] How can a mortal be **righteous** before God? (Job 9:2)

A little later in the dialogue Eliphaz asked Job a question,

[14] What is man, that he could be pure, or one born of woman, that he could be **righteous**? (Job 15:14)

David knew the sins of his heart and pled with God,

[1] O LORD, hear my prayer, listen to my cry for mercy; in your faithfulness and **righteousness** come to my relief.

[2] Do not bring your servant into judgment, for **no one living is righteous** before you. (Psalm 143:1-2)

The Gospel is truly good news! Jesus the perfect Son of God came down from heaven and lived a perfect life (a perfectly *righteous* life) on earth. He alone qualifies to be our 'savior' if he wanted to, and the good news is that *he wanted to take our place on the cross* -the innocent One for the guilty; the sinless One for sinners; the perfect One for the imperfect; *the righteous One for the unrighteous one!* Paul got it down to a sentence!

[21] God made him [Christ] who had no sin to be sin for us, **so that in him we might become the righteousness of God**. (2 Corinthians 5:21)

***This, I believe, is one of the key verses in Scripture.*** God, in Christ on the cross, took upon himself our sins so that in exchange we might be able to take on his imputed righteousness thus making us forever acceptable in his Beloved Son. What an incredible exchange!

> [5] God saved us, **not** because of **righteous** things we had done, but because of **his mercy.** (Titus 3:5)

> [8] It is by **grace** you have been saved, through faith—and this not from yourselves, it is the gift of God—

> [9] **not by [self-righteous] works**, so that no one can boast. (Ephesians 2:8-9)

It is only then that we can truly do good works for the glory of God.

> [10] We are God's workmanship, created in Christ Jesus to **do good works**, which God prepared in advance for us to do. (Ephesians 2:10)

We must never wavier from the truth that we do not do 'good works' to ***obtain*** our salvation, or to ***retain*** our salvation, but to ***express*** our salvation!

# God's Righteous Justice and Judgment Go Hand-in-Hand

> [4] God is the Rock, his works are perfect, and **all his ways are just.** A faithful God who does no wrong, **upright and just** is he. (Deuteronomy 32:4)

> [14] **Righteousness and justice** are the foundation of your throne; love and faithfulness go before you.
> (Psalm 89:14; 7:8, 11; 33:5; 96:13; 94:15, 97:2; Isa 11:4; Mic 7:9)

⁸ Let the LORD **judge** the peoples. **Judge me**, O LORD, according to **my righteousness**, according to my integrity, O Most High.

Even Nebuchadnezzar, the pagan king of Babylon came to understand that what God does is *right and just.*

³⁷ I, Nebuchadnezzar, praise and exalt and glorify the King of heaven, because **everything he does is right** and all his ways are just. And those who walk in pride he is able to humble. (Daniel 4:37)

## God Will Prove Himself Righteous and Just

When Vernon Grounds was the President of Denver Seminary every Christmas he would send a letter to all the school's graduates wherever they had located around the world to affirm his ongoing love for them, as well as attempt to encourage them knowing that many of them were serving the Lord in very difficult places. One year he wanted them to know he was confident God's *righteousness* would prevail even if at any particular time what they were going through was making it difficult to see how God could possibly prove himself *righteous.*

"I have quit worrying and fussing over the intractable problem of evil, confident that God's explanation will completely satisfy my mind and heart."

Give God time and space and he will prove to be both *righteous and just.* We read in the *future tense,*

¹⁵ Judgment **will again** be founded on **righteousness**, and all the upright in heart **will follow it.**
(Psalm 94:15; Prov 29:16; Isa 5:16)

This is just cause for *singing* God's praises as the *righteous judge.* *Righteousness* will win out in the end!

[13] **Sing** before the LORD, for he comes, he comes to **judge** the earth. He **will** judge the world in **righteousness** and the peoples in his truth. (Psalm 96:13; 98:9)

# God Loves Righteousness and Justice

[5] The LORD **loves righteousness and justice**; the earth is full of his unfailing love.
(Psalm 33:5; 45:4, 7; 145:17; 146:8)

# God in His Righteousness Expresses Wrath Against the Unrighteous

Ultimately, evil *never* wins out over good, due to God's *'righteous indignation'*.

[9] O **righteous** God, who searches minds and hearts, bring to an end the violence of the wicked and make **the righteous** secure.

[11] God is **a righteous judge**, a God who **expresses his wrath every day**. (Psalm 7:9, 11)

There is no perfect crime; no one ultimately gets away with murder. At the Last Judgment -if not before- God will have his day in court with the unrighteous and wicked.

[23] You may be sure that your sin will find you out. (Numbers 32:23)

How should we respond to this information? We would do well to learn our lesson anytime we sense our righteous God has a case against us. Here was what the Psalmist learned when he sensed he was being disciplined by God:

[67] Before I was afflicted I went astray, but now I obey your word. (Psalm 119:67)

[71] It was good for me to be afflicted so that I might learn your decrees. (Psalm 119:71)

[75] I know, O LORD, that your laws are **righteous**, and in faithfulness you have afflicted me. (Psalm 119:75)

# Our Response in Knowing God is Righteous, Just and Merciful

We need to make it our desire to

[20] walk in **the way of righteousness**. (Proverbs 8:20)

We can pray for God's mercy to overshadow God's judgment.

[1] O LORD, hear my prayer, listen to my cry for **mercy;** in your faithfulness and **righteousness** come to my relief.

[2] Do not bring your servant into **judgment,** for no one living is **righteous before you.**
(Psalm 143:1-2; 4:1; 7:8-9; 119:121)

James' response to this prayer would be this:

[13] **Mercy triumphs over judgment!** (James 2:13)

[32] God has bound all men over to disobedience so that he may have **mercy** on them all.

[33] Oh, the depth of the riches of the wisdom and knowledge of God! How unsearchable his judgments, and his paths beyond tracing out! (Romans 11:32-33; Isa 41:10)

Once when I was going through an unusually difficult and stressful time, I travelled to a seminary campus just to spend a day alone with the Lord in prayer and meditation. When I was praying about my situation I sensed the Lord's words from scripture coming to mind, *'I am with you!'* and the words, *'Trust me'.*

Shortly thereafter the Lord brought across my path a friend who was a seminary professor. "Doug, how are you doing?" He asked. "Terrible," I replied. He invited me into his office and together we talked and prayed, and the burden was lifted! The Lord brought to mind how in his strength I could give a *righteous response* to those who were causing me such pain and distress.

Joseph lived to see the day when his mean-spirited brothers crossed his path again. He was in a position to do them harm for the way they had treated him with such abusive jealousy and cruelty. Because *he served a righteous God*, he wanted to *reflect God's righteousness* by doing the *right* thing by them. He wanted them to know he had forgiven them, and longed to be reconciled. That day his brothers became the recipients of God's love, grace, mercy and righteousness flowing through their estranged little brother who just happened to have become the second in command in Egypt. Joseph said to his grateful brothers,

> [20] You intended to harm me, but God intended it for good to accomplish what is now being done, the saving of many lives. (Genesis 50:20)

## Righteousness vs Faith

Paul, in writing that *'the righteous will live by faith'* (Romans 1:17) was actually quoting from the Old Testament prophet Habakkuk which shows that 'righteousness' and 'faith' have been fused together for a long time.

> [4] The **righteous** will live by his **faith**
> (Habakkuk 2:4)

That '*the righteous live by faith*' is a key concept in Scripture. It has been God's message to the world for thousands of years. Consider Abraham who lived about 4000 years ago.

> [6] Abram **believed** the LORD, and he credited it to him as **righteousness**. (Genesis 15:6)

It's *at the point we 'believe the Lord'* that we begin to be *empowered by God to live a righteous life.* We have the indwelling presence of the Holy Spirit transforming our lives from the inside out. God has removed our heart of stone and transplanted it with soft heart of flesh so that we can know and love and serve our righteous God.

> [26] I will give you a **new heart** and put **a new spirit in you**; I will remove from you your heart of stone and give you a heart of flesh. (Ezekiel 36:26)

There are endless examples of faith-filled people who were considered by God to be 'Righteous' People. The first biblical example of **a righteous man** was Abel.

**Abel**

> By faith Abel offered God a better sacrifice than Cain did. By **faith** he was commended as **a righteous man**, when God spoke well of his offerings. And by faith he still speaks, even though he is dead. (Hebrews 11:4)

**Noah**

> [9] Noah was **a righteous man**, blameless among the people of his time, and he walked with God. (Genesis 6:9)

## Abraham

> [21] Was not our ancestor Abraham considered **righteous** for what he did when he offered his son Isaac on the altar? (James 2:21)

## Lot

> [7] He rescued Lot, **a righteous man**, who was distressed by the filthy lives of lawless men (2 Peter 2:7)

## Rahab

> [25] Was not even Rahab the prostitute considered **righteous** for what she did when she gave lodging to the spies and sent them off in a different direction? (James 2:25)

## David

David took a spiritual inventory of his life and he came to this conclusion:

> [20] The LORD has dealt with me according to **my righteousness**; according to the cleanness of my hands he has rewarded me.

> [21] For I have kept **the ways of the LORD**; I have not done evil by turning from my God. (Psalm 18:20-21)

Solomon prayed to God regarding his father David,

> [6] You have shown great kindness to your servant, my father David, because he was faithful to you and **righteous** and **upright in heart**. (1 Kings 3:6)

There are New Testament examples of **righteous people**.

**Joseph**

> <sup>19</sup> Joseph her husband was **a righteous man**
> (Matthew 1:19)

**Simeon**

> <sup>25</sup> There was a man in Jerusalem called Simeon, who was **righteous** and devout. (Luke 2:25)

**John the Baptist**

> <sup>20</sup> Herod feared John and protected him, knowing him to be **a righteous and holy man.** (Mark 6:20)

**Paul**

> <sup>10</sup> You are witnesses, and so is God, of how holy, **righteous** and blameless we were among you who believed. (1 Thessalonians 2:10)

## The saints in heaven

> <sup>8</sup> Fine linen, bright and clean, was given her to wear."
> (Fine linen stands for the **righteous acts of the saints**.)
> (Revelation 19:8)

May our names be added to these dear saints because we too have become people of faith, and walk righteously before he Lord!

## Blessings of Righteousness

Joy of all joys, God's willing to impute his righteousness to our account making us acceptable to him. In turn, he enables us to reflect *his righteous ways* in all we say and do by empowering us with his indwelling *righteous Holy Spirit!*

> [12] Surely, O LORD, you **bless the righteous**; you surround them with your favor as with a shield.
> (Psalm 5:12; 112:2-4; Prov 10:6-7)

The thousands who attended the funeral of Billy Graham, and the millions who watched on TV and online certainly underscored the truth of this scripture. The memories of this righteous man were many and they were all blessed! We sense God is present in those who are truly 'Righteous'.

> [5]**God is present** in the company of **the righteous**?
> (Psalm 14:5)

# God Hears the Prayers of the Righteous

> [15] The eyes of the LORD are on the **righteous** and his ears **are attentive to their cry.** (Psalm 34:15; 1 Pe 3:12)

It is a blessing to know the prayers of the *'righteous'* are heard and answered! David believed his prayer was heard.

> [1] Hear, O LORD, my **righteous** plea; **listen to my cry.** Give ear to **my prayer**— it does not rise from deceitful lips. (Psalm 17:1-2; 34:15, 17-18)

Solomon upon observing the result of his righteous father on his knees praying concluded that

> [29] The LORD is far from the wicked but *he hears* the *prayer of the* righteous.
> (Proverbs 15:29; cf. Ps 66:18)

# God's Love is a Blessing to Those He has Declared 'Righteous'

> [8] The LORD lifts up those who are bowed down, the LORD **loves** the **righteous**.
> (Psalm 146:8; Prov 15:9)

# Righteousness and Joy go Together

God Gives *Joy* to those to whom God imputes righteousness.

> [11] **Rejoice in the LORD** and be glad, **you righteous; sing**, all you who are upright in heart!
> (Psalm 32:11; 33:1; 64:10; 68:3; 97:11-12; 119:172)

> [28] The prospect of the **righteous** is **joy**, but the hopes of the wicked come to nothing.
> (Proverbs 10:28)

Bernard of Clairvaux (1091-1153) wrote the hymn 'Jesus, the Very Thought of Thee'. The very thought of Jesus brought him joy!

Jesus, the very thought of Thee
With sweetness fills the breast;
But sweeter far Thy face to see,
And in Thy presence rest.

Nor voice can sing, nor heart can frame,
Nor can the mem'ry find
A sweeter sound than Thy blest name,
O Savior of mankind!

O hope of every contrite heart,
**O joy of all the meek,**
To those who fall, how kind Thou art!
How good to those who seek!

> **Jesus, our only joy** be Thou,
> As Thou our prize will be;
> Jesus, be Thou our glory now,
> And through eternity.

'Joy' became the theme of one-time atheist C.S. Lewis turned Christian. He titled his autobiography, *'Surprised by Joy!'* ☺

# God's Leading Us in Paths of Righteousness is a Blessing

To know and do the will of God and thus be on the right 'path' is a *blessing* for the *'righteous'*.

> [3] He **guides me** in **paths of righteousness** for his name's sake. (Psalm 23:3; 5:8; Prov 11:5; Isa 26:7))

# God Meets the Daily Needs of the 'Righteous'

> [3] The LORD does **not let the righteous go hungry** but he thwarts the craving of the wicked.
> (Proverbs 10:3)

> [25] I was young and now I am old, yet I have never seen the **righteous** forsaken or their children begging bread.
> (Psalm 37:25)

These are the words of David, but I can also say the same words as I look back over my own life. I have never felt forsaken by God even when facing hard times. Facing hard times together with God has made all the difference. And it has also been the case that our children have never been forced to 'beg bread'.

> [17] The LORD **upholds the righteous**.
> (Psalm 37:17)

² Cast your cares on the LORD and he will sustain you;
he will **never let the righteous fall.**
(Psalm 55:22; Prov 12:7; 13:6; 12:13; 28:1)

⁵ You **come to the help** of those who gladly **do right**, who
remember **your ways.** (Isaiah 64:5)

I grew up in a poor pastor's home. One summer when I was about
ten years old and attending a summer church camp the talk of us PKs
(preacher kids) in the playground one day centered on comparing our
fathers' salaries. I felt ashamed when I had to share with everyone that their
fathers made 3 or 4 times as much money as my father.

My parents had very little, but we never missed a meal; we never
lacked anything we ever needed. I recall the day one of the members of our
church dropped off at our house a carton of eggs. What my parents soon
discovered was that there was a dollar bill folded and tucked under each
egg in the carton] (A dollar went a long ways in those days!)

Over the years, never being rich myself, I've learned by experience the
truth of David's words:

¹⁶ Better the little that the **righteous** have than the wealth
of many wicked. (Psalm 37:16)

My wife and I have many (what we call) '*God stories*' –times when
things came down to the wire, and the Lord stepped in at the critical
moment to meet the need. One winter's day I had a parking lot 'fender
bender'. The next day a check arrived in the mail that was the exact
amount needed for the car repair. (The check had been put in the mail
before the accident happened.) On another occasion the day our rent was
due a friend knocked on the door and put a check in our hands that was
the exact amount needed for the rent. Our friend had no idea how much
money we needed. Praise the Lord! It's as my wife often says, "God is
seldom early, but he's never late!" ☺

²⁸ The **righteous** will thrive like a green leaf…

³⁰ The fruit of the **righteous** is a tree of life.
(Proverbs 11:28, 30; 10:16; 12:12)

*Douglas Nelson*

# It is a Blessing that God Rescues and Delivers the Righteous

Fighting the Lord's battles David as a man of war often found himself praying,

> [17] The **righteous** cry out, and the LORD hears them; he **delivers** them from all their troubles.
> (Psalm 34:17-19; 140:1, 7, 13)

God's rescue of the '*righteous*' recorded by Solomon in his Proverbs is *proverbial* (pun intendedJ).

> [29] The **way of the LORD** is a **refuge** for the **righteous**, but it is the ruin of those who do evil.

> [30] The **righteous** will never be uprooted, but the wicked will not remain in the land.
> (Proverbs 10:29-30; 11:4, 8; 121:21)

# What Does 'Righteous Living' Look Like?

Living righteously has many facets.

### The Righteous are Generous

> [21] The wicked borrow and do not repay, but **the righteous give generously** (Psalm 37:21; 26)

### The Upright are Peaceful

> [37] Consider the blameless, observe the **upright**; there is a future for the **man of peace**.
> (Psalm 37:37)

-According to Solomon there seems to be no end to the number of good things that characterize the righteous.

[18] The *path* of **the righteous** is like the first gleam of dawn, shining ever brighter till the full light of day. (Proverbs 4:18)

[11] The *mouth* of **the righteous** is a fountain of life (Proverbs 10:11)

[20] The *tongue* of **the righteous** is choice silver. (Proverbs 10:20)

[21] The *lips* of **the righteous** nourish many. (Proverbs 10:21)

[23] The *desire* of **the righteous** ends only in good. (Proverbs 11:23)

[5] The *plans* of **the righteous** are just. (Proverbs 12:5)

[9] The *light* of **the righteous** shines brightly. (Proverbs 13:9)

[7] The **righteous** man leads a *blameless life.* (Proverbs 20:7)

[1] The **righteous** are as *bold as a lion.* (Proverbs 28:1)

[7] **The righteous** *care about justice* for the poor. (Proverbs 29:7)

# Be Thankful for God's Righteousness

It's the righteous who willingly sing praises to God for his righteousness! It's only right that they should! ☺

> [11] **Rejoice** in the LORD and be glad, **you righteous**; sing, all you who are **upright** in heart!
> (Psalm 32:11; 64:10; 97:12)

> [17] **I will give thanks** to the LORD because of **his righteousness** and will **sing** praise to the name of the LORD Most High.
> (Psalm 7:17; 51:14; 98:4-5, 9; 145:7; 119:172)

# Ultimately 'Heaven' is the Blessing of the Righteous

A home in Heaven is the ultimate *blessing* for those whom God calls *'righteous'* Those who are walking now in *'paths of righteousness for his Name's sake'* are interested in Heaven and the possibility of being in God's *righteous* presence forever!

> [3] He leadeth me in the *paths of righteousness* for his name's sake...

> [6] and I will dwell in the house of the LORD for ever.
> (Psalm 23:3-6 KJV)

> [28] In the **way of righteousness** there is life; along that path is **immortality**. (Proverbs 12:28)

At the end of time Jesus as Judge will separate the sheep from the goats; the *righteous from the unrighteous.*

[46] "Then they (the unrighteous) will go away to eternal punishment, but **the righteous to eternal life.**" (Matthew 25:46)

**To our Righteous God be the glory!**

CHAPTER 5

# The Way of God is Truth

J ohn in his heavenly vision heard everyone singing that *all of God's ways are true.*

> ³ They **sang the song** of Moses the servant of God and the song of the Lamb: "Great and marvelous are your deeds, Lord God Almighty. Just and **true are your ways**, King of the ages. (Revelation 15:3)

But we need to ask *'What is truth?'* Pilate asked this question when Jesus was standing on trial before him.

> ³⁷ "You are a king, then!" said Pilate. Jesus answered, "You are right in saying I am a king. In fact, for this reason I was born, and for this I came into the world, to testify to the truth. Everyone on the side of **truth** listens to me."
>
> ³⁸ "**What is truth?**" Pilate asked. (John 18:37-38)

It is sad to detect cynicism in Pilate's voice when standing before him was *Truth incarnate.* Jesus has gone on record:

> ⁶ "**I am** the way and **the truth** and the life. No one comes to the Father except through me. (John 14:6)

## Definition of 'Truth'

The dictionary is our friend when it comes to defining 'truth'

> "The quality of being in accordance with experience, facts, or reality; conformity with fact; agreement with a standard, rule, etc.; that which accords with fact or reality; a verified fact, principle…connotes correspondence with fact or with reality; a degree of plausibility sufficient to induce belief." (New World Dictionary)

Consider the value of truth with regard to its longevity.

The Battell Chapel was filled with 650 Yale students and guests when in an early fall evening Ravi Zacharias and Abdu Murray spoke on 'The Quest for Meaning in a Post-Truth Culture'. At one point in their duo-lecture they made reference to Winston Churchill and Martin Luther King Jr's comments affirming that "**Truth** is the **most valuable thing** in the world," and "**Truth…will have the final say.**"
(Kayla Bartsch, Christian Union, Fall 2017, p.7)

[8] He remembers his covenant forever, **the word he commanded, for a thousand generations**
(Psalm 105:8)

This is nothing other than what Jesus had been saying all along.

[35] Heaven and earth will pass away, but **my words will never pass away.** (Matthew 24:35)

[60] All your words are **true**; all **your righteous laws are eternal.** (Psalm 119:160)

Peter draws from the prophecy of Isaiah when defining *truth's longevity.*

[24] "All men are like grass, and all their glory is like the flowers of the field; the grass withers and the flowers fall,

[25] but **the word of the Lord stands forever.**" And this is the word that was preached to you.
(1 Peter 1:23-25, Isaiah 40:8)

# God is the Origin of Truth

Pastor Paul Beck said it well when preaching to his New York Congregation on the subject of Truth. "Truth is the self-expression of God!"

¹⁹ I, the LORD, speak the **truth; I declare what is right.**
(Isaiah 45:19)

Augustine wrote in his Confessions,

Where I found truth there found I my God –the 'Truth'
itself.

It was said that on President Harry Truman's desk in the Oval Office
sat a motto that read, 'The Buck Stops Here'. In the case of God, 'Truth
stops with God' in that God has the final word on 'truth'. And why not?
God is the Author of Truth. Isaiah asks the right questions:

¹³ Who has understood the mind of the LORD, or
instructed him as his counselor?

¹⁴ Whom did the LORD consult to enlighten him, and
who taught him the right way? Who was it that taught
him knowledge or showed him the path of understanding?
(Isaiah 40:13-14)

Martyn Lloyd Jones has a cogent thought.

You can never reason at Truth, you can never find it by
looking for it. **Truth is revealed** to us, all we do is to
reason about it after having seen it.
(D. Martyn Lloyd Jones: The First Forty Years, p. 92)

John of the Cross (1542-1591) in his 'Ascent of Mount Carmel' wrote,

We can trust God implicitly in his ability to speak, but
we cannot, first of all, trust in our ability to hear him
accurately...Though God does accommodate himself in
many ways to be able to communicate with us at all,
when it comes to knowing **his higher ways** we must
accommodate ourselves to him...**His ways**, purposes and

viewpoints are so much higher –to speak plainly, different from ours.
(David Hazad, 'You Set Me on Fire, pp. 114-116).

God lets us know in no uncertain terms,

[8] "My thoughts are not your thoughts, neither are your ways my ways," declares the LORD.

[9] "As the heavens are higher than the earth, so are my ways higher than your ways and my thoughts than your thoughts. (Isaiah 55:8-9)

[5] How great are your works, O LORD, how profound your thoughts. (Psalm 92:5)

The truth is that God has revealed more truth about himself and his ways in our world than we can absorb in a lifetime. John makes this abundantly clear just with reference to the truth God has revealed in and through his Son by sending him to earth.

[25] Jesus did many other things as well. If every one of them were written down, I suppose that even the whole world would not have room for the books that would be written. (John 21:25)

Isaac Newton, one of the world's greatest scientists once wrote,

I do not know what I may seem to the world, but, as to myself, I seem to have been only like a boy playing on the sea shore, and diverting myself now and then by finding a smoother pebble or a prettier shell than ordinary, while **the great ocean of truth** lay all undiscovered before me. (Charles Hummel, Galileo, p. 148)

[17] How precious to me are your thoughts, O God! How vast is the sum of them!

[18] Were I to count them, they would outnumber the grains of sand. When I awake, I am still with you. (Psalm 139:17-18)

God's words being eternally true are profound.

[33] Oh, the depth of the riches of the wisdom and knowledge of God! How unsearchable his judgments, and his paths beyond tracing out!

[34] "Who has known the mind of the Lord? Or who has been his counselor?"

[35] "Who has ever given to God, that God should repay him?"

[36] For from him and through him and to him are all things. To him be the glory forever! Amen. (Romans 11:33-36)

Because truth by definition is unchanging (2+2=4 is unchanging), this speaks to the fact that God the Author of truth is unchanging.

[6] "I the LORD do not change. (Malachi 3:6)

*Truth is* nothing less than the ***unchanging*** mind of God. God goes on record,

[19] God is not a man, that he should lie, nor a son of man, that he should change his mind. Does he speak and then not act? Does he promise and not fulfill? (Numbers 23:19)

God speaking through the Psalmist says,

[34] **I will not violate** my covenant **or alter** what my lips have uttered. (Psalm 89:34)

[19] **I, the LORD, speak the truth**; I declare what is right...

²³ By myself I have sworn, my mouth has uttered in all
integrity a word that will not be revoked.
(Isaiah 45:19, 23)

See how this plays itself out in 'nature' and what God calls the 'fixed
laws of heaven and earth'.

²⁵ I have…established my covenant with day and night and
**the fixed laws of heaven and earth**. (Jeremiah 33:25)

One example of unvarying truth with reference of the fixed laws of
nature are the fixed boundaries of the oceans which God has established.

²² I made the sand a boundary for the sea, **an everlasting
barrier it cannot cross.** The waves may roll, but they
**cannot prevail**; they may roar, but they **cannot cross** it.
(Jeremiah 5:22)

There may be high tides and fierce storms ('the Perfect Storm') -even
tsunamis- but no nation or continent has ever disappeared under the
ocean.

David committed his eternal destiny into the hands of the *God of
truth.*

⁵ Into your hands I commit my spirit; redeem me, O
LORD, the **God of truth**. (Psalm 31:5)

King David believed *God's truth* would lead him into the light and
out of the darkness of any problem he was struggling with.

⁴ **Show me your ways**, O LORD, teach me your paths;

⁵ **guide me in your truth** and teach me, for you are God
my Savior, and my hope is in you all day long.
(Psalm 25:4-5)

Note the parallel David drew between *God's ways* and *God's truth*. *God's way is the way of truth.*

> ¹¹ Teach me **your way**, O LORD, and I will walk in **your truth**. (Psalm 86:11)

Jesus prayed to the one he called 'the only *true* God'.

> ³ This is eternal life: that they may know you, the **only true God**, and Jesus Christ, whom you have sent. (John 17:3)

Shifting the scene to the courtroom, Isaiah notes that

> ¹⁶ He who takes an oath in the land will swear by **the God of truth**. (Isaiah 65:16)

To this day when someone enters the witness stand he is made to rest his hand on the Bible and swear that he will 'tell the truth, the whole truth and nothing but the truth, so help me God!' To lie in court is to invite a prison sentence. We are assured by the Psalmist that at the end of human history Truth is going to be front and center in God's courtroom.

> ¹³ Sing before the LORD, for he comes, he comes to judge the earth. He will judge the world in righteousness and the peoples in **his truth**. (Psalm 96:13)

## Christ is Truth Incarnate

After having lived for years with Jesus day and night right up through his death, resurrection and ascension John concluded that Jesus is *Truth incarnate.*

¹⁴ The Word became flesh and made his dwelling among us. We have seen his glory, the glory of the One and Only, who came from the Father, **full of grace and truth**. (John 1:14)

²⁰ We know also that the Son of God has come and has given us understanding, so that we may **know him who is true**. And we are **in him who is true**—even in his Son **Jesus Christ. He is the true God** and eternal life. (1 John 5:20)

Jesus revealed himself to his disciples as he who is

⁶ The way and **the truth** and the life. (John 14:6)

The Son of God is *Truth incarnate.* Jesus as *Truth* is unchanging as the Author of Hebrews has stated.

⁸ Jesus Christ *is the same yesterday and today and forever.* (Hebrews 13:8)

We *learn truth* from Jesus. Twenty-seven times in the Gospel of John alone Jesus prefaced what he wanted to say with the words, *'I tell you the truth...'* For example,

⁴⁷ **I tell you the truth**, he who believes has everlasting life. (John 6:47)

⁵⁸ "**I tell you the truth**," Jesus answered, "before Abraham was born, I am!" (John 8:58)

Irenaeus (d. 202 AD) wrote in his 'Against the Heresies'

There is no way we could have learned **the ways of God** unless our Teacher, **the Word**, had been made man. **For no one else could have shown us what the Father is**

**like**…He alone knows the mind of God and knows the **ways** of God and understands the wisdom of his **ways**. (You Give Me New Life, David Hazard, p. 72)

# The Holy Spirit Is the Spirit of Truth

The *Holy Spirit*, who is one with the Father and the Son is equally *true in all his ways*. Jesus identifies the Holy Spirit as the '*Spirit of Truth*'.

[26] The **Spirit of truth** who goes out from the Father, he will testify about me. (John 15:26)

[13] When he, the **Spirit of truth**, comes, he will **guide you into all truth**. He will not speak on his own; he will speak only what he hears, and he will tell you what is yet to come. (John 16:13; 14:16-17)

The *Spirit of Truth* is the antithesis of the 'spirit of falsehood'. John teaches how to distinguish between the Spirit of Truth and the spirit of error and falsehood.

[6] We are from God, and whoever knows God listens to us; but whoever is not from God does not listen to us. This is how we recognize the **Spirit of truth** and the **spirit of falsehood**. (1 John 4:6)

# The Word of God is True

The Author of Hebrews has gone on record that it is impossible for God to lie.

[18] It is impossible for God to lie. (Hebrews 6:18)

'*Truth*' is a word mentioned over 200 times in Scripture. Truth reverberates throughout the Word of God from Genesis to Revelation. How can it be otherwise considering the God of all Truth is the Author of Scripture. The Holy Bible is all about *the one true God* telling the *truth*! Even if no one else believes God's Word is true, Jesus believes! He prayed to his Father on the night of his betrayal,

> [17] Your **word** is **truth**. (John 17:17)

Paul has thrown out this challenge:

> [4] **Let God be true**, and every man a liar. As it is written: "So that you may be proved right when you speak and prevail when you judge." (Romans 3:4)

God's Word is not simply 'true'; it is '*TRUTH*' itself! Not just some of the words, but *every word* is *true* right down to the 'dotting of the 'i' and the crossing of the 't'.

> [18] I tell you the truth, until heaven and earth disappear, **not the smallest letter, not the least stroke of a pen**, will by any means disappear from the Law until everything is accomplished.
> (Matthew 5:18; Ps 33:4)

Truth by definition remains unchanging forever!

> [33] Heaven and earth will pass away, but my words will **never pass away.**
> (Luke 21:33)

> [8] The grass withers and the flowers fall, but **the word of our God stands forever.**
> (Isaiah 40:8; 1 Peter 1:25)

What lasts longest is what is the most valued. We know the sayings, 'A diamond is forever' and 'A diamond is a girl's best friend' which symbolizes marriage and a lasting relationship 'till death do us part!'

There is something that is longer lasting than a diamond; it's the eternal Word of God! Here was how much Solzhenitsyn valued the true words of Scripture:

"One word of truth outweighs the whole world." (John Stott, Involvement, p.1:107)

Scripture is a real treasure trove!

[14] I rejoice in following your statutes as one rejoices in **great riches**...

[72] The law from your mouth is **more precious** to me **than thousands of pieces of silver and gold**...

[127] I love your commands **more than gold, more than pure gold**. (Psalm 119:14, 72, 127)

I have in my possession what I like to call a 'Treasure Map'. It is a map of the surface of the moon with all its craters. You might ask, "How can a map of the moon be a treasure map?" Well it's not, except for one thing. If ever -God forbid- every Bible on earth were confiscated and destroyed, I have a map of where to locate a Bible on the moon!

I had the rare privilege of meeting Col. James Irwin who flew aboard the Apollo 15 moon mission, and was the first man to drive a 'Moon Buggy' on the surface of the moon. I had heard that he had taken a Bible to the moon on his mission, and I finally had the opportunity to ask him in person to verify the rumor. It was true, and he was more than willing to 'X' the spot on the map and sign his name identifying were he had left the Bible. He left it sitting on the 'Moon Buggy' Well, it's unlikely that every Bible on earth will be destroyed, but there's at least one copy of the Holy Bible that God has safely tucked away on the moon! Better yet, according to the Psalmist God's word is tucked away safe in heaven itself!

[89] Your word, O LORD, is eternal; it stands firm in the heavens. (Psalm 119:89)

We can also tuck away the Bible for safe keeping in our hearts! ☺

[11] I have hidden your word in my heart that I might not sin against you.
(Psalm 119:11)

Here's how one man came to value the Bible following a ship wreck. Missionary Alexander Duff was

> deaf to the frantic shouts of the crewmen trying to herd passengers off a sinking ship. All he could do was stare at hundreds of his books bobbing in the waves near the Cape of Good Hope, South Africa. How could he ever replace his painstakingly acquired 800 volume library? Once safe on the cold barren shore Duff watched a small object slowly wash ashore. He realized it was his Bible. Out of an entire ship's cargo, only one item was saved -the Bible. Duff felt God was telling him the Bible was worth more than all the rest of his possessions. (Global Prayer Digest, 11/7/84)

The Psalmist prayed:

[43] Do not snatch the **word of truth** from my mouth, for I have put my hope in your laws. (Psalm 119:43)

If there is ever a need to verify the truth claims of Scripture, Charles Spurgeon has said it best.

> The Word of God is like a lion. You don't have to defend a lion. All you need do is to let the lion loose and the lion will defend itself.
> (Quoted by Klaus Bockmuehl, The Challenge of Marxism, pp. 156-157)

We can *let God speak for himself*!

> [19] I have not spoken in secret, from somewhere in a land of darkness **I, the LORD, speak the truth**; I declare what is right. (Isaiah 45:19)

The *Word of God* is *an anvil* that has worn out every hammer that has ever hit it in an effort to destroy it.,

> [29] "Is not **my word** like fire," declares the LORD, "and like a hammer that breaks a rock in pieces?" (Jeremiah 23:29)

It's as Paul put it

> [8] We cannot do anything against the **truth**, but only for the **truth**. (2 Corinthians 13:8)

Ever since Old Testament times unbelievers have attempted to tamper with the Word of God.

> [36] Every man's own word becomes his oracle and so you distort the words of the living God, the LORD Almighty, our God. (Jeremiah 23:36)

God takes it in hand to guarantee that no one will ever be able to change Scripture because we *cannot change 'truth'*. Jesus put it this way:

> [36] You cannot make even one hair white or black. (Matthew 5:36)

In a beauty salon a white hair may be covered up with black dye, but a white hair is still a white hair as it becomes obvious in a month or so when hair growth discloses the hair's true color.

America's Founding Fathers acknowledged in the Declaration of Independence *that truth is self-evident*, and this is the foundation of human society.

"We hold these **truths to be self-evident**, that all men are created equal, that they are endowed by their Creator with certain unalienable rights, that among these are Life, Liberty and the pursuit of Happiness..."

Paul made it a point that it was *self-evident truth* he was setting forth before them.

[1] We have renounced secret and shameful ways; we do not use deception, nor do we distort the word of God. On the contrary, by **setting forth the truth plainly** we commend ourselves to every man's conscience in the sight of God. (2 Corinthians 4:2)

[4] As servants of God we commend ourselves in every way...

[7] in **truthful speech** and in the power of God...
(2 Corinthians 6:3-4, 7)

The Church is the very pillar and foundation of *truth*.

[15] The church of the living God [is] the **pillar and foundation of the truth**. (1 Timothy 3:15)

It is uniquely the Church's job in the world to uphold the 'pillar of truth' -the Bible. Billy Graham's life was exemplary in that he in his lifetime faithfully proclaimed the gospel truth of the Word of God to over 200 million people, as well as sharing the Gospel with every US President from Dwight Eisenhower to Donald Trump! Repeatedly he would say "The Bible says..." and then say what the Bible says resulting in countless thousands of people putting their faith in the *truth* of the life-transforming Gospel of Jesus Christ!

Paul reminds us that the words of Scripture are not just words. They are the true Words of God!

[13] We thank God continually because, when you received the word of God, which you heard from us, you accepted

it not as **the word of men**, but as it actually is, **the word of God,** which is at work in you who believe. (1 Thessalonians 2:13)

As such, God's Word is *trustworthy.*

⁷ All his precepts are **trustworthy.**

⁸ They are steadfast for ever and ever, done in **faithfulness** and uprightness. (Psalm 111:7-8)

Right to the last chapter of the Bible the focus is on the *trustworthy words* of our *trustworthy God.*

⁶ The angel said to me, "These words are **trustworthy and true.** The Lord, the God of the spirits of the prophets, sent his angel to show his servants the things that must soon take place." (Revelation 22:6)

God wants us to reflect the trustworthiness of the Word of God in our lives by living out the truths found in the scriptures.

²² Do not merely listen to the word, and so deceive yourselves. Do what it says (James 1:22)

# The Gospel is True

Paul is adamant that *the gospel of salvation in Christ is true.*

⁸ Even if we or an angel from heaven should preach a gospel other than the one we preached to you, let him be eternally condemned! (Galatians 1:8)

Paul's great concern was that everyone stick with the gospel of Christ so that

[5] the **truth of the gospel** might remain with you. (Galatians 2:5)

At one point Paul had to confront Peter for not living up to the truth of the gospel.

[14] When I saw that they were not acting in line with the **truth of the gospel**, I said to Peter in front of them all, "You are a Jew, yet you live like a Gentile and not like a Jew. (Galatians 2:14)

Paul defined the *gospel* as the *'word of truth'*. He reminded the Ephesian Christians of this.

[13] You also were included in Christ when you heard **the word of truth, the gospel of your salvation.** (Ephesians 1:13)

Paul reminded the Colossian Christians that **the gospel is** *true*.

[5] The faith and love that spring from the hope that is stored up for you in heaven and that you have already heard about in **the word of truth, the gospel**

[6] that has come to you. All over the world this **gospel** is bearing fruit and growing, just as it has been doing among you since the day you heard it and understood **God's grace in all its truth**. (Colossians 1:5-6)

And to the Thessalonian believers Paul sent the same message.

[13] We ought always to thank God for you, brothers loved by the Lord, because from the beginning God chose you to be saved through the sanctifying work of the Spirit and through **belief in the truth**.

¹⁴ He called you to this through **our gospel**, that you
might share in the glory of our Lord Jesus Christ.
(2 Thessalonians 2:13-14)

'A word is a word is a word', but when it is *the* 'word of God' it is a
*deep truth.* Paul urged Timothy who was teaching the Deacons of his
church to impress upon them that

⁹ They must keep hold of the **deep truths of the faith**
with a clear conscience.
(1 Timothy 3:9)

The truth of the matter is that if a person refuses to believe the *deep*
*truths of the gospel* he has forfeited his only hope of eternal salvation.

¹² Salvation is found in no one else, for **there is no other**
**name** under heaven given to men by which we must be
saved." (Acts 4:12)

The 'good news' of the gospel is this:

⁴ God our Savior…wants all men to be saved and to come
to a *knowledge of the* truth.
(1 Timothy 2:3-4)

According to Jesus this is all about coming out of the darkness of
our ignorance, the darkness of our sin and fears and into the light of his
presence to be saved.

¹⁹ This is the verdict: Light has come into the world, but
men loved darkness instead of light because their deeds
were evil.

²⁰ Everyone who does evil hates the light, and will not
come into the light for fear that his deeds will be exposed.

²¹ But **whoever lives by the truth comes into the light**, so that it may be seen plainly that what he has done has been done through God." (John 3:19-21)

Those who believe *the truth of the gospel of salvation in Christ* do not perish, rather, they are given entrance into heaven -into Paradise itself. A friend of my wife was on her death bed. After being unresponsive for 2 or 3 days family members were called to her bedside knowing that the end was near. Suddenly, to everyone's surprise she opened her eyes and with a far off look she spoke with her last breath, *'It's all really true!'* and then she passed into the presence of her Lord and Savior Jesus! To God be the glory!

# Truth is Freeing to Live By

³ Send forth your light and **your truth**, let them guide me; let them bring me to your holy mountain, to the place where you dwell. (Psalm 43:3)

³² I run in the path of your commands, for you have set my heart free.
(Psalm 119:32)

Some people walk around freely in our society but are imprisoned spirits due to the guilt of unconfessed sins, and the fear that the truth will find them out. By contrast, I have known people in prison who have come to believe the *truth* that Jesus Christ is their Savior, and it has transformed their lives by *setting their spirits free*! Although still incarcerated they have been set free by God from the guilt and consequences of their sins. It's the case that 'prison bars do not a prison make'. They tell of the freedom they have to share the gospel with inmates, participate in prison worship services, study the scriptures in depth, and pray.

³² You will know the **truth**, and the **truth will set you free.**"

³⁴ Jesus replied, "I tell you the **truth**, everyone who sins is a slave to sin...

[36] So if the Son sets you free, you will be free indeed.
(John 8:32, 34, 36)

Just *telling the truth* in itself *is freeing*! When I was a young child my father taught me many things that have stayed with me a lifetime. I remember him saying, "Dougie, tell the truth and you won't have to remember what you said!" That was a freeing concept for me. Tell the truth and God will bring back into your mind what you have said; tell a lie and you're on your own -without God's help. You have to remember every word you said, lest you slip up and get caught in your lie, which God has determined will happen sooner or later.

# God Looks for Truth in Us

Looking for truth in us is *God's way*!

[3] O LORD, do not **your eyes look for truth**?
(Jeremiah 5:3; Ps 51:6)

We know about 'truth in advertising' and hope merchants are telling us the truth about the products they are urging us to buy -especially if the product is a used car that looks in too good of a shape to be true. There were no used cars in biblical times (maybe used chariots), but they sold many things by weight, therefore the God of all Truth had a lot to say about not being a cheating merchant with dishonest scales.

[13] Do not have two differing weights in your bag—one heavy, one light.

[14] Do not have two differing measures in your house—one large, one small.

[15] You must have accurate and honest weights and measures, so that you may live long in the land the LORD your God is giving you.

*Douglas Nelson*

<sup>16</sup> For the LORD your God detests anyone who does these things, anyone who deals dishonestly.
(Deuteronomy 25:13-16; Lev 19:36, Prov 11:1; Ezk 45:10-11)

The merchants in Amos's day were delighted every time their religious holidays were over so they could reopen their shops and get back to enriching themselves by short changing their customers.

<sup>5</sup> "When will the New Moon be over that we may sell grain, and the Sabbath be ended that we may market wheat?"— **skimping the measure, boosting the price and cheating with dishonest scales.** (Amos 8:5)

The customer, too, can make an unfair profit by bartering with a merchant until he becomes willing to sell below cost rather than lose the sale completely.

<sup>14</sup> "It's no good, it's no good!" says the buyer; then off he goes and boasts about his purchase.
(Proverbs 20:14).

The *God of all truth* sees everything and calls us to account -even if it means a 'Last Judgment'.

<sup>13</sup> Nothing in all creation is hidden from God's sight. Everything is uncovered and laid bare before the eyes of him to whom **we must give account.** (Hebrews 4:13)

This certainly proved itself out in the early church when Peter exposed the lies of a husband and wife who had conspired to cheat the church out of some money by lying.

<sup>3</sup> Then Peter said, "Ananias, how is it that Satan has so filled your heart that you have **lied to the Holy Spirit** and have kept for yourself some of the money you received for the land? (Acts 5:3)

They weren't just lying to Peter or to the church, but they were lying to the living God.

## God Teaches Truth

Tertullian (155-240 AD) an early leader in the Church wrote:

Whatever you are to believe about God, you must **learn it from God himself**. If you do not obtain this knowledge from God, you will be unable to obtain it from any other person. For who is able to reveal that which God has hidden?

Desire to understand what God has disclosed to us. This was the Psalmist's desire of heart. He knew what to pray for, namely, discernment.

> [125] I am your servant; give me discernment that I may understand your statutes. (Psalm 119:125)

Animals differ from us in that they have no teachers; they do not sit in classrooms, they read no books. They operate on natural instinct. A favorite pastime of my wife and I have is to watch birds that fly to our birdfeeder. No one taught them how to fly yet they make perfect landings and take offs. We also have a birdhouse that becomes home every year to a wren family. It's fascinating to watch the 'father' bird day-after-day bring twigs to build a complex nest –at least it would be complex for me to build! ☺

We are not animals of instinct. There is information that *God wants to teach us* from Scripture. God makes note that this is a distinction between us and animals of instinct.

> [8] **I will instruct you and teach you** in the way you should go; I will counsel you and watch over you.

⁹ Do not be like the horse or the mule, which have **no understanding** but must be controlled by bit and bridle or they will not come to you.
(Psalm 32:8-9)

Consider another example. The ant doesn't learn from us, but God in his Word teaches us what we can learn from observing ants.

⁶ **Go to the ant**, you sluggard; consider its ways and be wise!

⁷ It has no commander, no overseer or ruler,

⁸ yet it stores its provisions in summer and gathers its food at harvest.

⁹ How long will you lie there, you sluggard? When will you get up from your sleep?

¹⁰ A little sleep, a little slumber, a little folding of the hands to rest—

¹¹ and poverty will come on you like a bandit and scarcity like an armed man. (Proverbs 6:6-11)

There is a lot I don't remember from my college days, but I remember Proverbs 6:10-11 'A little sleep, a little slumber, a little folding of the hands to rest— and poverty will come on you like a bandit and scarcity like an armed man.' I had just barely settled into my room in the freshmen dorm the first day I had arrived on campus when everyone got word the Dean of Men that evening wanted to meet all of us in the dorm lounge. Once he got everyone's attention he spoke to us on these verses about the need for us to study hard and not become lax; not to 'fold our hands' and 'slumber' in our classes. This was the talk we all needed in order to get off on the right foot in the new world of college academia. I learned something that evening from the self-motivated industrious **ant**! ☺

We might do well to liken God to a Dean of Men sitting us down to teach us things we desperately need to know if we are to function well in life. More than anything God wants to teach us *his ways,* so we can not only know about him, but also know him, believe in him, love him and serve him, because he is worthy. Moses prayed to God,

> [13] If you are pleased with me, **teach me your ways** so I may know you and continue to find favor with you. (Exodus 33:13)

This was a repeated prayer of David in scripture.

> [11] **Teach me your way, O LORD**, and **I will walk in your truth**; give me an undivided heart, that I may fear your name.
> (Psalm 86:11; 27:11; 143:8-10)

Are we eager to be 'taught by God' what he wants us to know about himself, about us, about life, about eternity? God is willing to be our Teacher.

> [17] "**I am the LORD your God, who teaches you** what is best for you, who directs you in the way you should go." (Isaiah 48:17)

If we think of God's Word the way the Psalmist did, we will be more than willing to be taught of God.

> [103] How **sweet are your words** to my taste, sweeter than honey to my mouth. (Psalm 119:103)

Once my wife and I were among 3000 people who attended a Christian conference in Washington DC at the Convention Center. The speaker set before us the challenge to make a vow to the Lord that we would spend time reading and meditating on the scriptures every day. That was over forty years ago and we haven't missed a day. Being in the Word is the best part of our day every day. The Lord teaches us daily from his Word; it's where we hear his Voice loud and clear☺

<sup></sup>¹⁵ I meditate on your precepts and consider **your ways.**

¹⁶ **I delight** in your decrees; I will not neglect your word. (Psalm 119:15-16)

***God's purpose for teaching*** us ***his ways disclosed in his Word*** is so that he might guide us into living meaningful, fulfilling, godly lives and thus bring glory to God.

¹⁰⁵ **Your word is a lamp** to my feet and a light for my path. (Psalm 119:105)

¹³⁰ The **unfolding of your words** gives **light**; it gives **understanding** to the simple. (Psalm 119:130)

Isaiah made this prophecy regarding the fact that ***till the end of time God will teach his ways.***

² In the last days...

³ Many peoples will come and say, "Come, let us go up to the mountain of the LORD, to the house of the God of Jacob. He will **teach us his ways,** so that we may **walk in his paths.**" (Isaiah 2:2-3)

# We can Know Truth

By contrast unbelievers will not let God teach them, because they don't believe there is any God. They assume what is 'invisible' is non-existent or at least unknowable. The ancient intellects of Athens, proved themselves to be agnostics when they erected a monument 'To the Unknown God'.

David states why unbelievers, agnostics, and atheists don't want there to be a 'God'. The reason is that they have a moral problem. They don't want any moral absolutes; no truth to hold them accountable for their thoughts, words or deeds.

> ¹ The fool says in his heart, "There is no God." They are **corrupt,** their deeds are **vile**; there is no one who does good. (Psalm 14:1)

> ¹⁴ They say to God, 'Leave us alone! We have no desire to know your ways. ¹⁵ Who is the Almighty, that we should serve him? What would we gain by praying to him?' (Job 21:14-15)

In a ***Peanuts*** comic strip Lucy is quizzing one of her friends about what he learned in school that day. "We studied the Copernicus Theory". "What's that?" Lucy asked. "It's the theory that the world revolves around the sun." "That's funny", Lucy said, "I always thought the world revolved around me!" ☺

It's sad to observe that there are people who think they are the fount of all of knowledge, and, therefore, if they say God doesn't exist he doesn't exist. But the truth is that we have access to information about God that didn't originate in this world, namely, the Heaven-sent inspired Word of God!

For example, this was the case of the young prophet Jeremiah, when he wrote from his heart words that didn't originate with him.

> ⁹ **The LORD reached out his hand and touched my mouth** and said to me, "Now, **I have put my words in your mouth.** (Jeremiah 1:9)

John Wesley along with his brother Charles were the founders of the Methodists which is now a worldwide denomination of churches. John put down in print his hunger and thirst for the Word of God to inform him about God; about life; about eternity!

To candid reasonable men I am not afraid to lay open what have been the inmost thoughts of the heart. I have thought: I am a creature of a day, passing through life as an arrow through the air. I am a spirit come from God and returning to God, just hovering over the great gulf till a few moments hence I am no more seen. I drop into an unchangeable eternity. I want to know one thing: the way to Heaven, how to land safe on that happy shore. God himself has condescended to teach the way. For this very end He came down from Heaven. He has written it in a book. Oh, give me that book. At any price, give me the Book of God. I have it! Here is knowledge enough for me. (Vernon Grounds, Radical Commitment, p. 50)

God desires that we desire to know all the *truth* about him and his ways he has recorded in the 'Book of God', that is, the Bible. J.B. Phillips in his classic book 'Your God is Too Small' writes:

"We can never have too big a conception of God." (p. 120)

Elihu's words fit well here.

2 "Bear with me a little longer and I will show you that there is more to be said in God's behalf."
(Job 36:2)

The Bible was designed by God to end our ignorance of the truth about him.

3 God our Savior…

4 wants **all men to be saved and to come to a knowledge of the truth**. (1 Timothy 2:3-4)

God wants us to know truth, especially the truth of the Gospel of salvation

²¹ I do not write to you because you do not **know the truth**, but because you do know it.
(1 John 2:21)

# We can Believe in the Truth -God's truth

There are people who are gullible, willing to believe everything without question. But there are also many people who are skeptical about everything; "Is it really true?" "It sounds too good to be true." The author of Job puts it well.

³ The ear tests words as the tongue **tastes** food.
(Job 34:3; 12:11)

The Author of Hebrews notes that there are people who have

⁵ **tasted** the goodness of **the word of God.**
(Hebrews 6:5)

² Like newborn babies, crave pure spiritual milk, so that by it you may grow up in your salvation,

³ now that you have **tasted** that the Lord is good.
(1 Peter 2:2-3)

⁸ **Taste** and see that the LORD is good; blessed is the man who takes refuge in him. (Psalm 34:8)

It is good to question those who question 'truth'. If someone says, "There is no truth." You might ask, "*Is that true?*" Or if someone says, "There are no absolutes." You might respond, "Are you *absolutely* sure?"☺ These are two questions Kelly Monroe Kullberg used to ask university students when she was a campus chaplain on an Ivy League campus in an effort to have them doubt their doubts. ('Finding God At Harvard') God gives us the ability to *recognize* and *believe truth.*

¹³ From the beginning God chose you to be saved through the sanctifying work of the Spirit and through **belief in the truth**. (2 Thessalonians 2:13)

Paul reminded Timothy that in 'later times' (which may be our times) how *critical* it will be *to know and believe the Truth as revealed by God* so as not to be deceived by hypocritical liars controlled by 'deceiving spirits'.

¹ The Spirit clearly says that in **later times** some will abandon the faith and follow **deceiving spirits** and **things taught by demons.**

² Such teachings come through **hypocritical liars**, whose consciences have been seared as with a hot iron. (1 Timothy 4:1-2)

Paul's warning was that no one be caught up in any form of spiritual darkness.

May we be able to say with David,

⁴ Even though I walk through the valley of the shadow of death, I will **fear no evil**, for you are with me; your rod and your staff, they comfort me. (Psalm 23:4)

The Lord's *rod* fends off every lie of the 'Evil One'; his *staff* points us in the right direction -the truth about God and the will of God. It is possible to believe the truth about God and God's Word even if at the moment we seem to be in a 'dark place.'

Clement of Alexandria (132-217) wrote these encouraging words.

Sometimes…God causes pain to enter our lives. You must seek Him during these times to see if He is using pain to teach and train you. If so, He will make it plain. If nothing else, the wise person knows that pain can cause you to press deeper into God –that is, into a more complete dependence upon Him- where you find sublime comfort of soul that lifts you above all anguish...For there our souls find rest, even when we cannot see where our Shepherd is leading us –even when the path ahead appears dark to our natural eyes. The more you come to rest in Him (and His Word), the more fully you will enter into Life- that is, the kind of spiritual life that even death cannot touch.

(Miscellaneous Teachings, David Hazard You Give Me New Life, pp. 90-91)

John Ramsey has written about his young daughter's kidnapping from her bedroom while he and his wife slept. The title of his book tells his story. 'The Other Side of Suffering: One Man's Journey from Devastation to Redemption'

> It was by *reading the Scriptures* and spending time in prayer that I came to discover we can become one with God's heart and mind, and the material world loses its grip on our thoughts. (p. 115)

When anyone believes in the truth of God's Word he falls heir to a spiritual strength that can enable him to endure anything. There are many stories coming from the persecuted Church. When Christians come under persecution and suffering the Scriptures become especially precious due to their sustaining power. Here is one story coming out of the French Revolution.

> "Political prisoners were herded into dungeons. In one place a prisoner possessed a Bible. His cell was crammed with men who wanted to hear the Word of God. Once each day for only a few moments a small shaft of light would come through a tiny window near the ceiling. The prisoners devised a plan whereby they would lift the owner of the Bible onto their shoulders and into the sunlight. There, in that positon, he would study the Scriptures.

Then they would bring him down and say, "Tell us now, friend, what did you read while you were in the light?'" (Hadden Robinson, Focal Point July-September 86)

# We Can Choose to Walk in the Truth

We can willingly choose to **walk in the truth** God has revealed regarding himself.

> ³ Your love is ever before me, and **I walk continually in your truth**. (Psalm 26:3)

David went on to say what this looks like

> ¹¹ **Teach me your way**, O LORD, and I will **walk in your truth;** give me an undivided heart, that I may fear your name. (Psalm 86:11)

Another Psalmist has written,

> ³⁰ I have chosen **the way of truth**; I have set my heart on your laws. (Psalm 119:30)

We can trust whatever God has said in the Scriptures he will do. It's walking in *the truth of God's Word* that *sustains* us and keeps hope alive!

> ¹¹⁶ **Sustain me** according to your **promise**, and I will live; do not let **my hopes** be dashed.
> (Psalm 119:116)

The aged beloved Apostle John thought of the members of his church as being his own 'dear children'. Nothing made him happier than to know that they chose to *walk in the truth.*

³ It gave me great **joy** to have some brothers come and tell about your **faithfulness to the truth** and how **you continue to walk in the truth.**

⁴ I have no greater **joy** than to hear that my children are **walking in the truth.** (3 John 1:3-4)

This same *joy* warms the hearts of fathers and mothers everywhere who are able to say this of their children. This is true in my case. My wife and I have **continual joy** knowing our children and grandchildren *'walk in the truth'*. Just today we received an email from one of our grandchildren that contained the words,

'I'm trying to stay strong and travel this new path with God at the helm. We'll see what he has in store for me!'

## We can Obey the Truth

It is true that we're saved by God's grace rather than by obeying all God's laws perfectly. God does not require us to obey all his moral laws as a *prerequisite* for salvation, nor to *retain* our salvation. Nevertheless, the word *'obey'* must remain in our Christian vocabulary if we ever hope to *express* our salvation.

¹⁵ "If you **love me**, you will **obey** what I command. (John 14:15)

To love the Lord is to love his Word. It's the *love* we have for our Savior that compels us to want to do what he tells us in his Word to do to *express* our salvation and our love for him. I dearly love my wife. As such, I enjoy expressing my love for her by *doing* everything I can that I know is meaningful and pleases her. To an even greater degree I long to please my Savior by doing what he says pleases him! And this is not hard in that what he wants me to do is always true; it's always the right thing to do.

With all of this in mind let's think of the New Testament word *'obey'* in terms of *heart-felt desire!* Paul urged the Galatian Christians not to listen to those who might try to get them to drop from their vocabulary the word 'obey' -as in 'obey the Lord's commands'. He said that to do so would be like running a race and someone purposely cutting in on you, tripping you up and thus putting you out of the competition.

> [7] You were running a good race. Who cut in on you and kept you from **obeying the truth**?
> (Galatians 5:7)

'*Obeying* the *truth*', makes everyone a winner whose life you touch.

> [22] Now that you have purified yourselves by **obeying the truth** so that you have **sincere love for your brothers**, **love one another deeply, from the heart.** (1 Peter 1:22)

We exhibit the *truths of Scripture* by the way in which we 'run the race' (*obey*). The scripture doesn't lack in giving us practical ways to obey scriptural truths so that our lives are a blessing to others. For example:

> [16] These are the things you are to do: **Speak the truth** to each other, and **render true and sound judgment** in your courts;
>
> [17] do not plot evil against your neighbor, and **do not love to swear falsely.** I hate all this," declares the LORD. (Zechariah 8:16-17)

# We Can Speak the Truth in Love.

Embedded in Paul's definition of love is the fact that love is all about being truthful to the one we say we love. I'm truthful to my wife whom I love; to her I'm an 'open book'!

> [6] **Love** does not delight in evil but **rejoices with the truth.**
> (1 Corinthians 13:6)

¹⁵ **Speaking the truth in love**, we will in all things grow
up into him who is the Head, that is, Christ…
(Ephesians 4:15)

# Truth Works

**Truth is powerful** when it is argued; it is even more
powerful when it is exhibited.
(John Stott, Involvement, p. 1:110)

Here is good news: *truth works* because it can be verified. Jesus, for example, was able to verify his truth claim that he was the Son of God -deity in flesh- by rising from the dead!

Yes, *truth works* because it can be verified. For example, There are an infinite number of possible answers to the equation 2+2, but there is only one right answer: '3'. Did I say '3'? I meant '4'. A State Lottery on one occasion sold 190 million tickets for a $243 million jackpot but only one ticket holder had the winning number on his ticket! Truth can be that narrow; that precise!

Punch in a phone number. Being close to getting the number correct doesn't work. Either it's totally right, and the phone rings, or it's totally wrong even if it is off only one digit, and the call doesn't go through. Inaccurate E-mail addresses are equally unforgiving.

Sports teams 'play by the rules'. In fact, any 'game' is nothing but a set of rules to be rigidly followed. Everyone knows that no team wins by breaking the Rules. Break the rules and there is a penalty; possibly even the forfeiture of the game. Either you play by the rules 'fair and square', or the game is over.

When it comes to telling the truth, lying does not work -at least not ultimately.

¹⁹ Truthful lips endure forever, but a lying tongue lasts
only a moment. (Proverbs 12:19)

*Truth is very narrow.* Perhaps this was why Jesus gave us the parable of two roads in the Sermon on the Mount. There is the ***narrow road of truth***, and the ***broad road paved with lies***!

[13] "Enter through the **narrow gate**. For wide is the gate and broad is the road that leads to destruction, and many enter through it.

[14] But small is the gate and **narrow the road that leads to life, and only a few find it.**
(Matthew 7:13-14)

Jesus himself is the 'Narrow Road' of truth.

[6] Jesus answered, "I am **the way** and **the truth** and the life. No one comes to the Father except through me.
(John 14:6)

[12] Salvation is found **in no one else**, for there is **no other name** under heaven given to men by which we must be saved." (Acts 4:12)

*'No one else' -Truth is that narrow!*

# Satan is the Father of Lies

Satan gives us options to truth. He has been attempting to offset the truth of God's Word with lies from the day he arrived in the Garden of Edom and deceived Adam and Eve by boasting he was offering them a better deal than what God was offering them. Jesus has exposed the Evil One as an inveterate liar.

[44] He was a murderer from the beginning, not holding to the truth, for there is no truth in him. When he lies, he speaks his native language, for **he is a liar** and the **father of lies**. (John 8:44)

Satan's objective is to convince people to *exchange* God's *Truth for a lie* by promising something better, but when all is said and done nothing he promises comes true.

²⁵ They **exchanged** the truth of God for a lie, and worshiped and served created things rather than the Creator—who is forever praised. Amen.
(Romans 1:25)

'Worship' is what Satan is after from us and especially from Jesus! The devil was so emboldened as to tempt the Son of God to worship him by disguising his lie as 'truth'.

⁶ He said to him, "I will give you all their authority and splendor, for it has been given to me, and I can give it to anyone I want to. [This was a lie]

⁷ So if you worship me, it will all be yours."
(Luke 4:6-7)

If the devil was so brazen as to tempt the Son of God we can be sure he will tempt us, also. Due to his pride and jealousy he wants to draw worship to himself -worship that rightly should go to God alone.

Satan's ploy is to suppress truth –to make truth look like a lie and a lie look like truth.

¹⁸ The wrath of God is being revealed from heaven against all the godlessness and **wickedness** of men who **suppress the truth** by their wickedness, (Romans 1:18)

What does 'suppression of truth' look like? Isaiah called the sinful people of his generation to account for attempting to twist lies into truth and truth into lies.

²⁰ Woe to those who call evil good and good evil, who put darkness for light and light for darkness, who put bitter for sweet and sweet for bitter.
(Isaiah 5:20)

In scripture we are encouraged to *love truth*!

<sup>19</sup>**love truth** and peace." (Zechariah 8:19)

Unfortunately, truth is hard to come by in our fallen world. It is depressing to turn on the news and hear story after story about people being caught in their lies -lies that have helped no one and have hurt many. Then there is 'Fake News' -news reported as true but is actually not true at all.

In Isaiah's day *truth* was in short order.

<sup>14</sup> Justice is driven back, and righteousness stands at a distance; **truth has stumbled in the streets**, honesty cannot enter.

<sup>15</sup> **Truth is nowhere to be found.** (Isaiah 59:14-15)

If you had walked the streets of Jerusalem in Jeremiah's day this is what it would have looked like:

<sup>1</sup> "Go up and down the streets of Jerusalem, look around and consider, search through her squares. If you **can find but one person who deals honestly and seeks the truth**, I will forgive this city.

<sup>2</sup> Although they say, 'As surely as the LORD lives,' still they are swearing falsely."

<sup>3</sup> O LORD, **do not your eyes look for truth**? You struck them, but they felt no pain; you crushed them, but they refused correction. They made their faces harder than stone and refused to repent. (Jeremiah 5:1-3)

<sup>14</sup> The visions of your **prophets were false** and worthless; they did not expose your sin to ward off your captivity. The oracles they gave you were **false and misleading**. (Lamentations 2:14)

According to John a lie is the antithesis of 'truth'

²¹ **No lie comes from the truth.** (1 John 2:21)

Paul warned the Corinthian church to be aware of false teachers -men who have played into the devil's hands.

¹⁴ **Satan himself masquerades as an angel of light.**

¹⁵ It is not surprising, then, if his servants masquerade as servants of righteousness. Their end will be what their actions deserve. (2 Corinthians 11:14-15)

*God* affirms again and again through his inspired spokesmen in Scripture that he always and *only tells the truth. God is not a liar.*

¹⁹ **God is not a man, that he should lie**, nor a son of man, that he should change his mind. Does he speak and then not act? Does he promise and not fulfill? (Numbers 23:19)

*Samuel* also went on record that God is not a liar.

⁹ He who is the **Glory of Israel** (i.e. **God**) **does not lie or change his mind**; for he is not a man, that he should change his mind." (1 Samuel 15:29)

The author of Hebrews goes so far as to say:

¹⁸ It is **impossible for God to lie.** (Hebrews 6:18)

God has sworn to tell the truth, sworn that he will keep his word. Here is an example out of Abraham's life.

¹³ When God made his promise to Abraham, since there was **no one greater for him to swear by, he swore by himself.** (Hebrews 6:13)

God also swore to David regarding the longevity of his kingship:

³⁵ Once for all, I have **sworn by my holiness** —and **I will not lie** to David—

³⁶ that his line will continue forever and his throne endure before me like the sun. (Psalm 89:35-36)

This was an incredible promise! Is God true to his word? It is now 3000 years later. Is 'his line continuing'? Yes it is, through Jesus the 'Son of David' who reigns forever as King of Kings and Lord of Lords. To God be the glory! Here are the prophetic words of scripture that state how God intended to make good his word of promise. With reference to Jesus Isaiah predicted that

⁷ Of the increase of his government and peace there will be no end. **He will reign on David's** throne and over his kingdom, establishing and upholding it with justice and righteousness **from that time on and forever**. The zeal of the LORD Almighty will accomplish this. (Isaiah 9:6-7)

The angel Gabriel announced to awestruck Mary, a direct descendant of David, that her virgin born son

³³ will reign over the house of Jacob **forever; his kingdom will never end."** (Luke 1:33)

Paul valued God's promises because they were true, and he knew they would come to pass.

²⁰ No matter how many **promises God has made**, they are "Yes" in Christ. (2 Corinthians 1:20)

God keeps all his promises, but here is something we need to keep in mind. God keeps his promises in his time -not our time. God, for example, promised to bring Judah back from her captivity to Babylon. But God through the prophet Jeremiah instructed them to settle down in Babylon, build houses, plant gardens, marry and have children, because the 'promise' wouldn't come to pass for 70 years.

<sup>10</sup> This is what the LORD says: "**When seventy years are completed** for Babylon, I will come to you and **fulfill my gracious promise** to bring you back to this place. (Jeremiah 29:10)

If a promise of God in his Word doesn't seem to be coming true for you, don't doubt God and his promise, rather consider the *timing* for the fulfillment of the promise. It will be at the right time -the time of God's choosing.

<sup>14</sup> "'The **days are coming**,' declares the LORD, '**when I will fulfill the gracious promise I made** to the house of Israel and to the house of Judah. (Jeremiah 33:14)

Here is an example of one of the many promises God has made to us in Scripture that we can claim by faith -but in God's time and under his terms and not ours. The day I was on my way to candidate to become the pastor of my first church the Lord brought to my attention a promise.

<sup>7</sup> God hath not given us the **spirit of fear**; but of power, and of love, and of a sound mind. (2 Timothy 1:7 KJV)

<sup>10</sup> Do not fear, for I am with you; do not be dismayed, for I am your God. I will strengthen you and help you; I will uphold you with my righteous right hand. (Isaiah 41:10)

I had been afraid, but from that point on I was not afraid. I can report that the Lord offset my weakness with his strength. I candidated and shortly afterward was invited to become their pastor. I can think of the many times through the ensuing years the Lord has strengthened me, helped me, and upheld me when I was weak, helpless and about to fall.

The Lord wants us to be totally committed to truth. To make this possible he makes 'truth' part of our 'spiritual armor' with which to fight the devil. He has buckled every piece of our spiritual armor altogether with the '*belt of truth*' thus making us invincible against Satan and his lies.

> [14] Stand firm then, with the **belt of truth** buckled around your waist. (Ephesians 6:14)

God's Word being *true* was also the conclusion of the Psalmist.

> [160] **All your words** are **true**; all your righteous laws are eternal. (Psalm 119:160)

# Reasons for Unbelief in the Truth

A spirit of rebellion against truth has always been pervasive. Here is but one example. Aldous Huxley wrote in 'Ends and Means' (p.312)

> I had motives for not wanting the world to have a meaning; consequently I assumed that it had none, and was able without difficulty to find satisfying reasons for this assumption...The philosopher who finds no meaning in the world...is concerned to prove that there is no valid reason why he personally should not do as he wants to do...For myself as, no doubt, for most of my generation the philosophy of meaninglessness was essentially an instrument of liberation...from a certain system of morality. We objected to morality because it interfered with our sexual freedom; we objected to the political and economic system...The supporters of these systems claimed that in some way they embodied the meaning (a Christian meaning, they insisted) of the world. There was one admirably simple method of confuting these people and at the same time justifying ourselves in our political and erotic revolt: we could deny that the world had any meaning whatsoever.

Huxley's words remind me of David's dire prediction in the Psalms.

¹ The fool says in his heart, "There is no God." They are corrupt, their deeds are vile; there is no one who does good. (Psalm 14:1-3)

Daniel's words apply here.

¹² Because of rebellion...**truth was thrown to the ground.** (Daniel 8:12)

The Evil One attempts to denigrate truth every way he can. He makes a 24/7 concerted effort to bombard us with an unending stream of covert and overt lies that he crafts together in the form of luring temptations, false accusations and bully threats. It's all by design to get back at God whom he hates by attempting to destroy in any way he can God's prized creation -us!

## Suppress Truth

¹⁸ The wrath of God is being revealed from heaven against all the godlessness and wickedness of men who **suppress the truth** by their wickedness, (Romans 1:18)

## Exchange Truth for a Lie

²⁵ They **exchanged the truth of God** for a lie, and worshiped and served created things rather than the Creator—who is forever praised. Amen. (Romans 1:25)

## Give No Attention to Truth

¹³ We have **not sought** the favor of the LORD our God by turning from our sins and giving **attention to your truth**. (Daniel 9:13)

## Reject Truth

[8] For those who are self-seeking and who **reject the truth** and follow evil, there will be wrath and anger. (Romans 2:8)

## Against Truth

[8] We cannot do anything **against the truth**, but only for the truth. (2 Corinthians 13:8)

## Robbed of Truth

[5] (There is) constant friction between men of corrupt mind, who have been **robbed of the truth**. (1 Timothy 6:5)

## Wander Away from Truth

[18] (They)…have **wandered away from the truth**. (2 Timothy 2:18)

## Despise Truth

God appointed Nathan the prophet to confront David following his act of committing adultery with Bathsheba.

[9] **Why did you despise the word of the LORD** by doing what is evil in his eyes? (2 Samuel 12:9)

To renounce truth for any reason is to despise God -the God of all Truth. Nathan brought it to David's attention that in *despising the word of God* he was actually *despising God himself* -which comes with consequences.

[10] Now, therefore, the sword will never depart from your house, **because you despised me** and took the wife of Uriah the Hittite to be your own.
(2 Samuel 12:10)

David repented and God forgave, but the Old Testament Scripture from David's time on is a sad record of tragedies that befell his descendants generation after generation beginning with his son Absalom.

## Oppose Truth

> [8] Just as Jannes and Jambres opposed Moses, so also these men **oppose the truth**—men of depraved minds, who, as far as the faith is concerned, are rejected. (2 Timothy 3:8)

## Turn away From Truth

> [4] They will **turn their ears away from the truth** and turn aside to myths. (2 Timothy 4:4)

Time and again following Paul's clear presentation of the truth of the Gospel of salvation in Jesus Christ some who listened turned away from the truth and turned on him. True to form in the concluding verses of Acts which records the last incident in Paul's life he is sharing the Gospel. Afterward some believed, but many turned away from the truth of the Gospel forcing Paul to declare that Isaiah's prophecy fit them:

> [26] "'Go to this people and say, "You will be ever hearing but never understanding; you will be ever seeing but never perceiving." (Acts 28:26)

## Dispute truth

> [2] Many will follow...shameful ways and will **bring the way of truth into disrepute.** (2 Peter 2:2)

## Walk in 'Darkness'

> [6] If we claim to have fellowship with him yet **walk in the darkness**, we **lie and do not live by the truth.** (1 John 1:6)

*Douglas Nelson*

## Self-deception

> [8] If we claim to be without sin, we **deceive ourselves** and **the truth is not in us.** (1 John 1:8)

## Lies do not come from Truth

> [21] I do not write to you because you do not know the truth, but because you do know it and because **no lie comes from the truth.** (1 John 2:21)

The God of all Truth has summed up in a sentence what he thinks of liars and truth tellers.

> [22] The LORD **detests** lying lips, but he **delights** in men who are **truthful.** (Proverbs 12:22)

John in Revelation learned *the fate of all liars* when he was informed who will be the residents of the lake of fire.

> [8] The cowardly, the unbelieving, the vile, the murderers, the sexually immoral, those who practice magic arts, the idolaters and **all liars**—their place will be in the fiery lake of burning sulfur. This is the second death." (Revelation 21:8)

No one should take these words lightly in that these words have appeared in every Bible that has ever been printed.

## Test Truth

Elihu said to Job:

> [3] **The ear tests words** as the tongue tastes food. (Job 34:3)

Paul stated it simply by saying,

²¹ **Test everything..** (1 Thessalonians 5:21)

When we test God's words what do we find?

⁵ "**Every word of God** is **flawless.** (Proverbs 30:5)

David defines *the truth of God's Word* in this picturesque way:

⁶ The **words of the LORD are flawless,** like silver refined
in a furnace of clay, purified seven times.
(Psalm 12:6; 2 Sam 22:31)

*God has a purpose* for every word he has ever said.

¹¹ My **word that goes out from my mouth**…will not
return to me empty, but **will accomplish** what I desire
and **achieve** the purpose for which I sent it.
(Isaiah 55:11)

¹² The **word of God** is living and active. Sharper than any
double-edged sword, **it penetrates** even to dividing soul
and spirit, joints and marrow; it judges the thoughts and
attitudes of the heart.
(Hebrews 4:12)

Is God willing for his words to be tested? Is God insulted if we demand proof his words are true? Do his prophesies actually come *true*? God always makes good on his word; always makes good on his promises. The Lord always does what he says he will do; in his time; in his way, for his glory; for our good! This was the point Joshua was making when he spoke to the newly formed nation of Israel shortly after they had conquered Canaan –the '*Promised Land*'.

⁴⁵ Not one of all **the LORD's good promises** to the house
of Israel failed; every one was fulfilled. (Joshua 21:45)

Centuries later, David had this to say about God's 'promises':

**The LORD is faithful to all his promises** and loving toward all he has made. (Psalm 145:13)

Solomon remained equally convinced that the promises God made to Israel had all come true.

[56] "Praise be to the LORD, who has given rest to his people Israel just as he promised. **Not one word has failed of all the good promises** he gave through his servant Moses. (1 Kings 8:56)

Although we may have confidence that God's words are true, trusting men who claim to be speaking God's words is something else. Moses said their words must be put to the test.

[21] You may say to yourselves, "How can we know when a message has not been spoken by the LORD?"

[22] If what a prophet proclaims in the name of the LORD does **not** take place or **come true**, that is a message the LORD has not spoken. That prophet has spoken presumptuously. Do not be afraid of him. (Deuteronomy 18:21-22)

The new Christians in Berea did their own *checking on Paul's words* that he claimed were inspired by God.

[11] They received the message with great eagerness and **examined the Scriptures** every day to see if what Paul said was **true**. (Acts 17:11)

They put Paul's words up against the known words of Scripture to see if there was a match. There was a perfect match, so they felt comfortable accepting Paul's words as the '*gospel truth*' -as being on equal par with the Holy Scriptures. Peter was among the first people to call Paul's teaching 'Scripture'.

<sup>16</sup> His letters contain some things that are hard to understand, which ignorant and unstable people distort, as they do the other Scriptures, to their own destruction. (2 Peter 3:16)

John noted that we are to *test the spirits* to know whether or not it is truly the Holy Spirit (the Spirit of Truth) and not a 'spirit of the antichrist' speaking lies through false prophets.

<sup>1</sup> Dear friends, **do not believe every spirit, but test the spirits** to see whether they are from God, because **many false prophets** have gone out into the world.

<sup>2</sup> This is how you can recognize the Spirit of God: Every spirit that acknowledges that Jesus Christ has come in the flesh is from God. (1 John 4:1-2)

It's the truth of God's Word that enables us to identify people who are deceitful liars and hypocrites. Their words and their lives never measure up to the truth of Scripture.

## Truth Protects

If you are driving down a highway and see a sign that says 'Road closed ahead. Bridge out!, these are *true* words designed to protect you from suddenly finding yourself flying off a collapsed bridge and into the river below. *God's Word* when believed and put into practice keeps us from 'going off the deep end' and wrecking our lives. God's *true* Word protects us from being deceived by the lies of the Evil One so that we stay on the straight and narrow way that leads to life rather then become sidetracked onto the broad way that leads to destruction.

<sup>13</sup> For wide is the gate and broad is the road that leads to destruction, and many enter through it.

[14] But small is the gate and narrow the road that leads to life, and only a few find it. (Matthew 7:13-14)

David believed the only protection he needed was his loving God's Truth.

[11] O LORD; may your love and **your truth always protect me**. (Psalm 40:11)

# Work for the Truth

May it be said of us what John said about his dear Christian friends.

[8] We ought therefore to show hospitality to such men so that we may **work together for the truth**. (3 John 1:8)

To work for *the truth* is *good work*, but sometimes it is *hard work -even dangerous work.*. Solzhenitsyn has written:

For the progress of **the truth** I am willing to suffer death. (Klaus Bockmuehl, Challenge of Marxism, p. 146)

It is hard work to have to *exhort anyone not to wander from the truth*. But it is good work.

[19] My brothers, if one of you should **wander from the truth** and someone should bring him back,

[20] remember this: Whoever turns a sinner from the error of his way will save him from death and cover over a multitude of sins. (James 5:19-20)

C.S. Lewis writes:

"A man cannot be always defending the truth; there must be a time to feed on it."
(Reflections on the Psalms, p. 17)

We *feed* on *God's way of truth revealed in Scripture* when we let it affect in a positive way all we think and say and do on behalf of the people God puts into our lives!

**To the God of all Truth be the Glory!**

CHAPTER 6

# The Way of God is Justice

# God's way is just

Paul has stated it as simply as possible:

⁶ **God is just.** (2 Thessalonians 1:6)

*'Just'* is simply *the way God is.* When God *acts justly* He is not doing so to conform to any external independent ruling, but, rather, he is simply being himself in every given situation.

Moses, the 'Law Giver' of the Old Testament understood that all *God's ways are just.*

⁴ He is the Rock, his works are perfect, and **all his ways are just.** A faithful God who does no wrong, upright and **just is he.** (Deuteronomy 32:4)

Elihu expanded on this thought with Job who due to his suffering may have questioned whether or not *God's way* on earth was just.

¹² It is unthinkable that God would do wrong, that the Almighty would **pervert justice…**

²¹ "His eyes are on the **ways of men**; he sees their every step.

²² There is no dark place, no deep shadow, where evildoers can hide.

²³ God has no need to examine men further, that they should **come before him for judgment.**

²⁶ He punishes them for their wickedness where everyone can see them,

²⁷ because they turned from following him and had **no regard for any of his ways.**
(Job 34:12, 21-23, 26-27)

> *God's way of justice is never perverted.* Rather, it's those who have
> *no regard* for *God's ways* who end up *perverting justice*!

> [13] The Lord says: "These people come near to me with their
> mouth and honor me with their lips, but **their hearts** are
> far from me. (Isaiah 29:13)

They said and did all the right things, but it was all only an attempt
to cover up their sinful behavior.

> [15] Woe to those who go to great depths to **hide their plans
> from the LORD**, who do their work in darkness and
> think, "**Who sees us? Who will know?**" (Isaiah 29:15)

Isaiah wrote about God's justice.

> [16] The LORD Almighty will be exalted by his **justice**, and
> the holy God will show himself holy by his righteousness.
> (Isaiah 5:16)

God's justice is as immoveable as a large mountain. Once when I was
flying over the Himalayas the pilot announced to everyone that if we
looked out the window we would see Mount Everest below us reaching up
to us almost 30,000 feet. That is a 'mighty mountain'.

God's justice is like the unfathomable ocean depths. I once lived in
Puerto Rico and came to understand that just off shore lay the 'Puerto
Rico trench' over 30,000 feet deep. God says his righteousness from which
comes his justice exceeds in might and scope the highest height and the
lowest depth on earth.

> [6] Your righteousness is like the **mighty mountains**, your
> justice like **the great deep**. O LORD, you preserve both
> man and beast. (Psalm 36:6)

Paul's grand doxology of praise affirms the greatness of God's
judgments.

³³ Oh, the depth of the riches of the wisdom and knowledge of God! **How unsearchable his judgments,** and his paths beyond tracing out! (Romans 11:33)

The prophet Zephaniah came to the conclusion that God is *just.*

⁵ The LORD…is righteous; he does no wrong. Morning by morning **he dispenses his justice,** and every new day he does not fail. (Zephaniah 3:5)

The Psalmist Asaph concludes:

⁷ It is God who **judges**: He brings one down, he exalts another. (Psalm 75:7)

Nebuchadnezzar was not a Jew and in fact exiled the Jews from Judah to Babylon for 70 years. However, this proud pagan world ruler came to this same conclusion concerning *God's justice,* when humbled by God.

³⁷ Now I, Nebuchadnezzar, praise and exalt and glorify the King of heaven, because **everything he does is right** and **all his ways are just.**
(Daniel 4:37)

# Justice is the Foundation of God's Throne

*Foundations* are basic. Nothing will remain standing for long if it doesn't have a solid foundation. There are pictures in the News of houses and bridges that have been washed away in floods because they didn't have a solid foundation. Asaph notes that the brutal, relentless storms of life have not been able to sweep away the world because God is its 'Foundation'.

² "I choose the appointed time; it is I who **judge uprightly**.

³ When the earth and all its people quake, it is **I who hold its pillars firm**… (Psalm 75:2-3; 89:14)

Rock solid faith in God's Word in the only foundation upon which to build a life capable of withstanding the storms of life.

> [24] Everyone who hears these words of mine and puts them into practice is like a wise man who built his house on the rock.

> [25] The rain came down, the streams rose, and the winds blew and beat against that house; yet it did not fall, because it had its **foundation on the rock**. (Matthew 7:24-25)

God's *just laws* speak of *fairness,* and it has been this way from the first day Noah walked out of the ark following the flood to repopulate the earth.

> [6] "Whoever sheds the blood of man, by man shall his blood be shed; for in the image of God has God made man. (Genesis 9:5-6)

God gave specific examples of what justice looks like.

> [23] You are to take life for life,

> [24] eye for eye, tooth for tooth, hand for hand, foot for foot. (Exodus 21:23-24; Lev 24:19-20)

Taking two eyes for one eye *isn't just*; the same for teeth, hands, feet. But an 'eye for an eye' is *just*! It may hurt, but *it is just; it is fair.* The penalty is to fit the crime, and never exceed it.

In the courts we can 'demand our pound of flesh', but we may just be expressing anger, an unforgiving spirit, bitterness, hardness of heart or worse. Jesus frowns on demanding *justice* as a way for seeking revenge. He says there is a better way.

> [38] "You have heard that it was said, 'Eye for eye, and tooth for tooth.'

<sup></sup>³⁹ But I tell you, Do not resist an evil person. If someone strikes you on the right cheek, turn to him the other also.

⁴⁰ And if someone wants to sue you and take your tunic, let him have your cloak as well.

⁴¹ If someone forces you to go one mile, go with him two miles.

⁴² Give to the one who asks you, and do not turn away from the one who wants to borrow from you. (Matthew 5:38-42)

Paul indicated what this should look like for Christians when someone has wronged them.

⁷ The very fact that you have lawsuits among you means you have been completely defeated already. Why not rather be wronged? Why not rather be cheated? (1 Corinthians 6:7)

This outpouring of underserved love on the guilty party paves the way for forgiveness, restitution, and reconciliation.

James reveals a secret. There is something more powerful than judgment; it's mercy!

¹³ **Mercy triumphs over judgment!** (James 2:13)

There is nothing in God's **justice** which forbids the exercise of His **mercy.** To think of God as we sometimes think of a court where a kindly judge, compelled by law, sentences a man to death with tears and apologies, is to think in a manner wholly unworthy of the true God. God is never at cross purposes with Himself. No attribute of God is in conflict with another."…Through the work of Christ in atonement, **justice is not violated but satisfied** when God spares a sinner.
(A.W. Tozar, The Knowledge of the Holy, p. 88, 94)

Jesus instructed Peter to be merciful and forgive the person who had offended him.

> [21] Peter came to Jesus and asked, "Lord, how many times shall I forgive my brother when he sins against me? Up to seven times?

Peter thought he was being magnanimous.

> [22] Jesus answered, "I tell you, not seven times, but **seventy-seven times.** (Matthew 18:21-22)

> [22] Jesus saith unto him, I say not unto thee, Until seven times: but, Until **seventy times seven.** (Matthew 18:22 (KJV)

You've got your pick depending on which translation you want to follow 77 or 490 times. We want everyone, including God, to be merciful to us, but as in Peter's case the Lord wants us to be merciful and non-judgmental toward anyone who has sinned against us. Jesus made this plain when teaching the 'Lord's Prayer'.

> [12] Forgive us our debts, as **we also** have forgiven our debtors. (Matthew 6:12)

Forgive and then let justice run its course. Jesus forgave the repentant thief on the cross, but the State wouldn't forgive. The death penalty was still upheld. There are incarcerated prisoners who have come to faith in the Lord as their Savior while serving time for their crimes. God has forgiven their sins but the State hasn't forgiven them. They are still serving 'hard time' for their crimes against society.

# God Delights in Justice

<sup>24</sup> I am the LORD, who exercises kindness, **justice** and righteousness on earth, for in these I **delight**," declares the LORD. (Jeremiah 9:24; Ps 67:4)

God knows his judgment will always be right; always fair; always just. An example was Sodom. Their sins and degradation had spiraled out of control. One day the Lord appeared to his friend Abraham and said,

<sup>20</sup> "The outcry against Sodom and Gomorrah is so great and their sin so grievous

<sup>21</sup> that I will go down and see if what they have done is as bad as the outcry that has reached me. If not, I will know." (Genesis 18:20-21)

Abraham had one concern.

<sup>23</sup> Abraham approached him and said: "Will you sweep away the righteous with the wicked?

<sup>25</sup> Far be it from you to do such a thing—to kill the righteous with the wicked, treating the righteous and the wicked alike. Far be it from you! **Will not the Judge of all the earth do right?"**
(Genesis 18:23, 25)

Abraham knew of at least four righteous people in the city, his nephew Lot, his wife and two daughters.

<sup>7</sup> He rescued Lot, a righteous man, who was distressed by the filthy lives of lawless men

[8] (for that righteous man, living among them day after day, was tormented in his righteous soul by the lawless deeds he saw and heard) (2 Peter 2:7-8)

God extracted Lot and his family from that wicked city shortly before divine judgment fell on the rest of the citizens of Sodom for whom God's 'grace period' had run out.

To say that God delights in justice is to say he *delights* in *equity, righteousness and truth.*

[10] The LORD reigns. The world is firmly established, it cannot be moved; he will **judge** the peoples **with equity…**

[13] Sing before the LORD, for he comes…**to judge** the earth. He will judge the world **in righteousness** and the peoples **in his truth.** (Psalm 96:10, 13)

To say that *God's delights in justice* is to also say the opposite, namely, that *God does not delight in injustice* or in any form of evil.

[4] You are **not a God who takes pleasure in evil**; with you the wicked cannot dwell…

[10] Declare them guilty, O God! Let their intrigues be their downfall. Banish them for their many sins, for they have rebelled against you. (Psalm 5:4, 10)

*God judges everyone* on an equal playing field.

[6] God will **give to each person** according to what he has done. (Romans 2:6)

God as Judge shows *no partiality* or *favoritism.* Peter had been prejudice against the Gentiles, but he learned this was not the case with his Lord who was the Savior of the Jews *and* the Gentiles.

³⁴ I now realize how true it is that **God does not show favoritism**...

³⁵ but accepts men from every nation who fear him and do what is right. (Acts 10:34 35)

# God Loves Justice

God not only *delights* in justice, he *loves justice*! This is God's way!

⁷ The LORD is righteous, he **loves justice**
(Psalm 11:7; 33:5)

Referring to God as 'King' the Psalmist has written:

⁴ The King is mighty, he **loves justice**— you have established equity; in Jacob you have **done what is just** and right. (Psalm 99:4)

God is more than willing to speak for himself on the subject! Speaking through the pen of the prophet Isaiah God has said:

⁸ **I, the LORD, love justice**; I hate robbery and iniquity. In my faithfulness I will reward them and make an everlasting covenant with them.
(Isaiah 61:8)

God not only loves justice but he **loves those who are just**!

²⁸ The LORD **loves the just** and will not forsake his faithful ones. They will be protected forever, but the offspring of the wicked will be cut off.
(Psalm 37:28, 30)

God throws out a challenge to everyone,

²⁴ **Let justice roll** on like a river, righteousness like a never-failing stream! (Amos 5:24)

John Perkins let the words '*Let Justice Roll Down*' turn into the title of his autobiography. Growing up in the Southern part of America he was treated unjustly time and again -even by those who were committed to upholding law and order. He eventually left the area, and moved to another part of the country for the safety of himself and his family. But the Lord put it into his heart to return to help others who were still being treated unjustly. Over several years he has helped many people find self-worth and dignity by spearheading just treatment by the authorities, as well as creating 'Coops' and meaningful employment for many disenfranchised people.

When our children were young teens we started reading John's story after dinner each evening. When I learned John was coming to our city to speak on the university campus, I invited him into our home to meet our family. He was willing to come to dinner. The impression of this humble, godly and 'justice loving' man made on our family was profound.

Although Moses was not a 'king' of the newly freed Hebrew slaves, he was nevertheless their God-appointed leader, ruler and *judge* as was noted by Stephen just moments before he was martyred.

³⁵ "This is the same Moses whom they had rejected with the words, 'Who made you ruler and **judge**?' He was sent to be their ruler and deliverer by God himself, through the angel who appeared to him in the bush. (Acts 7:35)

During Old Testament times God empowered Kings to speak on his behalf and their word was law. God empowered King Solomon with wisdom to render a stunning court decision.

²⁸ When all Israel heard the verdict the king had given, they held the king in awe, because they saw that he had **wisdom from God** to **administer justice**. (1 Kings 3:28)

The visiting Queen of Sheba shared what she observed in Solomon.

⁸ Praise be to the LORD your God, who has delighted in you and placed you on his throne as king to rule for the LORD your God. Because of the love of your God for Israel and his desire to uphold them forever, **he has made you king over them, to maintain justice and righteousness.**"
(2 Chronicles 9:8)

*God also appointed judges* who made rulings and rendered decisions on his behalf.

⁸ If cases come before your courts that are **too difficult for you to judge**—whether bloodshed, lawsuits or assaults—take them to the place the LORD your God will choose.

⁹ Go to the priests, who are Levites, and to **the judge who is in office** at that time. Inquire of them and they will give you the verdict.
(Deuteronomy 17:8-9)

*Jesus was concerned for justice.* He gave this parable to enable people to understand that God is just in all his decisions.

³ There was a widow in that town who kept coming to him with the plea, **'Grant me justice** against my adversary.'…

⁷ **Will not God bring about justice** for his chosen ones, who cry out to him day and night? Will he keep putting them off?

⁸ I tell you, **he will see that they get justice**, and quickly."
(Luke 18:3, 7-8)

# God Cannot be Bribed

'PAY FOR PLAY' is not limited to gamblers in casinos, at race tracks and sporting events. It's a saying, unfortunately, that also identifies people who want to bribe lawmakers to do them business favors -thus corrupting government officials. The question is this: Can we bribe God as our lawgiver to do us favors or to ward off judgment? The answer is one word: 'NO'! God's 'way' is justice, never bribery, graft or corruption.

> [17] The LORD your God is God of gods and Lord of lords, the great God, mighty and awesome, who shows **no partiality** and **accepts no bribes.**

> [18] He defends the cause of the fatherless and the widow, and loves the alien, giving him food and clothing.
> (Deuteronomy 10:17-18; Job 34:19; Ps 96:10)

God does not accept bribes; neither does he want us to accept bribes, but to judge fairly.

> [2] "Do not follow the crowd in doing wrong. When you give testimony in a lawsuit, **do not pervert justice** by siding with the crowd,..

> [8] "**Do not accept a bribe**, for a bribe blinds those who see and twists the words of the righteous. (Exodus 23:2, 8)

> [17] **Do not show partiality in judging**; hear both small and great alike. Do not be afraid of any man, for **judgment** belongs to God.
> (Deuteronomy 1:17; 16:18-20)

God had this indictment that he levied against the corrupt justices in Malachi's day.

> [9] I have caused you to be despised and humiliated before all the people, because you have not followed my ways but have shown partiality in matters of the law. (Malachi 2:9)

Samuel appointed his two sons to be judges in Israel, but they didn't walk in the way of righteousness as their father did.

<sup>1</sup> When Samuel grew old, he appointed his sons as **judges for Israel**...

<sup>3</sup> But his sons did not walk in his ways. They turned aside after dishonest gain and **accepted bribes and perverted justice.** (1 Samuel 8:1, 3)

Isaiah graphically stated how unjust people had become in his day.

<sup>3</sup> Your hands are stained with blood, your fingers with guilt. Your lips have spoken lies, and your tongue mutters wicked things.

<sup>4</sup> **No one calls for justice**; no one pleads his case with integrity. They rely on empty arguments and speak lies; they conceive trouble and give birth to evil...

<sup>8</sup> The way of peace they do not know; **there is no justice in their paths.** They have turned them into crooked roads; no one who walks in them will know peace.

<sup>9</sup> So **justice is far from us**, and righteousness does not reach us. We look for light, but all is darkness; for brightness, but we walk in deep shadows...

<sup>11</sup> We all growl like bears; we moan mournfully like doves. **We look for justice, but find none**; for deliverance, but it is far away...

<sup>14</sup> So **justice** is driven back, and righteousness stands at a distance; truth has stumbled in the streets, honesty cannot enter.

<sup>15</sup> Truth is nowhere to be found, and whoever shuns evil becomes a prey. (Isaiah 59:3-4; 8-9, 11, 14-15)

At the end of the Old Testament God is still reprimanding his people for operating a corrupt judicial system

> [9] I have caused you to be despised and humiliated before all the people, because you have not followed **my ways** but have **shown partiality in matters of the law.**
> (Malachi 2:8-9)

In New Testament times according to Peter nothing had changed with regard to the Lord judging impartially.

> [17] Since you call on a **Father** who **judges each man's work impartially,** live your lives as strangers here in reverent fear. (1 Peter 1:17)

Injustice reached its lowest point when Jesus, innocent of any wrongdoing, was condemned by false witnesses and sentenced to be crucified.

> [23] This man was handed over to you by God's set purpose and foreknowledge; and you, with the help of **wicked men, put him to death by nailing him to the cross.** (Acts 2:23)

**God Upholds the Cause of the Oppressed**

The LORD looked and was displeased that there was no justice so *he took matters into his own hands to turn things around.*

> [16] He saw that there was no one, he was appalled that there was no one to intervene; so his own arm worked salvation for him, and his own righteousness sustained him.

> [17] He put on righteousness as his breastplate, and the helmet of salvation on his head; he put on the garments of vengeance and wrapped himself in zeal as in a cloak.

[18] According to what they have done, so will he repay wrath to his enemies and retribution to his foes. (Isaiah 59:16-18)

God wants us as transformed believers to **walk in the way of justice**, and be as pure in our dealings with one another as new driven snow! Eric Metaxas has written about William Wilberforce and his tireless effort in the early 1800s to convince Parliament to end the British slave trade.

Perhaps the most obvious sign of Wilberforce's conversion to the Christian faith was that it changed the way he looked at everything. Suddenly he saw what he was blind to before; that God was **a God of justice and righteousness** who would judge us for the way we treated others; that every single human being was made in God's image and therefore worthy of profound respect and kindness; that God was 'no respecter of persons' and looked upon the rich and poor equally.

('**7** Men and the Secret to Their Greatness', p. 45)

[6] He will make your righteousness shine like the dawn, **the justice of your cause** like the noonday sun. (Psalm 37:6)

The good news is that God is for the oppressed, the downtrodden -the underdog. The title of Psalm 102 reads

"A prayer of an afflicted man. When he is faint and pours out his lament before the LORD."

[1] Hear my prayer, O LORD; let my cry for help come to you.

[2] Do not hide your face from me when I am in distress. Turn your ear to me; when I call, answer me quickly. (Psalm 102:1-2)

God's answer to such a prayer is not disappointing. It comes in the next Psalm.

> ⁶ The LORD works righteousness and **justice for all the oppressed.** (Psalm 103:6; 140:12; 146:7)

The Psalmist in Psalm 94 prays that God as Judge will ultimately redress wrongs.

> ² Rise up, **O Judge** of the earth; pay back to the proud what they deserve…
>
> ¹⁵ **Judgment will again be founded on righteousness,** and all the upright in heart will follow it. (Psalm 94:2, 15)

Does the Lord want us to side with the oppressed, the marginalized and the downtrodden of our world, to work for their justice? The answer needs to be a resounding '*Yes*'!

> ³ This is what the LORD says: **Do what is just and right.** Rescue from the hand of his oppressor the one who has been robbed. Do no wrong or violence to the alien, the fatherless or the widow, and do not shed innocent blood in this place. (Jeremiah 22:3)

Recall the words of Jesus to his disciples while eating a meal with them in Bethany.

> ⁷ The poor you will always have with you, and you can help them any time you want. (Mark 14:7)

## God Will Establish Justice

Just today I received an email from a Washington DC Christian lawyer who writes,

The corruption and lawlessness (here) is deeper than you think...the facts are shocking.

God has no choice but to hold everyone accountable for their actions if he is to maintain justice. God has outlined what unjust people need to do.

<sup>15</sup> Each of you must turn from your wicked ways and reform your actions. (Jeremiah 35:15)

What often is the case -at least at first- is this:

<sup>23</sup> A wicked man accepts a bribe in secret to **pervert the course of justice**. (Proverbs 17:23)

God through Moses laid down this regulation for human courts of law.

<sup>18</sup> Appoint judges and officials for each of your tribes in every town the LORD your God is giving you, and **they shall judge the people fairly.** (Deuteronomy 16:18)

<sup>16</sup> If a malicious witness takes the stand to accuse a man of a crime,

<sup>17</sup> the two men involved in the dispute must stand in the presence of the LORD before the priests and the judges who are in office at the time.

<sup>18</sup> The judges must make a thorough investigation, and if the witness proves to be a liar, giving false testimony against his brother,

<sup>19</sup> then do to him as he intended to do to his brother. You must purge the evil from among you.

<sup>20</sup> The rest of the people will hear of this and be afraid, and never again will such an evil thing be done among you.

[21] Show no pity: life for life, eye for eye, tooth for tooth, hand for hand, foot for foot.
(Deuteronomy 19:16-21)

From the very beginning of his reign as Israel's king Solomon prayed that **justice** would be **the rule of the land.**

[22] "When a man wrongs his neighbor and is required to take an oath and he comes and swears the oath before your altar in this temple,

[23] then hear from heaven and act. Judge between your servants, **repaying the guilty** by bringing down on his own head what he has done. **Declare the innocent not guilty** and so establish his innocence.
(2 Chronicles 6:22-23)

# Definition of justice

It is never wrong to do right and it is never right to do wrong. The issue revolves around determining what is 'right' vs what is 'wrong'. Solomon sought for the answer in the right place. He came before God who is the Author of all that is 'right'. Solomon began his reign as the King of Israel by praying and asking for a wise and *discerning heart.*

[9] Give your servant a **discerning heart** to govern your people and to **distinguish between right and wrong.**
(1 Kings 3:9)

A person who is qualified to judge and bring about justice must be able to discern between right and wrong, and give a right ruling. How did the Lord respond to Solomon's prayer?

[10] The Lord was pleased that Solomon had asked for this...

[12] I will do what you have asked. **I will give you a wise and discerning heart**, so that there will never have been anyone like you, nor will there ever be.
(1 Kings 3:10, 12)

Early in his reign he made such *just* judgments that everyone

[28] held the king in awe, because they saw that he had **wisdom from God to administer justice**. (1 Kings 3:28)

Solomon's great wisdom to discern good from evil, and right from wrong was only a dim reflection of Jesus whom Paul identified as

[24] **wisdom of God**. (1 Corinthians 1:24)

Paul was only confirming what Jesus had already said.

[42] The Queen of the South will rise at the judgment with this generation and condemn it; for she came from the ends of the earth to listen to Solomon's wisdom, and now **one greater than Solomon is here**. (Matthew 12:42)

# Jesus is just

To *judge justly* one must live justly within the **boundaries of truth**. Even Jesus' detractors were forced to acknowledge he was qualified to render true and just decisions on any subject because of his moral integrity.

[14] "Teacher, we know **you are a man of integrity**. You aren't swayed by men, because you pay no attention to who they are; but **you teach the way of God in accordance with the truth**. (Mark 12:14)

Ken Gire has noted that

**Jesus brought justice to the world** not through loud proclamations or forceful demonstration. He did it with the upmost gentleness.
(The North Face of God, p. 153)

Consider Isaiah's prophecy regarding how Jesus would bring about justice on earth.

[1] "Here is my servant, whom I uphold, my chosen one in whom I delight; I will put my Spirit on him and he will bring **justice** to the nations.

[2] **He will not shout or cry out, or raise his voice in the streets.**

[3] **A bruised reed he will not break, and a smoldering wick he will not snuff out.** In faithfulness **he will bring forth justice.**
(Isaiah 42:1-3)

Here is an example out of the Gospels of Jesus bending down and quietly writing with his finger in the dust before giving his decision regarding a woman standing before him surrounded by men accusing her of adultery and demanding her death.

[6] Jesus bent down and started to write on the ground with his finger.

[7] "If any one of you is without sin, let him be the first to throw a stone at her.

[8] He stooped down and wrote on the ground

[9] At this, those who heard began to go away one at a time, the older ones first, until only Jesus was left, with the woman still standing there.

¹⁰ Jesus straightened up and asked her, **"Woman, where are they? Has no one condemned you?"**

¹¹ "No one, sir," she said. "Then **neither do I condemn you**," Jesus declared. "Go now and leave your life of sin." (John 8:6-11)

Jesus said why his Father sent him down from Heaven.

⁷ God did not send his Son into the world to condemn the world, but to save the world through him. (John 3:17)

God himself has gone on record.

¹¹ 'As surely as I live', declares the Sovereign LORD, 'I take **no pleasure in the death of the wicked, but rather that they turn from their ways and live.** Turn! Turn from your evil ways!' (Ezekiel 33:11)

The Lord is merciful to humble, repentant sinners. Once while I was directing a Christian coffee house ministry in Massachusetts, a young man began coming to the coffee house where he heard the gospel of salvation. Eventually he accepted the Lord as his Savior, and it soon became evident he was transformed by the Lord into a new creation. What came to light was that he had been on the run from the Law for a crime he had committed in Florida. He became willing to return to Florida and give himself up to the authorities knowing they would book him, put him in prison and probably 'throw away the key'. With fear and trembling he made his way back to Florida and gave himself up. That was the last we heard from him -for about two weeks. Then, he walked through the door of the coffee house a 'free man'. The authorities found a technicality in the law that enabled them to release him from his charges rather than sentence him.

It remains the Lord's longing that ultimately everyone (even the repentant thief on the cross in his last breath) will reach out to him in faith for salvation and thus mercifully escape the Last Judgment of eternal condemnation! If we 'throw ourselves on the mercy of Heaven's court' we will not be disappointed! The Lord wants to be able, by his own doing, to present us one day in the court of Heaven as *'blameless'*.

> [8] He will keep you strong to the end, so that you will **be blameless on the day of our Lord Jesus Christ.**
> (1 Corinthians 1:8; 1 Thess 3:13; Jude 1:24-25)

The Gospel good news is that

> [1] There is now **no condemnation** for those who are in Christ Jesus. (Romans 8:1)

As such, our resurrected and ascended Lord Jesus Christ, the Son of God, is our Defense Attorney pleading our case at the Bar of Justice in Heaven.

> [34] Who is he that condemns? **Christ Jesus**, who died—more than that, who was raised to life—**is at the right hand of God and is also interceding for us.**
> (Romans 8:34; Heb 7:25; 1 Jn 2:1)

In case you have ever wondered what Jesus is doing right now in Heaven, he is interceding for you and me! This is very good news indeed! ☺

# When it Seems God is not Just

At any particular moment it can seem like God is not just when he is not immediately calling people to account for their sinful actions, and it seems like people are 'getting away with murder' and 'perfect crimes' are being committed and going undetected. David prayed fervently to the Lord,

> [12] Arise, LORD! Lift up your hand, O God. Do not forget the helpless.

¹³ Why does the wicked man revile God? Why does he say to himself, "He won't call me to account". (Psalm 10:12-13)

The Prophet Habakkuk had his questions.

² **How long**, O LORD, must I call for help, but you do not listen? Or cry out to you, "Violence!" but you do not save?

³ **Why** do you make me look at injustice? **Why** do you tolerate wrong? Destruction and violence are before me; there is strife, and conflict abounds.

⁴ Therefore the law is paralyzed, and **justice never prevails**. The wicked hem in the righteous, so that **justice is perverted**. (Habakkuk 1:2-4)

Both David and Jesus (who quoted David on the cross) felt abandoned by God at the darkest moment of their lives, yet they steadfastly put their trust in God.

¹ **My God, my God, why have you forsaken me**? Why are you so far from saving me, so far from the words of my groaning?

² O my God, I cry out by day, but you do not answer, by night, and am not silent. (Psalm 22:1-2; Matthew 27:46; Mark 5:34)

God cautions us not to prematurely conclude in any particular situation that he has not acted justly. He asked Job:

⁸ "Would you discredit my justice? Would you condemn me to justify yourself? (Job 40:8)

This is not a position you want to put yourself in, rather, always give God the benefit of the doubt that he knows what he is doing and he is always doing the right thing.

> God can only judge fairly, wisely, and rightly: there is no partiality, deceit, or bias in Him. And our holy God judges not on superficial externals. Certain judgments may not look 'right' to us, but this matter of God's right judgments calls for a spiritual EKG for you and for me and for every Christ-follower...Only God sees and knows what is really in the heart of man...When all is said and done, we can be confident that 'the Judge of all the earth' will do what is right!
> (O.S. Hawkins, The Believer's Code, March 8, p. 79)

**Consider that God can use adverse circumstances to *test us* with the goal that the 'test' strengthen us.**

When things aren't going the way we planned it doesn't mean they aren't going the way God all along has determined they should go especially when it is Christians suffering unjustly for their faith. Whenever we see a wrong that isn't being righted don't conclude God's judgment is askew. Nik Ripken has interviewed over 600 Christians in 40 nations who have suffered unimaginable forms of suffering, and who have also witnessed many a martyr's death. Speaking on behalf of those who are called upon to suffer for their faith in the Lord he writes,

> Through our pilgrimage, we have been challenged biblically to believe that God can use even unspeakable pain for His purposes. And we are able now to say with confidence that God uses persecution and suffering for His purposes. Exactly **why** God uses persecution and suffering is a holy mystery, but the fact that He **does** use persecution and suffering is a certainty...(We have begun) to garner valuable insights about persecution,

about **the ways of God**, and about how the church…
thrives -especially in persecution…

According to the Bible, persecution is normal, simply a
natural by-product of faith.
('The Insanity of Obedience', p. 12, 22)

Recall Jesus' prediction,

> [22] All men will hate you because of me.
> (Matthew 10:22)

When we're tempted to pray "God judge them" the Lord wants us to
love and forgive those who hate us even though *it may seem unreasonable*
if not impossible at the time of suffering.
Jesus stayed the course (and has set the course for us)

> [2] Let us fix our eyes on Jesus, the author and perfecter of
> our faith, who **for the joy set before him endured the
> cross**, scorning its shame, and sat down at the right hand
> of the throne of God.
>
> [3] Consider him who **endured such opposition from
> sinful men, so that you will not grow weary and lose
> heart.** (Hebrews 12:2-3)

Here are the words found on Jesus' lips as he approached the 'finish
line' having been nailed to the cross in excruciating pain.

> [34] "Father, forgive them, for they do not know what they
> are doing." (Luke 23:34)

Nik notes that persecuted Christians he has interviewed also find
themselves praying,

> "God, forgive us as we forgive others!" and "God, glorify
> your Name!" (Ibid., p. 26)

The truth is that God wants to ***test us not to weaken us but to strengthen us,*** and to enhance our character. Whenever God 'tests' us we can know two things: we're in good company in that the record stands that God tested all the saints in Scripture, whether it's Daniel being thrown to the lions, or Paul being beaten time and again within an inch of his life. Second, testing is good for us when it is God doing the testing. This turned out to be the case during the Israelites' 40 year stay in the wilderness.

> [2] Remember how the LORD your God led you all the way in the desert these forty years, to humble you and to **test** you in order to know what was in your heart, whether or not you would keep his commands...

> [16] He gave you manna to eat in the desert, something your fathers had never known, to humble and to **test** you so that in the end it might go well with you.
> (Deuteronomy 8:2, 16)

> [3] The crucible for silver and the furnace for gold, but **the LORD tests the heart**. (Proverbs 17:3)

> [10] **You, O God, tested us**; you refined us like silver.

> [11] You brought us into prison and laid burdens on our backs.

> [12] You let men ride over our heads; we went through fire and water, **but you brought us to a place of abundance.**
> (Psalm 66:10-12)

I recall when I was a young child hearing my father sing as a solo in church the old hymn 'God Leads Us Along' based on Isaiah 43:2.

God Leads Us Along

Sometimes on the mount where the sun shines so bright
God leads His dear children along

Sometimes in the valley, in darkest of night
God leads His dear children along

Some through the waters, some through the flood
Some through the fire, but all through the blood
Some through great sorrow, but God gives a song
In the night season and all the day long
    -George A. Young (1903)

[2] When you pass through the waters, I will be with you; and when you pass through the rivers, they will not sweep over you. When you walk through the fire, you will not be burned; the flames will not set you ablaze. (Isaiah 43:2)

[10] See, I have refined you, though not as silver; **I have tested you in the furnace of affliction.**

[11] For my own sake, **for my own sake, I do this.** (Isaiah 48:10-11)

Are we willing to acknowledge it's within God's purview to 'test' us? No one is exempt from God's testing. If Paul wasn't -and he wasn't- neither will we be exempt.

[19] **I served the Lord with great humility** and with tears, **although I was severely tested** by the plots of the Jews....

[24] However, I consider my life worth nothing to me, if only I may finish the race and complete the task the Lord Jesus has given me—the task of testifying to the gospel of God's grace. (Acts 20:19, 24)

Are we willing like the saints of old to *give God permission to 'test' us?*

[2] **Test me**, O LORD, and try me, examine my heart and my mind. (Psalm 26:2)

²³ Search me, O God, and know my heart; **test me** and know my anxious thoughts.
(Psalm 139:23; 1 Chron 29:17; Jer 11:20)

The Lord wants us to understand what his will is in allowing trials and testing in our life.

¹⁷ Understand what the Lord's will is. (Ephesians 5:17)

If you ever wanted to know the 'will of God' for your life, this is it!

¹⁸ Give thanks **in all circumstances**, for **this is God's will for you in Christ Jesus**.
(1 Thessalonians 5:18)

²⁰ Always give thanks to God the Father **for everything**, in the name of our Lord Jesus Christ. (Ephesians 5:20)

'*In*' and '*for*' are such little words, but they are easier spoken than lived out when it comes to giving thanks for the 'in's' and 'for's' of life when they engulf you in seemingly overwhelming circumstances. I once heard someone say, "I thanked the Lord *for* my helplessness so that I might trust *in* him." What might we say in similar circumstances?

Although it never seems soon enough for us, in the process of time God gets his work done, and *sorrows turn to joy*.

⁵ Weeping may remain for a night, but rejoicing comes in the morning. (Psalm 30:5)

This scripture verse was the assurance the Lord gave me the long night I spent in a hospital's 'Fathers Lounge' in Denver praying and pacing for hours awaiting the delivery of our first child. Jesus' words rung true for me at 6:30 AM the next morning!

²¹ Blessed are you who weep now, for you will laugh.
(Luke 6:21)

Habakkuk, while standing in the rubble of what had once be his beautiful homeland, came to this conclusion,

> [17] Though the fig tree does not bud and there are no grapes on the vines, though the olive crop fails and the fields produce no food, though there are no sheep in the pen and no cattle in the stalls,
>
> [18] **Yet I will rejoice in the LORD, I will be joyful in God my Savior.**
>
> [19] **The Sovereign LORD is my strength**; he makes my feet like the feet of a deer, he enables me to go on the heights. (Habakkuk 3:17-19)

When Job surveyed the overall futility of his situation he reached a surprising conclusion. *It's the 'end of the story that tells the story'.* At least this was how it worked out for Job. His ordeal in experiencing the onslaught of Satan indeed strengthened his faith and deepened his character. Although he had to live through forty-one chapters of his life, in chapter 42 he came out ultimately a winner and not a looser.

> [10] After Job had prayed for his friends, the LORD made him prosperous again and gave him **twice as much** as he had before…
>
> [12] The LORD **blessed the latter part of Job's life more than the first…** (Job 42:10, 12)

Since *God's ways do not change* we can *expect 'testing' of the saints* right up till the end of time. But 'testing' is not without its rewards.

> [6] In this you greatly rejoice, though now for a little while you may have had to suffer grief in **all kinds of trials.**
>
> [7] These have come so that your faith—of greater worth than gold, which perishes even though refined by

fire—may be proved genuine and may result in praise, glory and honor **when Jesus Christ is revealed.** (1 Peter 1:6-7)

[12] Blessed is the man who **perseveres under trial**, because when he has **stood the test,** he will receive the crown of life that God has promised to those who love him. (James 1:12)

# God Judges with Righteousness

It's true that the 'wheels of justice grind slow' but they are grinding and in the end Justice will prevail -even if it means there has to be a 'Last Judgment' at the end of human history when God once and for all puts everything right! Paul reminds us that it may take till *the Last Judgment* before justice is fully served on those who persist in their wickedness.

[6] God is just: **He will pay back trouble** to those who trouble you

[7] and give relief to you who are troubled, and to us as well. **This will happen when the Lord Jesus is revealed from heaven** in blazing fire with his powerful angels. (2 Thessalonians 1:6-7)

Knowing God's Judgment Day is coming we are assured that *God is just even if at the moment if may not seem to be the case.* When it looks like everyone is committing 'the perfect crime' -they aren't. God will ultimately call them to account at Heaven's Bar of Justice where Jesus himself will sit as Judge. This was a point Peter made when sharing the Gospel with Cornelius a God-fearing Roman Centurion.

[42] **Jesus** commanded us to preach to the people and to testify that **he is the one** whom God appointed as **judge** of the living and the dead. (Acts 10:42)

This day is coming at the end of time. It will be God's judgment day. Having been given a vision of this coming Judgment Day Daniel described what he saw.

> [9] "As I looked, "thrones were set in place, and the Ancient of Days took his seat. His clothing was as white as snow; the hair of his head was white like wool. His throne was flaming with fire, and its wheels were all ablaze.
>
> [10] A river of fire was flowing, coming out from before him. Thousands upon thousands attended him; ten thousand times ten thousand stood before him. **The court was seated, and the books were opened.** (Daniel 7:9-10)

What John saw in a vision over 500 years later coincided with what Daniel saw.

> [12] I saw the dead, great and small, standing before the throne, and books were opened. Another book was opened, which is the book of life. The dead were **judged** according to what they had done as recorded in the books. (Revelation 20:12)

Perhaps David was thinking of God's Judgment Day when he wrote,

> [10] The righteous will be glad when they are avenged, when they bathe their feet in the blood of the wicked.
>
> [11] Then men will say, "Surely **the righteous still are rewarded; surely there is a God who judges the earth.**" (Psalm 58:1-2, 10-11)

There will come a point of no return when everything will be ripe for judgment, and God's court will be in session!

⁹ **O righteous God**, who searches minds and hearts, bring to an end the violence of the wicked and make the righteous secure. (Psalm 7:9)

¹³ They will sing before the LORD, for he comes, he comes to judge the earth. **He will judge the world in righteousness** and the peoples in his truth. (Psalm 96:13; 7:9; 98:9; Isa 11:3-4; 26:9)

# God Disciplines With Justice

The prophet Hosea, however, noted that even before the Last Judgment God holds everyone accountable for their evil words and deeds. He lets nothing go unaddressed.

⁹ They have sunk deep into corruption...**God will remember** their wickedness and punish them for their sins. (Hosea 9:9; Ezk 6:10; Jer 21:14)

Listen to the words of the repentant thief on the cross to the unrepentant thief on the cross next to him.

⁴¹ We are **punished justly**, for we are **getting what our deeds deserve**. (Luke 23:41)

God disciplines with justice, but we can be sure of one thing, God has never wanted to be put in this position. *Hear the pathos in God's voice* coming from Isaiah's pen.

¹⁸ **If only** you had paid attention to my commands, your peace would have been like a river, your righteousness like the waves of the sea. (Isaiah 48:18)

*Hear the pathos in the Son of God's voice.*

<sup></sup>³⁴ How often I have longed to gather your children together, as a hen gathers her chicks under her wings, but you were not willing!

³⁵ Look, your house is left to you desolate
(Luke 13:34-35)

Paul has exhorted us **not to 'grieve the Holy Spirit'.**

³⁰ Do not grieve the Holy Spirit of God, with whom you were sealed for the day of redemption. (Ephesians 4:30)

God longs to restore repentant sinners to his favor.

¹⁷ **I will restore you to health** and heal your wounds, declares the LORD.
(Jeremiah 30:17; 31:27-28; 32:36-38; 33:6, 8; 36:19, 25-27)

³² Though he brings grief, he **will show compassion**, so great is his unfailing love.

³³ For he does not willingly bring affliction or grief to the children of men. (Lamentations 3:32-33)

# Act Justly

From the beginning days of the nation of Israel Moses demanded justice in the courts.

¹⁶ I charged your judges at that time: Hear the disputes between your brothers and **judge fairly**, whether the case is between brother Israelites or between one of them and an alien.

¹⁷ **Do not show partiality in judging**; hear both small and great alike. Do not be afraid of any man, for judgment

belongs to God. Bring me any case too hard for you, and I will hear it. (Deuteronomy 1:16-17)

Isaiah heard the Lord's voice ringing in his ears!

[1] **Maintain justice and do what is right.**
(Isaiah 56:1)

God, for example, wants *just dealings in the marketplace* whether it's a Mom and Pop store or, a superstore chain, or an international business conglomerate. It's been this way ever since the days of Moses.

[35] "'Do not use dishonest standards when measuring length, weight or quantity.

[36] Use honest scales and honest weights...I am the LORD your God. (Leviticus 19:35-36)

[13] Do not have two differing weights in your bag—one heavy, one light.

[14] Do not have two differing measures in your house—one large, one small.

[15] You must have accurate and honest weights and measures, so that you may live long in the land the LORD your God is giving you.

[16] For the LORD your God detests anyone who does these things, anyone who deals dishonestly.
(Deuteronomy 25:13-16; Prov 11:1; 16:11; Mic 6:11)

Spiritually transformed *Christians do not need the law to force them to act justly* as is the case with the ungodly who need policemen, judges and soldiers to hold them in check from succeeding in their wicked schemes. Godly people do what the law requires not because they have to, but because they want to from the heart.

⁵ The plans of the righteous are **just**.
(Proverbs 12:5)

Paul made a profound statement to Timothy.

⁹ We…know that **law is made not for the righteous but for lawbreakers** and rebels, the ungodly and sinful, the unholy and irreligious; for those who kill their fathers or mothers, for murderers,

¹⁰ for adulterers and perverts, for slave traders and liars and perjurers—and for whatever else is contrary to the sound doctrine

¹¹ that conforms to the glorious gospel of the blessed God, which he entrusted to me.
(1 Timothy 1:8-11)

When all is said and done may we be able to say:

¹²¹ I have done what is **righteous** and **just**.
(Psalm 119:121; Prov 8:20)

Then we can *anticipate God's blessing.*

³ **Blessed** are they who maintain **justice**, who constantly **do what is right.** (Psalm 106:3; 112:5)

# The Last Word on 'Justice'

John in Revelation heard everyone singing in Heaven about *God's just ways.*

³ The song of Moses the servant of God and the song of the Lamb: "Great and marvelous are your deeds, Lord

God Almighty. **Just** and true **are your ways, King of the ages**. (Revelation 15:3)

In his vision of heaven John heard a deafening roar when all Heaven's countless citizens with united voice affirmed that God is just, and all his ways are just!

[1] I heard what sounded like **the roar of a great multitude in heaven shouting**: "Hallelujah! Salvation and glory and power belong to our God,

[2] for **true and just are his judgments**." (Revelation 19:1-2)

**To God be the Glory that He is Just in all his Ways!**

CHAPTER 7

# The Way of God is Love

# God is Love

The *God of love in the New Testament* is the one and same *loving God who appeared in the Old Testament* from beginning to end. The love of God is the major theme of *both* the Old and New Testament. The key New Testament scripture is John 3:16

> [16] **God so loved the world** that he gave his one and only Son, that whoever believes in him shall not perish but have eternal life. (John 3:16)

That *God is love, is loving and is loveable* was also the major theme during all the days of the Old Testament. In just one chapter alone the Psalmist of Psalm 136 states twenty six times, *'His love endures forever'*! Thirty two times the authors of the Old Testament highlight the fact that *God's love is unfailing* beginning with Exodus 15 and ending with Lamentations 3:32.

> [13] "In your **unfailing love** you will lead the people you have redeemed. In your strength you will guide them to your holy dwelling. (Exodus 15:13)

> [32] Though he brings grief, he will show compassion, so great is his **unfailing love**. (Lamentations 3:32)

The word 'love' appears 305 times in the Old Testament, and 200 times in the New Testament

> The most basic truth in all the universe, lying open in the pages of Scripture for all to see (is that) the foundation... for all existence throughout all creation is nothing more or less than this: God really is just what the Bible says of him: **God is Love'**!
> ('A God to Call Father', Michael Phillips, p. 216)

*Love is God's 'way'* with us! Our hope for meaningful and fulfilling life rests in God's *love* for us.

<sup>18</sup> The eyes of the LORD are on those who fear him, on those whose **hope is in his unfailing love**, (Psalm 33:18)

<sup>22</sup> May **your unfailing love rest upon us**, O LORD, even as we put our hope in you.
(Psalm 33:22)

Augustine writes in his 'Homilies on the 1<sup>st</sup> Epistle of John,

You should think only one thought, if you wish to perceive God and become like Him, day by day, **'God is love'**.

Who doesn't know that *love is the most powerful force on earth*?

<sup>13</sup> These three remain: faith, hope and **love**. But **the greatest of these is love**. (1 Corinthians 13:13)

Speaking to the *greatness of God's love* David put it this way.

<sup>17</sup> The LORD is righteous in all his ways and **loving toward all he has made**. (Psalm 145:17)

'*All*' is a little word with a huge meaning when having anything to do with God –*especially his love* for *all he has made*, and how he responds to *all who love him*. A.W. Tozar has made this point.

**Love**…is not something God has and which may grow or diminish or cease to be. His **love is the way God is**, and when he loves he is simply being himself.
(The Knowledge of the Holy, p. 24)

After a lifetime of ministry as a Pastor Glen Evans wrote,

I must remember that while **God always deals with me** from righteousness, it is always **through love**…**Love** makes it possible for a righteous God and sinful people to find a common ground of meeting…Because I know

**I can trust His ways**...how thrilled I am to be serving a God who is absolutely right in all He does, yet absolutely tender in how He does it! Let His name be praised!" (Glen Evans, Daily With the King', September 19, 'Finding God's Way Delightful')

Doubting God could *love unlovable people* was something Moses pondered when leading his newly freed rag tag Hebrew slaves out of Egypt and in route to the Promised Land. When he asked God how he could love them, basically the only answer he gave Moses was *'I love you 'cause I love you...'* They had nothing to merit his love, but he loved them anyway.

⁷ The LORD did not set his affection on you and choose you because you were more numerous than other peoples, for you were the fewest of all peoples.

⁸ But it was because **the LORD loved you** and kept the oath he swore to your forefathers that he brought you out with a mighty hand and redeemed you from the land of slavery, from the power of Pharaoh king of Egypt.

⁹ Know therefore that the LORD your God is God; he is the faithful God, **keeping his covenant of love** to a thousand generations of those who love him and keep his commands. (Deuteronomy 7:7-9)

A 'thousand generations' is a long time. These words are comparable to Psalmist saying that 'God's love endures forever' (Ps 136:1-26).

God's love is not just the purest and highest form of love in the universe, He reaches down from heaven to whisper to us **'I have loved you with an everlasting love; therefore with loving kindness have I drawn you'.** (Eastward Missions, 11/27/16)

The words *loving* and *kindness* were first fused together into one word *'lovingkindness'* in the 1535 Coverdale translation, and was then fused together 26 times in the 1611 King James Version of the Bible. Here are a few examples:

> [7] Shew thy marvellous **lovingkindness**,.
> (Psalm 17:7 KJV)

> [7] How excellent *is* thy **lovingkindness**, O God (Psalm 36:7 KJV)

> [11] Withhold not thou thy tender mercies from me, O LORD: let thy **lovingkindness** and thy truth continually preserve me. (Psalm 40:11 KJV)

What is humbling to know is that God would extend 'loving-kindness' to us, because he would be just in condemning us as sinners and consigning us to eternal banishment from his sight. It's as I heard someone say once, 'I don't know how the likes of God could ever like the likes of me!' But the good news that takes up most of the space in the Bible is that God knows we're sinners yet loves us anyway -in spite of ourselves. It's as someone has said,

> Love is 'God's bright star in Man's dark night'.

Jeremiah lived in dreadful times, yet he took courage in knowing that God had not abandoned his love for Israel.
> [3] The LORD appeared to us in the past, saying: **"I have loved you with an everlasting love;** I have drawn you with **loving-kindness.** (Jeremiah 31:3)

Nehemiah in the following generation rehearsed in a prayer that although God should have abandoned Israel to suffer the consequences of their sins, instead he *continued to love them.*

> [17] You are a forgiving God, gracious and compassionate, slow to anger and **abounding in love.** Therefore **you did not desert them.** (Nehemiah 9:17)

The truth that *God is love* is equally *the theme of the New Testament*. If there was ever anyone who was qualified to speak to the fact that 'God is love' it was the Apostle John who was known by everyone in his day as 'the disciple **Jesus loved**' (John 13:23, 19:26, 20:2, 21:7, 20). His first of three letters might easily be called the 'Epistle of Love'. John mentioned the words love, loved and loving 38 times. Two times he plainly stated that 'God is Love'.

> [8] Whoever does not love does not know God, because **God is love...**
>
> [16] We know and rely on the love God has for us. **God is love**. Whoever lives in love lives in God, and God in him. (1 John 4:8, 16)

> In only one passage throughout all of God's Word does any biblical writer take it upon himself to fully define God's **being**...The writer was the disciple John. 'God **is** Love'. This was the highest summation of God's *being*! (Michael Phillips, 'A God to Call Father', p. 217)

Don Osgood majors on this thought in his book, 'Listening for God's Silent Language: Hearing God Speak in the Unexpected Places of Life'.

> **God is love**, so **when he loves us he gives us himself**. He can't give us love without giving us himself. That is why we can't give love without giving ourselves. (p.35)

> The Creator...didn't create love and then leave. **He is love**. He came to earth and died and rose again –all because of love. He sent ...his Holy Spirit who makes it possible for us to love each other. He gave me parents to love, a wife to love, children to love. Wherever love is, He is!. (p. 55)

John concludes his Gospel by stating that we could never record enough words to fully describe all the Son of God did by coming to earth to demonstrate God's love. •

> [25] Jesus did many other things as well. If every one of them were written down, I suppose that even the whole world would not have room for the books that would be written. (John 21:25)

Authors have tried! Walk into the library of a Christian seminary and you'll see thousands of books lining the shelves all attempting to describe the love of God expressed through his Son Jesus Christ!

Paul ran out of words when telling us how much God loves us.

> [38] I am convinced that neither death nor life, neither angels nor demons, neither the present nor the future, nor any powers,
>
> [39] neither height nor depth, nor anything else in all creation, will be able to separate us from the **love of God that is in Christ Jesus our Lord.** (Romans 8:38-39)

Paul has noted that in becoming God's 'new creation' (2 Corinthians 5:17) we have become *benefactors of God's loving-kindness.*

> [3] At one time we too were foolish, disobedient, deceived and enslaved by all kinds of passions and pleasures. We lived in malice and envy, being hated and hating one another.
>
> [4] But when the **kindness and love of God** our Savior appeared,

[5] he saved us, not because of righteous things we had done, but because of his mercy. He saved us through the washing of rebirth and renewal by the Holy Spirit. (Titus 3:3-5)

Giving good gifts is an expression of loving-kindness. Our kind and loving Heavenly Father is the giver of good gifts!

[11] If you, then, though you are evil, know how to give good gifts to your children, how much more will your Father in heaven give good gifts to those who ask him! (Matthew 7:11)

This was another way for Jesus to say we have been given the 'good gift of the Holy Spirit'!

[13] If you then, though you are evil, know how to give good gifts to your children, how much more will your Father in heaven give the Holy Spirit to those who ask him!" (Luke 11:13)

Let the fact that God loves you *quiet your anxious soul.*

[17] The LORD your God is with you, he is mighty to save. He will take great delight in you, **he will quiet you with his love...**

Whenever I come to my senses and confess any sin I have owned up to and sought forgiveness, I sense God 'quieting me with his love'. This is so precious!

Those who love God want to sing his praises, but it's also true that God loves us and *wants to sing our praises!*

[17] ... **he will rejoice over you with singing."** (Zephaniah 3:17)

All because he loves us!

# God the Father is Love

Consider *God the Father's love for us.*

[1] How great is the **love the Father** has lavished on us, that we should be called children of God! And that is what we are! The reason the world does not know us is that it did not know him. (1 John 3:1)

[21] He who loves me will be **loved** by my **Father**, and I too will **love** him and show myself to him." (John 14:21)

[23] Jesus replied, "If anyone loves me, he will obey my teaching. My **Father** will **love** him, and we will come to him and make our home with him. (John 14:23)

# God the Father Loves his Son

Just how long has the Father loved his Son? Did it begin at his baptism *("This is my Son, whom I love")*. However old creation is, the Father's love for his Son is older still.

[24] "Father, I want those you have given me to be with me where I am, and to see my glory, the glory you have given me because **you loved me before the creation of the world.** (John 17:24)

As hard as it is to wrap the mind around, there was someone else the Father loved before the creation of the world, namely, *us* (and in your case, *you*)!

[3] Praise be to the God and Father of our Lord Jesus Christ, who has blessed us in the heavenly realms with every spiritual blessing in Christ.

[4] For he **chose us** in him **before the creation of the world** to be holy and blameless in his sight. **In love**

[5] he predestined us to be adopted as his sons through Jesus Christ, in accordance with his pleasure and will— (Ephesians 1:3-5)

# God the Son is Love

'Like Father; like Son'

[9] "As the **Father** has **loved** me, **so have I loved you.** (John 15:9)

Consider the godly love that was (and still is) exhibited in Jesus the Son of God. There is no greater expression of love then for someone who loves to the point of being willing to shed his life's blood for the one whom he loves. John began writing his book of Revelation by identifying Jesus as the one who

[5] **loves us** and has freed us from our sins **by his blood.** (Revelation 1:5)

It was *his own blood* Jesus the Son of God was consecrating when he blessed the cup before sharing it with everyone at the Last Supper.

[27] Then he took the cup, gave thanks and offered it to them, saying, "Drink from it, all of you.

[28] This is **my blood** of the covenant, which is poured out for many for the forgiveness of sins. (Matthew 26:27-28)

Paul is an example of a man who was willing to live for Christ who had died for him.

[20] The life I live in the body, I live by faith in **the Son of God**, who **loved me** and **gave himself for me.**
(Galatians 2:20)

We cannot fail to be moved by the heroism of Father Maximillian Kolbe, the Polish Franciscan, in the Auschwitz concentration camp. When a number of prisoners were selected for execution, and one of them shouted that he was a married man with children, Father Kolbe stepped forward and asked if he could take the condemned man's place. His offer was accepted by the authorities, and he was placed in an underground cell, where he was left to die of starvation.
(John Stott, 'The Cross of Christ', p. 136)

[8] God demonstrates **his own love** for us in this: While we were still sinners, Christ died for us. (Romans 5:8)

Feel the pathos in these words prophetically coming from the mouth of the Lord.

[10] "They will **look on me, the one they have pierced.**"
(Zechariah 12:10)

John affirmed that the Son of God fulfilled this ancient prophecy on the cross where his hands, his feet, and his side were pierced.

[37] Scripture says, "They will look on the one they have pierced." (John 19:37)

Paul, for one, was overwhelmed by his awareness of the **love of Christ** in that he considered himself to have been the world's 'worst sinner'.

[14] The grace of our Lord was poured out on me abundantly, along with the faith and **love** that are **in Christ Jesus.**

[15] Here is a trustworthy saying that deserves full acceptance: Christ Jesus came into the world to save sinners—of whom **I am the worst.**

[16] But for that very reason I was shown mercy so that in **me, the worst of sinners**, Christ Jesus might display his unlimited patience as an example for those who would believe on him and receive eternal life. (1 Timothy 1:14-16)

For Paul, the love of Christ for him, indeed for the whole world, was unfathomable. He was *lost for words to describe the magnitude of Christ's love.*

[35] Who shall separate us from the **love of Christ?** Shall trouble or hardship or persecution or famine or nakedness or danger or sword?...

[37] No, in all these things we are more than conquerors through him who loved us.

[38] For I am convinced that neither death nor life, neither angels nor demons, neither the present nor the future, nor any powers,

[39] neither height nor depth, nor anything else in all creation, will be able to separate us from **the love of God that is in Christ Jesus our Lord.**
(Romans 8:35-39)

Paul's prayer was that the love of Christ might prevail in our lives as Christians.

[17] I pray that you, being rooted and established in **love,**

[18] may have power, together with all the saints, to grasp how wide and long and high and deep is **the love of Christ,**

[19] and to know **this love that surpasses knowledge**—that you may be filled to the measure of all the fullness of God. (Ephesians 3:17-19)

Once the noted theologian Karl Barth who had written several books on Scripture and theology was asked what was the greatest thing he had learned from all his studies. He replied:

> *Jesus loves me,*
> *This I know,*
> *For the Bible tells me so!*

There are ever ***deepening levels of intimacy*** God wants us to experience as he expresses his love for us. Awareness of the full scope of God's love for us in Christ should take our breath away!

# Servant

It is a privilege to be a servant of the Lord. John the Baptist, for one, knew what an honor it was, and said so.

> [7] "After me will come one more powerful than I, the thongs of whose sandals **I am not worthy** to stoop down and untie." (Mark 1:7)

# Servant to Friend

> [15] I no longer call you servants, because a servant does not know his master's business. Instead, I have **called you friends**, for everything that I learned from my Father I have made known to you. (John 15:15)

# Friend to Brother

[11] Both the one who makes men holy and those who are made holy are of the same family. So Jesus is not ashamed to call them **brothers**. (Hebrews 2:11)

[35] Whoever does God's will is **my brother and sister and mother**." (Mark 3:35)

# Brother to Bride of Christ

[31] "For this reason a man will leave his father and mother and be united to his **wife,** and the two will become one flesh."

[32] This is a profound mystery—but I am talking about **Christ and the church**. (Ephesians 5:31-32)

# Bride of Christ to Body of Christ

[30] We are **members of his body**. (Ephesians 5:30)

[20] On that day you will realize that I am in my Father, and **you are in me**, and **I am in you**. (John 14:20)

[15] If anyone acknowledges that Jesus is the Son of God, **God lives in him and he in God.**

[16] And so we know and rely on the love God has for us. God is love. **Whoever lives in love lives in God, and God in him.** (1 John 4:15-16)

In turn, experiencing God's love for us in Christ becomes the incentive for us to *love one another.*

[12] My command is this: **Love each other as I have loved you**. (John 15:12)

[34] "A new command I give you: **Love one another. As I have loved** you, so you must love one another.

[35] By this all men will know that you are my disciples, if you **love one another**."
(John 13:34-35)

# God the Holy Spirit is Love

[5] God has poured out his **love** into our hearts by **the Holy Spirit,** whom he has given us. (Romans 5:5)

Paul commended the Colossian Christians' for their poured out *love in the Spirit.*

[7] Epaphras, our dear fellow servant, who is a faithful minister of Christ on our behalf,

[8] (has) told us of your **love in the Spirit**. (Colossians 1:7-8)

The evidence of the indwelling presence of the Holy Spirit of God in the heart and life of a Christian is the 'fruit of the Spirit' beginning with '**love**'.

[22] The fruit of the Spirit is **love,** joy, peace, patience, kindness, goodness, faithfulness,

[23] gentleness and self-control. Against such things there is no law.(Galatians 5:22-23)

All nine fruit are equally available and precious, but 'love' tops the list! Paul appealed to the 'love of the Spirit' as an incentive for people to pray for him.

[30] I urge you, brothers, by our Lord Jesus Christ and by the **love of the Spirit**, to join me in my struggle by **praying to God for me**. (Romans 15:30)

# God's Love is Unconditional

God loves us all ***unconditionally***. This truth is wrapped up in the word 'whoever'.

[16] God **so loved the world** [anyone, everyone] that he gave his one and only Son, that **whoever [anyone, everyone]** believes in him shall not perish but have eternal life. (John 3:16; 1 Jn 4:16)

If you ever wanted to find your name in the Bible, here it is: **WHOEVER!** Substitute your name for 'whoever'. 'Whoever' is generic for 'everyone' -even YOU ☺

We don't have to do anything to qualify to become a recipient of his love. We don't have to look good, feel good, or be good to earn God's love. We don't have to do something to merit his love. We can never put God in our debt so that he owes us his love. The truth is that God knows all about us…and loves us anyway! David Jerimiah recently said in a TV message,

God loves us too much to leave us the way we are! This is how we come to understand that his love for us all is ***unconditional***.

Billy Graham has stated it this way:

**No matter what sin you have committed**, or how terrible, dirty or shameful it may be, **God loves you**. This love of God is immeasurable, unmistakable and unending. (Billy Graham, Day By Day, December 2007)

[20] Praise be to God, who has **not** rejected my prayer or **withheld his love** from me! (Psalm 66:20)

Could there be a more comforting truth than this? God will never withhold his love from us for any reason! God sees value in even the worst of us. Consider the thief on the cross who by his own admission was worthy of nothing but death. Nevertheless he cried out to Jesus with his last breath for mercy. Jesus didn't withhold his love from him; he mercifully saved him.

> [42] "Jesus, remember me when you come into your kingdom."

Jesus demanded no conditions before answering his request. He simply said,

> [43] "I tell you the truth, today you will be with me in paradise." (Luke 23:42-43)

There is no better place to be the moment after you die than to be with our loving Lord in Paradise!

## God's Love is Unfailing

> [76] May your **unfailing love** be my **comfort**, according to your promise to your servant.
> (Psalm 119:76)

God's *unfailing love* is a *refuge* in the storms of life.

> God's love is just as real in times of adversity as in times of blessing. (Bridges, 'Trusting God', p.110)

> [7] How priceless is your **unfailing love**! Both high and low among men find **refuge** in the shadow of your wings.
> (Psalm 36:7)

> [12] In your **unfailing love**, silence my enemies; destroy all my foes, for I am your servant.
> (Psalm 143:12; 31:21; 61:7; 94:17-19)

Even in the midst of the demise of their nation through war both Isaiah and Jeremiah remained convinced God would show them compassion and *unfailing love* even if their captors didn't. Isaiah penned these words as coming from the mouth of the compassionate, loving God.

> [10] Though the mountains be shaken and the hills be removed, yet my **unfailing love** for you will not be shaken nor my covenant of peace be removed," says the LORD, who has compassion on you. (Isaiah 54:10)

Jeremiah, the 'weeping prophet' writes with eyes brimming with tears,

> [32] Though he brings grief, he will show compassion, so great is his **unfailing love.** (Lamentations 3:32)

The ultimate good news of scripture is that God is eternal. God is love. Therefore, his *love is eternal.*

> [1] I will **sing of the LORD's great love forever**; with my mouth I will make your faithfulness known through all generations.

> [2] I will declare that **your love stands firm forever**, that you established your faithfulness in heaven itself. (Psalm 89:1-2; 100:5; 107:1, 106:1; 117:2; 118:1-4; 136:1)

*'In God We Trust'* is perhaps the most printed sentence in the English language in that the words appear on every bill minted by the US Treasury, and every coin punched out in our Philadelphia, Denver, San Francisco and West Point mints right down to the penny. On a typical day the mints produce about 30 million coins. I have a (very incomplete) penny collection dating back to 1910 and I read the words on a 1910 penny: 'In God We Trust'.

What is it about God that we 'trust'? Is it not his unfailing love?

> [5] **I trust in your unfailing love**; my heart rejoices in your salvation. (Psalm 13:5)

[10] Many are the woes of the wicked, but the LORD's **unfailing love** surrounds the man who **trusts** in him. (Psalm 32:10; 52:8; 143:8)

More than anything, what sustains us in affliction is not the hope it will end, *but God's unending love in the midst of affliction* no matter what.

[7] I will **be glad and rejoice in your love**, for **you saw my affliction** and knew the anguish of my soul. (Psalm 31:7)

God's love is just as real in times of adversity as it is in times of blessing…We can believe that God loves us even when it's not evident due to adversity…The experience of God's love, and comfort it is intended to bring, is dependent upon our believing the truth about God's love as it is revealed in scripture.
(Jerry Bridges, The Pursuit of Holiness, p. 110. 147, 155)

God's *unfailing love is like a HUGE 'Rock'* -God's *unfailing protective refuge* for us to hide behind in times of trial, affliction or persecution.

[4] Trust in the LORD forever, for the LORD, the LORD, is **the Rock eternal.** (Isaiah 26:4)

I enjoy 'praying the scriptures' every day. One of the scriptures I pray back to the Lord is Psalm 19:14

[14] May the words of my mouth and the meditation of my heart be pleasing in your sight, **O LORD, my Rock** and my Redeemer. (Psalm 19:14)

I draw a lot of strength for whatever I may face on any particular day from the truth that my loving God is to me an unfailing ROCK of defense. I think of a spiritual that was sung quite often in the churches of my childhood.

**Jesus is a rock** in a weary land,
A weary land, a weary land;
My Jesus is a rock in a weary land
A shelter in the time of storm.

Yes, the Lord's *unfailing love* is our *impregnable refuge* against whatever the Evil One throws our way. As I write these words, Lord willing, my wife and I will be traveling halfway around the world a week from now to conduct a conference. We will be flying into dangerous air space and ministering in an area of the world that is very unstable politically at the moment. We go, believing the Lord to be our refuge. (If you are reading these words, you will know that we completed our mission and made it back home so I could continue to write this book. To God be the glory! J)

[10] The name of the LORD is **a strong tower**; the righteous
**run to it and are safe**.
(Proverbs 18:10; Ps 73:26; 84:11)

# God's Love is Unlimited

To know God in the biblical sense is to be personally acquainted with his qualities such as **love**, mercy and righteousness. Those are the **qualities that have no limits, no ends.**
(Glen Evans, Daily With the King, July 16)

The *earth* is a very big place. A.W. Tozar, using the size of the earth as his example, illustrates the immense volume of God's love for us.

God's love is measureless. It is more: it is boundless…His love is something he is and because he is infinite that love can enfold the whole created world in itself and have room for ten thousand times ten thousand worlds besides.
(The Knowledge of the Holy, p. 53)

⁵ The LORD loves righteousness and justice; the **earth is full of his unfailing love**. (Psalm 33:5)

⁶⁴ The **earth is filled with your love**, O LORD; teach me your decrees. (Psalm 119:64)

But what is this 'ten thousand times ten thousand worlds besides' that Tozar has mentioned? The Authors of Scripture compare the magnitude of God's love for us with the size of the universe with its billions of galaxies. The universe is no small place, yet it dwarfs in size when compared with the magnitude of God's love for us -for you and for me! God once challenged Abraham to count the number of stars knowing it was an impossible assignment.

⁵ He took him outside and said, "Look up at the heavens and count the stars—if indeed you can count them." (Genesis 15:5)

As a love gift God promised to give him more descendants than the number of stars he could see in the clear night sky.

God not only knows the total number of stars, but he also has a **name** (a unique purpose) for every star.

⁴ He determines the number of the stars and **calls them each by name**. (Psalm 147:4)

²⁶ Lift your eyes and look to the heavens: Who created all these? He who brings out the starry host one by one, and **calls them each by name**. Because of his great power and mighty strength, not one of them is missing. (Isaiah 40:26)

I was introduced to the measureless and boundless 'love of God' at a very young age listening to my father's powerful bass voice singing solos in church about God's love. One song was his favorite and he sang it as often as he had opportunity as a solo, or in a men's quartet in a church service or live on the radio. The song soon became my favorite, also, not simply because it was my father singing it, but because of the profundity of the words describing the vastness of God's love. God's love reached me through this song.

> Could we with ink the ocean fill
> And were the skies of parchment made
> Were every stalk on earth a quill
> And every man a scribe by trade.
>
> To write the love of God above
> Would drain the ocean dry
> Nor could the scroll contain the whole
> Though stretched from sky to sky.
> -Frederick M. Lehman (1868-1953)

[5] Your **love**, O LORD, **reaches to the heavens**, your faithfulness to the skies.
(Psalm 36:5; 103:11; 108:4)

*God likes the word 'abounding'* when it comes to describing the scope of his love for us.

[6] He passed in front of Moses, proclaiming, "The LORD, the LORD, the compassionate and gracious God, slow to anger, **abounding in love and faithfulness.**
(Exodus 34:6)

[5] You are forgiving and good, O Lord, **abounding in love** to all who call to you.
(Psalm 86:5, 15; 103:8; Joel 2:13; Neh 9:17)

The good news of God's concept of abounding love flows through the New Testament, too.

[17] I pray that you, being rooted and established in **love**,

[18] may have power, together with all the saints, to **grasp how wide and long and high and deep** is the **love of Christ,**

[19] and to know this **love that surpasses knowledge**—that you may be filled to the measure of all the fullness of God. (Ephesians 3:17-19; 1 Tm 1:14)

[We are] far more loved and accepted than we ever hoped. (Tim Keller, Preaching, p. 139)

## God's Love Always Perseveres

[7] **Love always perseveres…**

[8] **Love never fails.** (1 Corinthians 13:7-8)

Johnathan Edwards' wife, Sarah, wrote in 'The Narrative' on the occasion of her 32nd birthday,

My safety and happiness, and eternal enjoyment of **God's immutable love seemed as durable and unchangeable as God himself.** (p. 17)

## God in His Love Saves Us

God repeatedly makes his point in Scripture that he is a gracious and *loving 'Savior'.*

[11] I, even I, am the LORD, and **apart from me there is no savior.**" (Isaiah 43:11; 45:21)

It is fitting that we readily acknowledge that God indeed is our 'Savior'.

> [9] We trusted in him, and he **saved us**. This is the LORD, we trusted in him; let us rejoice and **be glad in his salvation.**" (Isaiah 25:9)

> [5] You are **God my Savior**, and my hope is in you all day long. (Psalm 25:5; 71:15; 98:3)

# There are Two Ways God 'Saves' Us as an Expression of His Love

### -God Saves Us Out of Our Troubles

David prayed:

> [6] **Save us** and help us with your right hand, that those you love may be delivered. (Psalm 108:6)

God wants to **save us out of our troubles** and we do have troubles on a world scale. Consider this clarion call for help in 1946 coming from Albert Einstein who made the atomic bomb a reality.

> The unleased power of the atom has changed everything except our modes of thinking, and thus we are drifting towards unparalleled catastrophe...A new type of thinking is essential if mankind is to survive.
> (Albert Einstein, in a telegram asking prominent persons for funds for the Atomic Scientists' Emergency Committee, cited in the NY Times, 5/25/46)

As far back as David's time nations have been in crisis and in need of *saving.*

⁵ You answer us with awesome deeds of righteousness, O
God our **Savior, the hope of all the ends of the earth**
**and of the farthest seas.** (Psalm 65:5)    ·

Paul has affirmed that God has placed a *restraint on evil* in the world
to *save the world* from being totally destroyed by evil men.

⁷ For the secret power of lawlessness is already at work; but
**the one who now holds it back will continue to do so**
**till he is taken out of the way.**
(2 Thessalonians 2:7)

I pray daily that God will not remove his 'restraint' that is holding
back the floodgates of evil from inundating the whole world in an atomic
holocaust that could fulfill John's prophetic words in Revelation:

¹⁹ The cities of the nations collapsed.
(Revelation 16:19)

At the moment if every nuclearized nation unleashed all their weapons
of mass destruction, indeed, all the cities of the nations would collapse.

No one less than God can restrain Satan whose self-assumed mission
is to find a way to annihilate mankind from the face of the earth. The
Lord, however, holds him back as is indicated in the first two unfolding
chapters in Job's story. God set the limits on Satan.

¹² Everything [Job] has is in your hands, but **on the man**
**himself do not lay a finger.** (Job 1:12)

⁶ He is in your hands; but you must **spare his life."**
(Job 2:6)

The rest of the book of Job told how in the process of time God did
spare Job's life by rescuing him out of all the trials and tribulations Satan
had heaped upon him.

Do not we also want to be *saved* out of our *daily troubles*? Aren't we
more than willing to pray with the Psalmist,

> ¹⁵⁹ **Preserve my life, O LORD, according to your love.**
> • (Psalm 119:159)

Isn't it true that the reason we have lived as long as we have is because God in his love has done everything necessary to preserve our lives? He has *saved* us from accidents and diseases and more. He's provided us with everything necessary to sustain our lives: air, water, food, shelter, work, and this is just the beginning! It's not that we haven't had our share of unpleasant circumstances to work through, but the point I'm making is this: at this moment, at least, we are still here -me writing this line and you reading this line. Let's praise the Lord together! He has saved us thus far from Satan's intentions for us which Jesus has said are these:

> ¹⁰ to steal and kill and destroy (John 10:10)

Once I sat down and drew up a list of all the times I could remember when the Lord saved me from injury, or illness that could have resulted in death. To my amazement the list was quite long -a couple pages single-spaced. The list contained everything from surviving pneumonia as an infant, to choking on a marble as a toddler, to nearly being thrown out of a car as a toddler when the door flew open while rounding a curve, to nearly being hit by a train as a teenager walking on railroad tracks, to avoiding car crashes, to recovering from appendicitis, to coming back from death's door from a quadruple heart bypass operation... It's as someone has said, "The blessing of being old is that you didn't die young!"☺

In the Psalms David and the Psalmists were constantly crying out to God in prayer to save them from all manner of seemingly unresolvable difficulties and life threatening situations. Here are some examples of their *cries for God to save them,* because of his great love.

> ⁴ Turn, O LORD, and deliver me; **save** me because of your **unfailing love.** (Psalm 6:4; 31:16)

> ¹³ Be pleased, O LORD, to **save me**; O LORD, come quickly to help me...
> (Psalm 40:13; 27:1, 9; 42:11; 60:5; 69:13; 71:2-4; 80:2-3; 85:7; 109:26; 116:4; 119:41, 94-95, 123, 166; 174)

What did these Psalmists who prayed for salvation conclude once the dust had settled?

> [39] The **salvation of the righteous comes from the LORD**; he is their stronghold in time of trouble.

> [40] **The LORD helps them and delivers them**; he delivers them from the wicked and saves them, because they take refuge in him. (Psalm 37:39-40)

> [16] I call to God, and the LORD **saves** me.
> (Psalm 55:16; 57:3; 62:1-2; 68:19-20; 118:14-16; 138:7; 145:19; 149:4)

The next time you see yourself in an impossible situation and in ***need of the loving Lord to save you*** consider turning to these scriptures and pray them back to the Lord as fervently and believingly as the Psalmists did. They weren't disappointed; you won't be either. If we learn nothing else from these Psalmists it is that crying out for God to save us is not a once in a lifetime prayer. They repeatedly experienced new trials and tribulations, so they repeatedly appealed to God in prayer for salvation out of difficult situations.

Once King Saul's son Jonathan and his armor-bearer came across an encampment of Philistine soldiers. The two of them were tempted to remain in hiding because they were so outnumbered, but Jonathan said to his young companion,

> "Nothing can hinder the LORD from **saving**, whether by many or by few." (1 Samuel 14:6)

Perhaps he was thinking of Gideon who defeated an army of thousands with just 300 men.

The words were easy to say, but not so easy to live out. Did God honor their faith and save them from being overpowered by the Philistines? Here was how the story unfolded.

Douglas Nelson

> [12] The men of the outpost shouted to Jonathan and his armor-bearer, "Come up to us and we'll teach you a lesson." So Jonathan said to his armor-bearer, "Climb up after me; **the LORD has given them into the hand of Israel.**" ...
>
> [20] They found the Philistines in total confusion, striking each other with their swords.
> (1 Samuel 14:12, 20)

Years later God acknowledged to the prophet Isaiah that he was still the only '*Savior*' there is.

> [11] I, even I, am the LORD, and apart from me there is no **savior**. (Isaiah 43:11)

God does '*save*' us one way or another. Either God saves us *from* a calamity; saves us *in* the calamity, or saves us *out of* the calamity. Daniel's three friends got it right when they were given the ultimatum from king Nebuchadnezzar to renounce their faith in God by bowing to a 90 foot high gold plated statute of himself or be thrown into a blazing fiery furnace. They knew that one way or another God would deliver them from the blast furnace. They replied to the king's ultimatum,

> [17] If we are thrown into the blazing furnace, **the God we serve is able to save us** from it, and he will rescue us from your hand, O king.
>
> [18] But **even if he does not**, we want you to know, O king, that **we will not serve your gods** or worship the image of gold you have set up."
> (Daniel 3:17-18)

Did God 'save' them from becoming 'toast'?

> [23] These three men, firmly tied, **fell into the blazing furnace**.

²⁴ Then King Nebuchadnezzar leaped to his feet in amazement and asked his advisers, "Weren't there three men that we tied up and threw into the fire?" They replied, "Certainly, O king."

²⁵ He said, "Look! I see four men walking around in the fire, unbound and unharmed, and the fourth looks like a son of the gods."

²⁶ Nebuchadnezzar then approached the opening of the blazing furnace and shouted, "Shadrach, Meshach and Abednego, servants of the Most High God, come out! Come here!" So **Shadrach, Meshach and Abednego came out of the fire,**

²⁷ and the satraps, prefects, governors and royal advisers crowded around them. They saw that the fire had not harmed their bodies, nor was a hair of their heads singed; their robes were not scorched, and there was no smell of fire on them.
(Daniel 3:23-27)

It's as someone has quipped, 'They wouldn't **bow**; wouldn't **bend**; wouldn't **burn**!'☺

New Testament saints were equally reliant upon the Lord to *save* them in the midst of their difficulties. Paul knew what it was to sense the Lord's powerful presence in the heat of trial.

¹⁷ *The Lord stood at my side and gave me strength*... and I was delivered from the lion's mouth. (2 Timothy 4:17)

⁸ We do not want you to be uninformed, brothers, about the hardships we suffered in the province of Asia. We were under great pressure, far beyond our ability to endure, so that we despaired even of life.

[9] Indeed, in our hearts we felt the sentence of death. But this happened that we might not rely on ourselves but on God, who raises the dead.

[10] He has **delivered** us from such a deadly peril, and he will deliver us.
(2 Corinthians 1:8-10; 11:15-33)

On board ship headed to Rome in the midst of a fierce Northeaster storm Paul said to the frantic crew and passengers,

[23] Last night an angel of the God whose I am and whom I serve stood beside me

[24] and said, 'Do not be afraid, Paul. You must stand trial before Caesar; and **God has graciously given you the lives of all** who sail with you.'

[25] So **keep up your courage, men, for I have faith in God** that it will happen just as he told me.
(Acts 27:23-25)

The ship was wrecked, but everyone on board was *saved*!

[42] The soldiers planned to kill the prisoners to prevent any of them from swimming away and escaping.

[43] But the centurion wanted to spare Paul's life and kept them from carrying out their plan. He ordered those who could swim to jump overboard first and get to land.

[44] The rest were to get there on planks or on pieces of the ship. In this way **everyone reached land in safety.**
(Acts 27:42-44)

Perhaps Jerry Bridges was thinking of scriptures like these when he wrote:

"God's love is just as real in times of adversity as it is in times of blessing." (Trusting God, p. 110)

George Dawson who lived from 1821 to 1876 once prayed:

"Almighty God...grant unto us that **in all trouble** of this our mortal life we may flee to the knowledge of your **loving kindness** and tender mercy; that so, sheltering ourselves therein the storms of life may pass over us and not shake the peace of God that is within us."
('The Meaning of Prayer', H. E. Fosdick, p. 41)

God may, and often does save us from trouble in the nick of time, but there are other times when the Lord saves us by letting us go through the trial and coming out unscathed. Recall this was what occurred with Shadrach, Meshach and Abednego, but this was also the case with our Lord as he faced the cross and prayed in the Garden of Gethsemane:

> [39] Going a little farther, he fell with his face to the ground and prayed, "My Father, **if it is possible, may this cup be taken from me**. Yet not as I will, but as you will."

Jesus prayed to escape the trial if it were possible; if it were God's will. But he determined that it wasn't his Father's will for him to escape the trial of the cross in light of what hanging on the cross would accomplish, namely, salvation for everyone who believes. So Jesus went back to prayer and modified his words.

> [42] He went away a second time and prayed, "My Father, if **it is not possible for this cup to be taken away <u>unless</u> I drink it**, may your will be done."
> (Matthew 26:39, 42)

**He was willing to go through the trial.** The result is that the world has a Savior! 'The Lamb of God who takes away the sin of the world.' (John 1:29).

We might ask, what better thing might happen if we simply let God see us *through the trial* to the other side confident something better is waiting for us on the far side of the trial? Are we willing to follow suit and follow in the footsteps of Jesus? Are we willing to say, "God, not my will, but yours be done!"

> 21 To this you were called, because Christ suffered for you, leaving you an example, that you should follow in his steps. (1 Peter 2:21)

Jesus was not disappointed in his Father for wanting him to endure the 'trial' rather than run from it. He was so willing to do his Father's will that he counted it all JOY!

> 2 Let us fix our eyes on Jesus, the author and perfecter of our faith, who for the **joy** set before him endured the cross, scorning its shame, and sat down at the right hand of the throne of God.
>
> 3 Consider him who endured such opposition from sinful men, so that **you will not grow weary and lose heart.** (Hebrews 12:2-3)

Who can say what God plans to accomplish in our lives -what 'joy' awaits us- if only we're willing to 'tie ourselves to the mast' and head into the 'storm'?

# -God Also Saves Us From the Consequences of Our Sins

As it turns out God saving us out of the difficulties of life (often of our own making) however he sees fit, as important as this is, is only a metaphor for God's willingness to *save us from suffering the consequences of our sins.* Yes, our loving God wants to save us out of the trials and troubles of life that come our way (strengthening our character and deepening our walk with the Lord), but even more God wants to *offer us and the whole world eternal salvation* from the consequences of our sins that would otherwise condemn us to Hell.

In both the Old and New Testaments *our loving Lord* has made the promise of *salvation* from the guilt and consequences of sin resulting in eternal life for all who believe! In the Old Testament David held out hope of *salvation issuing in eternal life* for him personally.

> [9] My heart is glad and my tongue rejoices; my body also will rest secure,

> [10] because **you will not abandon me to the grave**, nor will you let your Holy One see decay.

> [11] You have made known to me the path of life; you will fill me with joy in your presence, with **eternal pleasures** at your right hand. (Psalm 16:9-11)

> [4] Even though I walk through **the valley of the shadow of death**, I will fear no evil, for you are with me; your rod and your staff, they comfort me…

> [6] Surely goodness and love will follow me all the days of my life, and **I will dwell in the house of the LORD forever.** (Psalm 23:4, 6)

> [3] It is as if the dew of Hermon were falling on Mount Zion. For there **the LORD bestows his blessing, even life forevermore.** (Psalm 133:3)

Isaiah understood the longevity of the 'salvation' God was offering him.

> [6] My **salvation will last forever.** (Isaiah 51:6)

The New Testament has a lot to say about the *loving offer of salvation* resulting in coming into *possession of eternal life?*

¹⁶ **God so loved the world** that he gave his one and only Son, that whoever believes in him shall **not perish but have eternal life.** (John 3:16; 36)

²⁴ "I tell you the truth, whoever hears my word and believes him who sent me **has eternal life** and will not be condemned; he has crossed over from death to life. (John 5:24; 6:40; 10:28; 17:3)

²⁵ This is what he promised us—even **eternal life.** (1 John 2:25; 5:11, 13)

²³ For the wages of sin is death, but **the gift of God is eternal life in Christ Jesus our Lord.** (Romans 6:23)

God is more than willing that none perish but that everyone have eternal life, but first of all he has to *save us from the guilt and consequences of our sins*, and this is no small thing! In honesty you may have to say, "I've met the enemy and it is I!" You may be your own worst enemy in that you have sinned, and are in need for someone to save you from the guilt and consequences of your sins, because you've come to the conclusion you can't save yourself. The good news is that everyone has access to such a 'Savior' -God himself. Although our sins have separated us from God, he remains near at hand to reach out to us the moment we pray wanting to be saved.

David was a man who reached out to God believing he would save him.

⁴ My guilt has overwhelmed me like a burden too heavy to bear.

⁵ My wounds fester and are loathsome because of my sinful folly.

⁶ I am bowed down and brought very low; all day long I go about mourning…

²¹ O LORD, do not forsake me; be not far from me, O my God.

²² Come quickly to help me, **O Lord my Savior.**
(Psalm 38:4-6, 21-22)

Scripture pictures God like a great army general putting on his battle gear and forging into battle to save those who have been captured by the enemy and are crying out to be rescued -saved.

⁸ **Save me** from all my transgressions. (Psalm 39:8)

¹⁶ He saw that there was no one, he was appalled that there was no one to intervene; so his own arm **worked salvation** for him, and his own righteousness sustained him.

¹⁷ He put on righteousness as his breastplate, and the **helmet of salvation** on his head; he put on the garments of vengeance and wrapped himself in zeal as in a cloak. (Isaiah 59:16-17)

¹⁷⁶ I have strayed like a lost sheep. **Seek your servant**, for I have not forgotten your commands.
(Psalm 119:176)

¹⁰ The Son of Man **came to seek and to save** what was lost." (Luke 19:10)

Saving us out of our daily troubles is one thing, but saving us from the guilt and consequences of our sins has proven to be the harder rescue operation for the Lord. The Lord made this plain the day he forgave the sins of a paralytic lying before him on a stretcher. He asked everyone,

⁵ Which is easier: to say, 'Your sins are forgiven,' or to say, 'Get up and walk'?

> [6] But so that you may know that the Son of Man has authority on earth to forgive sins...." Then he said to the paralytic, "Get up, take your mat and go home."
> (Matthew 9:5-6)

Everyone got it wrong. The people watching thought it was easier to say 'Your sins are forgiven'. After all, anyone can say that. To them the harder thing would be for Jesus to say 'Rise up and walk.' However, for Jesus the harder thing was to say 'Your sins are forgiven', because it meant dying on the cross for it to be so!

In the New Testament we learn the truth that God's ultimate plan was to do the hard work of the cross, to enable him to *save everyone* who is willing by faith to be saved from the guilt and consequences of their sins.

Isaiah's prophecy regarding God's provision of our *salvation from sin* was so graphic that it's as though he was standing at the foot of Christ's cross.

> [4] Surely he took up our infirmities and carried our sorrows, yet we considered him stricken by God, smitten by him, and afflicted.
>
> [5] But he was **pierced for our transgressions**, he was **crushed for our iniquities**; the punishment that brought us peace was upon him, and by his wounds we are healed.
>
> [6] We all, like sheep, have gone astray, each of us has turned to his own way; and the LORD has **laid on him** the iniquity of us all. (Isaiah 53:4-6)

An *obstacle* in the Lord *saving us from our sins* is *our unwillingness* to admit we are sinners -lost and in need of 'saving'. Solomon states it well.

> [2] All a man's ways **seem innocent** to him. (Proverbs 16:2)

Solomon has given us an example.

[20] "This is the way of an adulteress: She eats and wipes her mouth and says, **'I've done nothing wrong.'** (Proverbs 30:20)

Tim Keller unmasks the uncanny way we are all experts at hiding our truly wretched condition from ourselves and thus are never willing to own up to anything that is wrong in our lives.

> [Never] underestimate our human ability to avoid conviction of sin. Every heart has scores of time-tested subterfuges and excuses by which it can somehow rationalize away any direct confrontation with its own wickedness.
> (Tim Keller, Preaching, p. 185)

Before God can bless sinners with eternal salvation they need to own up to their wickedness. God's first task is to bring us to accept that

[23] all have sinned and fall short of the glory of God, (Romans 3:23)

and be confronted with the fact that

[23] the wages of sin is death.

Then it becomes God's joyful task to inform 'sinners' that

the **gift of God** is eternal life in Christ Jesus our Lord. (Romans 6:23)

Mary, the Mother of our Lord, on the very night of his conception acknowledged that she herself was a sinner and in need of a 'Savior'.

[46] Mary said: "My soul glorifies the Lord

[47] and my spirit rejoices in **God *my* Savior**, (Luke 1:46-47)

Douglas Nelson

The words of this song of praise by Buddy Greene and Mark Lowry are precious.

> Mary did you know that your baby boy would one day walk on water?

> Mary did you know that your baby boy would **save** our sons and daughters?

> Did you know that your baby boy has come to make you new?

> This child that you've delivered, will soon deliver you

An angel appeared to Joseph in a dream and said of Mary,

> [21] She will give birth to a son, and you are to give him **the name Jesus.**

> **He** will **save** his people **from their sins.**
> (Matthew 1:21)

Jesus whose name means '**God saves**' came into the world as '*our Savior*' on that 'first Christmas' so long ago! When it was time for his birth an angel appeared to shepherds watching their flocks by night in the fields surrounding Bethlehem. His resounding good news was that the Son of God -Mary's son Jesus- the '*Savior*' had just been born.

> [11] Today in the town of David a **Savior** has been born to you; he is Christ the Lord. (Luke 2:11)

Years later people who heard Jesus speak and observed his every move came to this conclusion:

> [42] We have heard for ourselves, and we know that this man really is the **Savior of the world.**"
> (John 4:42)

The Author of Hebrews adds this detail:

> [25] **He is able to save completely** those who come to God through him, because he always lives to intercede for them. (Hebrews 7:25)

At the risk of life and limb Peter declared before the whole Sanhedrin (the full assembly of the elders of Israel) when on trial,

> [30] The God of our fathers raised Jesus from the dead— whom you had killed by hanging him on a tree.

> [31] God exalted him to his own right hand as Prince and **Savior that he might give repentance and forgiveness of sins.** (Acts 5:30-31)

John, who was closer to Jesus than anyone, reached the same conclusion.

> [14] We have seen and testify that the Father has sent his Son to be the **Savior of the world.** (1 John 4:14)

One night Jesus said to Nicodemus an inquirer,

> [17] God did not send his Son into the world to condemn the world, but to **save** the world through him. (John 3:17)

Jesus said regarding his *mission* in the world,

> [47] I did not come to judge the world, but to **save** it. (John 12:47)

Peter came to the conclusion early on in the book of Acts that

> [12] **Salvation** is found in no one else, for there is no other name under heaven given to men by which we must be saved." (Acts 4:12)

A little later in Peter's life is the story of an angel confirming to Cornelius, a Roman Centurion, that God would send someone to him in response to his prayers who would give him a message he needed to hear.

> [14] He will bring you a message through which you and all your household will be **saved.**' (Acts 11:14)

The Lord sent Peter to Cornelius' door to share *the gospel of salvation.*

On the first leg of his first missionary journey Paul spoke in the Pisidian Antioch synagogue. He reviewed the history of Israel, and ended with the story of *David* noting that

> [23] from this man's descendants God has brought to Israel the **Savior Jesus**, as he promised.
> (Acts 13:23)

Paul and Barnabas were invited back to speak again on the next Sabbath, and this time brought to everyone's attention that the **salvation God provided was not only for the Jews, but also for Gentiles** –actually, for anyone and everyone on the face of the earth. Paul said to everyone assembled that he and Barnabas were fulfilling an ancient prophecy of Isaiah.

> [47] This is what the Lord has commanded us: "'I have made you a light for the Gentiles, that you may bring **salvation to the ends of the earth.**'"
> (Isaiah 49:6)

> [48] When the Gentiles heard this, they were glad and honored the word of the Lord; and all who were **appointed for eternal life** believed.
> (Acts 13:47-48)

Once I had the privilege of serving as a pastor of an international English-speaking church in a Southeast Asian country. For me, at least, it was so far from where I had come from that I liked to tell my friends that although I wasn't living at the *'ends of the earth'*, I could see the 'ends of the earth' from there ☺ My joy while living there was worshiping with Christians from over 40 nations, and rejoicing with people who responded to the Gospel by accepting the Lord Jesus Christ as their personal 'Savior'! On one occasion I had the privilege of baptizing seven new believers in an outdoor jacuzzi!

In the end of the Bible, John continued to affirm that Jesus is the *Savior of the world.*

> [14] We have seen and testify that the Father has sent his Son
> to be the **Savior of the world.** (1 John 4:14)

Unfortunately, not everyone is willing to believe this truth -not even those who stood at the foot of the cross while Jesus was in the very act of saving the world! (How close can you come to the truth and still miss it?) They stood there mocking him -convinced that if he couldn't save himself from the cross he couldn't save anyone –much less the whole world.

> [35] The people stood watching, and the rulers even **sneered at him.** They said, **"He saved others; let him save himself** if he is the Christ of God, the Chosen One."
>
> [36] The soldiers also came up and **mocked him.** They offered him wine vinegar
>
> [37] and said, "If you are the king of the Jews, **save yourself"**…
>
> [39] One of the criminals who hung there **hurled insults** at him: "Aren't you the Christ? **Save yourself and us!"** (Luke 23:35-37, 39)

The truth is that Jesus *saved* others by *not saving* himself. Dying on the cross sacrificially as the 'Lamb of God' was what qualified him to become *our* Savior!

John the Baptist was the first to recognize that Jesus was not merely his cousin, but the 'Lamb of God'.

[29] The next day John saw Jesus coming toward him and said, "Look, the **Lamb of God**, who **takes away the sin of the world!** (John 1:29)

When Paul and Silas first ventured into Europe they were beaten and chained to a wall in a Philippian prison. That night a powerful earthquake loosened their chains from the wall. Shaking in his boots the terrified Jailor asked them, "What must I do to be **saved**?" They responded:

[31] "Believe in the Lord Jesus, and **you will be saved**—you and your household." (Acts 16:31)

Paul never varied from this message. For example, he shared in his letter to the Romans

[9] If you confess with your mouth, "Jesus is Lord," and believe in your heart that God raised him from the dead, *you will be* saved.

[10] For it is with your heart that you believe and are justified, and it is with your mouth that you confess and *are saved...*

[13] "Everyone who calls on the name of the Lord *will be saved.*" (Romans 10:9-10, 13)

Paul was moved in spirit by the very thought that he had a *Savior*!

[15] Here is a trustworthy saying that deserves full acceptance: **Christ Jesus came into the world to save sinners**—of whom **I am the worst.**
(1 Timothy 1:15)

We may not be the 'worst of sinners', but isn't it still true that we, too, like Paul, need a Savior?

³ At one time **we too** were foolish, disobedient, deceived and enslaved by all kinds of passions and pleasures. We lived in malice and envy, being hated and hating one another.

⁴ But when the kindness and **love of God our Savior** appeared,

⁵ **he saved us**, not because of righteous things we had done, but because of his mercy. **He saved us** through the washing of rebirth and renewal by the Holy Spirit, (Titus 3:3-5)

This is all about confession of sin -confession of soul. (Yes, 'confession is good for the soul'!) Confession is the willingness to be honest and humble before God about what we have done that is sinful in his sight. It's as David Jeremiah said in one of his TV messages:

Confession is to say the same thing about sin God does!

Whenever we have opportunity to *share the Gospel of Salvation* with anyone there are any number of scripture verses you may want to use. Here, for example, is a set of verses all coming out of Romans called **The Roman Road** to salvation.

²³ **All have sinned** and fall short of the glory of God, (Romans 3:23)

⁸ God demonstrates his own love for us in this: While we were still sinners, **Christ died for us.** (Romans 5:8)

²³ The wages of sin is death, but **the gift of God is eternal life** in Christ Jesus our Lord. (Romans 6:23)

⁹ If you confess with your mouth, "Jesus is Lord," and believe in your heart that God raised him from the dead, you will be **saved.**

[10] For it is with your heart that you believe and are justified, and it is with your mouth that **you confess and are saved.** (Romans 10:9-10)

[1] **There is now no condemnation** for those who are in Christ Jesus. (Romans 8:1)

[1] Since we have been justified through faith, **we have peace with God** through our Lord Jesus Christ, (Romans 5:1)

Jesus didn't suffer and die simply at the hands of the soldiers who surrounded his cross. Because *'Christ died for us'* we have to own up to the fact that we were there, too, inflicting pain and death on him —nailing and crushing him with our sins. O.S. Hawkins graphically portrays us surrounding the cross and what we did to him as sinners.

We hated Him. We spit in His face. We beat Him with a leather strap until His back was a bloody pulp. We stripped Him naked and mocked Him. We put a scarlet robe on Him and smashed a crown of thorns on His brow. And then we laughed and laughed and laughed.

Finally, we took His hands -those same hands that once had calmed storms, stroked children's heads, multiplied the loaves and fishes, formed the spittle for the blind man's eyes, and clasped themselves in prayer in the garden- and we nailed them fast to a cross.

Then we took those same feet that had walked miles to bring healing and truth, that had walked on the sea, and we nailed them to a cross.
(The Believer's Code, June 9, p. 176)

Will you sing with me?

On a hill far away, stood an old rugged Cross

The emblem of suff'ring and shame
And I love that old Cross where the dearest and best
For a world of lost sinners was slain...

So I'll cherish the old rugged Cross
Till my trophies at last I lay down
I will cling to the old rugged Cross
And exchange it some day for a crown.
                    -George Bennard (1873-1958)


One Scripture verse alone (John 3:16) when believed has led a countless number of people into an eternal relationship with *Jesus their loving Savior.*

[16] "God so loved the world that he gave his one and only Son, that whoever believes in him shall not perish but have eternal life. (John 3:16)

**The Way of God is Love. To God be the glory**☺

CHAPTER 8

# The Way of God is Grace

# Grace Defined

G race is one of God's wonderful **ways** by which he has made himself
known to us through Scripture. John of the Cross (1542-1591) brings
'grace' to the forefront by writing

> This is the **era** of **grace** and the **gospel** –that is the
> **way** God has chosen to bring our souls under his good
> rulership.
> (Ascent on Mount Carmel, Book 2, Chapter 22)

God fully disclosed his *grace* by the entrance of his Son into the world
to become our 'Savior'.

> [14] The Word became flesh and made his dwelling among
> us. We have seen his glory, the glory of the One and Only,
> who came from the Father, **full of grace** and truth.
> (John 1:14)

J.I. Packer in his classic book 'Knowing God' says simply,

> "Knowing God is a matter of **grace**." (p. 36)

He defines 'God's grace' this way:

> The **grace of God** is love freely shown towards guilty
> sinners, contrary to their merit. (Ibid., p. 120)

The 'grace of God' is not just a New Testament concept in that
everyone in the Old and New Testaments were sinners and desperately
in need of the grace of God. *Noah was the first person recorded in
Scripture who found grace with God.*

> [8] Noah found **grace** in the eyes of the LORD.
> (Genesis 6:8 (KJV))

We should banish from our minds forever the erroneous notion that justice and judgment characterize the God of the Old Testament, while mercy and **grace** belong to the Lord of the Church in the New Testament…The Old Testament is indeed a book of Law, but…before the great flood **Noah 'found grace** in the eyes of the Lord' and after the Law was given God said to **Moses**, 'You have **found grace** in my sight'.
(A.W. Tozar, The Knowledge of the Holy, p. 97, 101-102)

David pondered the *grace of God* when he and Bathsheba's infant son sickened and died.

22 "While the child was still alive, I fasted and wept. I thought, 'Who knows? The LORD may be **gracious** to me and let the child live.'
(2 Samuel 12:22)

David broached the subject of God's **grace** again in the Psalms.

8 The LORD is compassionate and **gracious**, slow to anger, abounding in love. (Psalm 103:8; 145:8)

In the belly of a fish Jonah learned this truth about God's graciousness.

2 I knew that you are a **gracious** and compassionate God, slow to anger and abounding in love, a God who relents from sending calamity. (Jonah 4:2)

The Psalmist of Psalm 111 concluded that if God was great enough to have created heaven and earth, surely it was not beyond his *ability to be gracious* toward the people he created.

2 Great are the works of the LORD; they are pondered by all who delight in them…

⁴ He has caused his wonders to be remembered; the LORD
is **gracious** and compassionate.
(Psalm 111:2, 4)

The prophet Joel was also an Old Testament spokesman for *God's grace*. He affirmed that *grace was most needed* when people sinned and were in need of forgiveness -God's *gracious* forgiveness!

¹³ Return to the LORD your **God,** for he **is gracious** and
compassionate, slow to anger and abounding in love, and
he relents from sending calamity. (Joel 2:13)

In Isaiah's day when the nation of Judah was on the brink of war with Babylon God still longed that he might be able to be **gracious** to his sinful people.

¹⁸ The LORD longs to be **gracious** to you; he rises to
show you compassion. For the LORD is a God of justice.
Blessed are all who wait for him!

¹⁹ O people of Zion, who live in Jerusalem, you will weep
no more. **How gracious he will be when you cry for
help**! As soon as he hears, he will answer you.
(Isaiah 30:18-19)

King Hezekiah backed Isaiah's words by pleading with his nation,

⁹ If you return to the LORD, then your brothers and your
children will be shown compassion by their captors and
will come back to this land, for the LORD **your God is
gracious and compassionate**. He will not turn his face
from you **if you return to him**. (2 Chronicles 30:9)

Did the people respond to the king's plea and return to the Lord? Sadly, they rejected God's gracious offer and so things went from bad to worse for them.

[10] The couriers went from town to town in Ephraim and Manasseh, as far as Zebulun, (with the King's urgent plea) but the people scorned and ridiculed them.
(2 Chronicles 30:10)

Upon Judah's return from her 70 year Babylonian captivity Ezra the priest rejoiced at the very thought that *God had acted graciously* toward his sinful people.

[8] Now, for a brief moment, the LORD our God has been **gracious** in leaving us a remnant and giving us a firm place in his sanctuary, and so our God gives light to our eyes and a little relief in our bondage.

[13] Our God, **you have punished us less than our sins have deserved** and have given us a remnant like this.
(Ezra 9:8, 13)

That is the grace of God. Nehemiah, Ezra's contemporary, understood the need for the *grace of God* while living in desperate times. He prayed,

[17] You are a forgiving God, **gracious** and compassionate, slow to anger and abounding in love. Therefore you did not desert them.
(Nehemiah 9:17)

Paul Tournier has focused on the fact that God's grace pure and simple is a *gift* to us.

There comes a day when everyone understands that all is of **grace,** that the whole world is a **gift** of God; a completely generous gift since no one forced him to it. We see each flower, each drop of water, each minute of our life as a gift of God. He gives them to all, both to those who know him and to those who are ignorant of him. But beyond that, though his gifts are completely disinterested, he is far from disinterested in those who are their recipients; he loves us,

each one of us in particular, personally. He gives with joy and he rejoices in our occasions of joy.
('The Meaning of Gifts', p. 59)

# -God is Gracious in All His Ways

The question is whether or not God is willing to show *grace* toward people who in their sins have turned away from him. Idol worshippers were certainly people who had turned away from God, and while they remained 'turned away' they spurned God's grace by doing so. At least this was the conclusion Jonah came to while pondering many things in the belly of the huge fish that had swallowed him.

> [8] "Those who cling to worthless idols **forfeit the grace** that could be theirs.
> (Jonah 2:8)

But there is good news! Moses heard God's response on the Holy Mount. Anyone who repents becomes the recipient of God's grace.

> [6] He passed in front of Moses, proclaiming, "The LORD, the LORD, the compassionate and **gracious God**, slow to anger, abounding in love and faithfulness,
>
> [7] maintaining love to thousands, and forgiving wickedness, rebellion and sin. "(Exodus 34:6-7)

To Jonah's surprise, when he preached to the wicked Assyrians who lived in Nineveh that if they didn't repent within 40 days God would bring judgment down upon their city, they did repent, and God showed them his amazing grace.

> [10] When God saw what they did and how they turned from their evil ways, he had compassion and did not bring upon them the destruction he had threatened.
> (Jonah 3:10)

The Psalmist writes with conviction of soul,

> [15] You O Lord, are a compassionate and **gracious** God, slow to anger, abounding in love and faithfulness. (Psalm 86:15)

> [5] The LORD <u>is</u> **gracious** and righteous; our God is full of compassion. (Psalm 116:5)

Not '*could be* gracious' nor '*may be* 'gracious', but '*is* **gracious**'!

Isaiah the prophet of Judah who had a direct line to God, understood that *God is gracious*.

> [18] The LORD longs to be **gracious** to you; he rises to show you compassion. (Isaiah 30:18)

'*Grace*' is especially **a New Testament word**. Christianity is all about God's *saving grace* that comes through his gracious Son Jesus Christ.

> [8] It is by **grace** you have been saved, through faith—and this not from yourselves, **it is the gift of God**—

> [9] not by works, so that no one can boast. (Ephesians 2:8-9)

> [20] Where sin abounded, **grace did much more abound**: (Romans 5:20 (KJV)

> [11] The **grace of God** that brings salvation has appeared to all men. (Titus 2:11)

# -The Son of God is Gracious

John Bunyan (1628-1688) the author of 'Pilgrim's Progress' wrote from a prison cell his autobiography which he titled '**Grace Abounding to the Chief of Sinners, or The Brief Relation of the Exceeding Mercy of God in Christ to his Poor Servant John Bunyan**' (1666). John first became aware that salvation is not by works (as he was attempting to do unsuccessfully) but salvation comes by faith in the **gracious finished work of Jesus Christ on the cross**.

> Poor wretch as I was! I was all this while ignorant of Jesus Christ; and going about to establish my own righteousness; and had perished therein, had not God in mercy showed me more of my state by nature.

> But upon a day, the good providence of God called me to Bedford, to work on my calling; and in one of the streets of that town, I came where there were three or four poor women sitting at a door, in the sun, talking about the things of God; and being now willing to hear them discourse, I drew near to hear what they said…I heard but understood not; for they were far above, out of my reach. Their talk was about a new birth, the work of God on their hearts, also how they were convinced of their miserable state by nature; they talked how God had visited their souls with His love in the Lord Jesus, and with what words and promises they had been refreshed, comforted, and supported, against the temptations of the devil…They also discoursed of their own wretchedness of heart, and of their unbelief; and did contemn, slight and abhor their own righteousness, as filthy, and insufficient to do them any good.

> And, methought, they spake as if joy did make them speak; they spake with such pleasantness of scripture language, and with such **appearance of grace** in all they said, that

they were to me, as if they had found a new world; as if they were people that dwelt alone, and were not to be reckoned among their neighbours. (Numb. xxiii. 9)

At the first church council meeting held in Jerusalem it was determined once and for all that it is not obedience to the Law of God, but *faith in the grace of God* shown in and through the Lord Jesus that has resulted in eternal salvation for both Jews and Gentiles.

[11] We believe it is through **the grace of our Lord Jesus** that we are saved. (Acts 15:11)

Surely this is worth giving thanks to God -forever!

[4] **I always thank God** for you because of his **grace given you in Christ Jesus.** (1 Corinthians 1:4)

In all Paul's inspired writings *the grace of God as seen in Jesus Christ* was a major theme. For example:

[4] I always thank God for you because of his **grace given you in Christ Jesus.** (1 Corinthians 1:4)

[9] You know the **grace of our Lord Jesus Christ**, that though he was rich, yet for your sakes he became poor, so that you through his poverty might become rich. (2 Corinthians 8:9)

[9] He has saved us and called us to a holy life—not because of anything we have done but because of his own purpose and **grace.** This **grace was given us in Christ Jesus** before the beginning of time. (2 Timothy 1:9)

Paul was fully aware of the *grace of the Lord Jesus Christ* being operable in his everyday life.

<sup>10</sup> **By the grace of God I am what I am**, and **his grace to me was not without effect**. No, I worked harder than all of them—yet not I, but the **grace of God** that was with me. (1 Corinthians 15:10; 2 Cor 1:12; 2 Cor 12:9)

Paul ended his letters the way he began them -focusing on the grace of God.

<sup>20</sup> The **grace of our Lord Jesus** be with you. (Romans 16:20; 2 Cor 13:14; Gal 6:18; Eph 6:24; Phil 4:23)

Paul has noted that we have a great eternal future awaiting us because of the **grace of our Lord Jesus Christ!**

<sup>6</sup> God raised us up with Christ and **seated us with him in the heavenly realms in Christ Jesus,**

<sup>7</sup> in order that in the coming ages he might show the **incomparable riches of his grace**, expressed in his kindness to us **in Christ Jesus**. (Ephesians 2:6-7; 2 Thess 2:16)

# -The Holy Spirit is gracious

It is a complement when anyone says of another person that he or she has a 'gracious spirit'. *Does God have a 'gracious spirit'?* God speaking through the Old Testament prophet Zechariah answers in the affirmative!

<sup>10</sup> **I will pour out** on the house of David and the inhabitants of Jerusalem a **spirit of grace** and supplication. (Zechariah 12:10)

God spoke repeatedly of this 'pouring out' of his gracious Spirit. Just as God pours out water on thirsty land to sustain life and to quench thirst, he has determined to ***pour his gracious Holy Spirit*** into our lives to give us spiritual life and to quench the thirst of our souls.

[3] I will pour water on the thirsty land, and streams on the dry ground; **I will pour out my Spirit on your offspring, and my blessing** on your descendants.
(Isaiah 44:3; Ezk 39:29; Joel 2:28-29;)

Has this prophecy come to pass? It began to come to pass when Jesus began his public ministry. One day Jesus arrived at the annual Jewish 'Feast of Tabernacles' in Jerusalem, having traveled on foot over seventy miles from Nazareth. At the strategic moment of the climax of this weeklong feast he positioned himself in the middle of the Temple Plaza as priests were symbolically pouring out water from a golden pitcher before the thousands of assembled worshipers.

On the last day of the feast… it was the priests' practice of bringing water in a golden pitcher…from the Pool of Siloam and pouring it out at the altar.
(The Wycliffe Bible Commentary, Everett F. Harrison, p. 1089)

[37] Jesus stood and said in a loud voice, "If anyone is thirsty, let him come to me and drink.

[38] Whoever believes in me, as the Scripture has said, **streams of living water** will flow from within him."

Here, John inserted into the text an explanation of what Jesus was referring to.

[39] By this **he meant the Spirit**, whom those who believed in him were later to receive. Up to that time the Spirit had not been given, since Jesus had not yet been glorified.
(John 7:37-39)

Jesus, by standing in front of the Temple and saying what he said, was a reminder of Ezekiel's vision of what will one day occur on the Temple Mount.

¹ I saw water coming out from under the threshold of the temple toward the east (for the temple faced east). The water was coming down from under the south side of the temple, south of the altar.

² He then brought me out through the north gate and led me around the outside to the outer gate facing east, and the water was flowing from the south side.

³ As the man went eastward with a measuring line in his hand, he measured off a thousand cubits and then led me through water that was ankle-deep.

⁴ He measured off another thousand cubits and led me through water that was knee-deep. He measured off another thousand and led me through water that was up to the waist.

⁵ He measured off another thousand, but now it was a river that I could not cross, because the water had risen and was deep enough to swim in—a river that no one could cross. (Ezekiel 47:1-5)

This 'living water' flowing from the Temple was the prediction of the coming of the **Holy Spirit** to fill the Church to overflowing with spiritual gifts and fruit of the Spirit from the Day of Pentecost till now!

¹ When the day of Pentecost came, they were all together in one place...

⁴ All of them were filled with the Holy Spirit...

¹⁶ This is what was spoken by the prophet Joel:

¹⁷ "'In the last days, God says, **I will pour out my Spirit on all people**. Your sons and daughters will prophesy,

your young men will see visions, your old men will dream dreams.

[18] Even on my servants, both men and women, **I will pour out my Spirit in those days,** and they will prophesy. (Acts 2:1, 4, 16-18)

# God is Gracious to the Humble

Of all the sins God hates he hates pride the most, in that it was the original sin committed by Lucifer. Pride was what caused Lucifer's fall from God's grace and from God's Heaven. The Son of God may have been referring to this prehistoric event when he said:

[18] I saw Satan fall like lightning from heaven. (Luke 10:18)

There is a familiar saying: 'Pride goes before a fall'.

[18] **Pride goes before destruction**, a haughty spirit before a fall. (Proverbs 16:18; Ps 147:6)

[34] God mocks proud mockers but gives **grace to the humble**. (Proverbs 3:34)

If anyone ever could have been justly proud would it not have been God himself? After all, he *is* God Almighty? He is the creator of heaven and earth. No one is his equal! But **God is not proud. God is humble.**

[15] This is what the high and lofty One says— he who lives forever, whose name is holy: "**I live** in a high and holy place, but also **with him who is contrite and lowly in spirit,** to revive the spirit of the lowly and to revive the heart of the contrite. (Isaiah 57:15)

***God offers grace to those who humble themselves.*** This is the way it's always been. For example, consider Ezra's prayer to God shortly after returning with a contingent of Jews from a humbling seventy year exile in Babylon.

> [8] "Now, for a brief moment, the LORD our God has been **gracious** in leaving us a remnant and giving us a firm place in his sanctuary, and so our God gives light to our eyes and a little relief in our bondage. (Ezra 9:8)

Jesus, the Son of God, is the personification of ***grace and humility.***

> [5] Your attitude should be the same as that of Christ Jesus:
>
> [6] Who, being in very nature God, did not consider equality with God something to be grasped,
>
> [7] but **made himself nothing**, taking the very nature of a servant, being made in human likeness.
>
> [8] And being found in appearance as a man, **he humbled himself** and became obedient to death— even death on a cross! (Philippians 2:5-8)

Jesus throws out this challenge to any and all who would follow him,

> [29] Take my yoke upon you and learn from me, for **I am gentle and humble in heart**, and you will find rest for your souls.
>
> [30] For my yoke is easy and my burden is light."
> (Matthew 11:29-30)

God is gracious toward those who want to ***reflect his humility.***

> [9] He **guides the humble** in what is right and teaches them **his way.**
> (Psalm 25:9; Isa 66:2; Lk 1:52)

If ever there was a humble person it was Moses.

> [3] Moses was a very **humble** man, more **humble** than anyone else on the face of the earth. (Numbers 12:3)

This was not his estimation of himself or he would have disqualified himself of the title, rather, this was God's estimation of Moses.

Saul of Tarsus is an example of a proud man who became willing to humble himself before the Lord.

> [9] **I am the least of the apostles** and do not even deserve to be called an apostle, because I persecuted the church of God.

> [10] But **by the grace of God** I am what I am, and **his grace** to me was not without effect. No, I worked harder than all of them—yet not I, but the **grace of God** that was with me. (1 Corinthians 15:9-10)

Young men especially seem to struggle with pride. Peter has given some sound advice to them.

> [5] Young men...be submissive to those who are older. All of you, **clothe yourselves with humility** toward one another, because, "God **opposes the proud** but gives **grace to the humble.**"

> [6] **Humble yourselves**, therefore, under God's mighty hand, that he may lift you up in due time...

> [12] I have written to you briefly, encouraging you and testifying that **this is the true grace of God**. Stand fast in it. (1 Peter 5:5-6, 12)

If young men took Peter's advice perhaps there would be fewer fatalities on our roads. I cringe whenever I see young arrogant drivers speed past me thinking they are the 'king of the road'. One day when I was going the speed limit on an interstate highway a young motorcyclist popping a wheelie sped past me balancing on one wheel. I was afraid of what I might have found waiting for me down the road.

James urged his readers to *prefer grace* and humility *over pride.*

⁶ **He gives us more grace**. That is why Scripture says: "**God opposes the proud** but **gives grace to the humble**."

⁷ Submit yourselves, then, to God...

10 Humble yourselves before the Lord, and he will lift you up. (James 4:6-7, 10)

The awareness of *God's measureless grace* in Christ Jesus set Annie Johnson Flint's heart to singing. Although she suffered severe physical affliction, Annie penned these words affirming the grace of God as being more than sufficient to match any crisis with joyful trust.

**He giveth more grace** when the burdens grow greater,
He sendeth more strength when the labors increase;
To added afflictions He addeth His mercy,
To multiplied trials, His multiplied peace.

His love has no limits, **His grace has no measure**,
His power no boundary known unto men;
For out of His infinite riches in Jesus
He giveth, and giveth, and giveth again.
      -Annie Johnson Flint (1862-1932)

# Salvation is God's Grace in action

The good king Hezekiah pled with his people to return to the Lord.

⁹ **If you return to the LORD**, then your brothers and your children will be shown compassion by their captors

and will come back to this land, for the LORD your **God is gracious** and compassionate. **He will not turn his face from you if you return to him**. (2 Chronicles 30:9)

Hezekiah's words were backed up by the words of the prophet Hosea.

[1] Return, O Israel, to the LORD your God. Your sins have been your downfall...

[2] Return to the LORD. Say to him: "Forgive all our sins and receive us **graciously**. (Hosea 14:1-2)

Grace is all about God's willingness to accept us the moment we're willing to repent and turn to him. E. Stanley Jones, a missionary for many years in the 1900's, wrote in his autobiography,

I don't have to persuade God to forgive me...It is a matter of my turning and my acceptance. He accepts me in and when I accept His acceptance. I do not have to overcome His reluctance. I have to lay hold on His highest willingness!
(On My Way Rejoicing p. 22)

God's 'highest willingness' is God's amazing grace!

'I like the way... Dr. Vernon Grounds amplified the overwhelming wonder of *God's grace* -pushing language to its limits in the process. At a conference where he was the keynote speaker he encouraged everyone by saying that because of the *saving grace of God in Jesus his Son* we are:

Eternally purposed
Uniquely formed
Sacrificially redeemed
Irrevocably justified
Personally indwelt
Sovereignly needed
Incalculably valued

Unconditionally loved
Inconceivably blessed

[17] If, by the trespass of the one man [Adam], death reigned through that one man, **how much more** will those who **receive God's abundant provision of grace** and of the gift of righteousness reign in life through the one man, Jesus Christ. (Romans 5:17)

Abounding sin is the terror of the world; **abounding grace** is the hope of the world.
(A.W.Tozar, 'The Knowledge of the Holy', p. 53)

Recall the title of John Bunyan's autobiography:

*'Grace Abounding to the Chief of Sinners, The Brief Relation of the Exceeding Mercy of God in Christ to his Poor Servant John Bunyan'*

The *grace of God* exceeds to an infinite degree the magnitude of our sins.

[20] The law was added so that the trespass might increase. But **where sin increased, grace increased** *all the more*,

[21] so that, just as sin reigned in death, so also **grace might reign through righteousness** to bring eternal life through Jesus Christ our Lord.
(Romans 5:20-21)

I recall as a child that the rafters of our church shook when we as a congregation sang at the top of our voices, and from the depths of our hearts the great hymn *'Wonderful Grace of Jesus'*.

**Wonderful Grace of Jesus**, greater than all my sin;
How shall my tongue describe it,
Where shall its praise begin?

Taking away my burden, setting my spirit free;
For the Wonderful Grace of Jesus reaches me!

Wonderful **the matchless Grace of Jesus,**
Deeper than the mighty rolling sea;
Higher than the mountain, sparkling like a fountain,
**All sufficient Grace** for even me...
        -Haldor Lillenas (1885-1959)

Yes, we are *saved and justified by the matchless grace of Jesus alone!*

[24] We are justified freely by his **grace** through the redemption that came by Christ Jesus.
(Romans 3:24)

Let's not ever forget what Christ had to endure for God to be able to offer us *redeeming grace.*

[9] We see Jesus, who was made a little lower than the angels, now crowned with glory and honor because **he suffered death**, so that **by the grace of God he might taste death for everyone.**
(Hebrews 2:9; Rom 5:1-2; Tit 3:7)

[7] In him **we have redemption** through his blood, the **forgiveness of sins**, in accordance with the **riches of God's grace** (Ephesians 1:7)

In the 16th century Martin Luther rediscovered the truth that by *grace we are justified* by *faith alone* in the Lord Jesus Christ!

We say that there is nothing in us that can deserve **grace**, and the forgiveness of sins. But we proclaim that we receive the **grace** solely and altogether by the free mercy of God...(We) do not become righteous by works but solely by **grace** and by faith in Christ.
(Luther, Lectures on Galatians, 1:58-59)

In the 17<sup>th</sup> century Bible commentator Matthew Henry wrote:

> We shall not fall under the curse of the Law if we submit to the **grace of the Gospel**.
> (Matthew Henry's Commentary 4:305)

Paul was a grateful recipient of God's amazing and undeserved *grace*.

> ¹⁴ The **grace of our Lord** was poured out on me abundantly, along with the faith and love that are in Christ Jesus.
> (1 Timothy 1:14)

He refused to claim any other basis for his salvation than God's grace.

> ²¹ I do not set aside the **grace of God**, for <u>if</u> **righteousness could be gained through the law, Christ died for nothing**!" (Galatians 2:21)

This may be among the most significant verses of scripture. *If* we could have said and or done anything to contribute to our salvation then Christ would have died unnecessarily! But Christ didn't die unnecessarily! He's the sole means of our salvation. Without his death on the cross there is nothing we could ever do to achieve our eternal salvation; nothing at all!

When Peter and John were hauled into court in an effort to pressure them to disavow this truth Peter stood before the court and said:

> ¹² Salvation is found in no one else [other than in Jesus Christ], for there is no other name under heaven given to men by which we must be saved." (Acts 4:12)

Sometime later at the very first church council in Jerusalem Peter and all the Founding Fathers concurred with this fundamental truth once and for all.

> ¹¹ We believe it is through the **grace** of our Lord Jesus that we are saved. (Acts 15:11)

Paul became a noted spokesman all over the world for this great truth -the saving *grace* of God in Christ. For example, he said to the leaders of the Ephesian church,

> [24] I consider my life worth nothing to me, if only I may finish the race and complete the task the Lord Jesus has given me—the **task of testifying to the gospel of God's grace.** (Acts 20:24)

> [32] I commit you to God and to the word of his **grace**, which can build you up and give you an inheritance among all those who are sanctified. (Acts 20:32)

Here, then, is the good news: *Grace is God's way* of bringing salvation to us.

> [11] **The grace of God** that **brings salvation** has appeared to all men. (Titus 2:11)

Paul, however, asked the question that would naturally come into everyone's mind.

> [1] What shall we say, then? Shall we go on sinning so that **grace** may increase? (Romans 6:1)

Paul' answer was a resounding 'NO'!

> [2] **By no means!** We died to sin; how can we live in it any longer?...

> [14] Sin shall not be your master, because you are not under law, but **under grace.**

> [15] What then? Shall we sin because we are not under law but **under grace?**
> **By no means!** (Romans 6:2; 14-15)

**Grace** is not justification of the sin, but the justification
of the sinner.
(Dietrich Bonhoeffer, The Cost of Discipleship, p. 52)

Have you ever sung this great hymn of the Church?
**Marvelous grace** of our loving Lord,
**Grace that exceeds our sin and our guilt**!
Yonder on Calvary's mount outpoured,
There where the blood of the Lamb was spilled.

Sin and despair, like the sea waves cold,
Threaten the soul with infinite loss;
Grace that is greater, yes, grace untold,
Points to the refuge, the mighty cross.

**Marvelous, infinite, matchless grace**,
Freely bestowed on all who believe!
You that are longing to see His face,
Will you this moment His **grace** receive?

**Grace, grace, God's grace,**
**Grace** that will pardon and cleanse within;
**Grace, grace, God's grace,**
**Grace** that is greater than all our sin!
–Julia H. Johnston (1849-1919)

# God's Grace Rests Upon the Church

Once I was a part of a planning team to start a new church plant. One of the first things we did was to take a survey in the community. We listed out on a sheet of paper about thirty possible names for the new church and asked people which name was the most appealing to them. The most chosen name was the one that had the word '*Grace*' in it. People in the community liked identifying 'grace' with the church. To them it was a warm and inviting name.

*Douglas Nelson*

The grace of God has been associated with the Church from the days of the New Testament. The first Christians were converted Jews living in and around Jerusalem. They were the first to realize that they were saved not because they were Jews; not because they kept God's Law perfectly (they didn't and couldn't), but because of the *grace* God had provided by offering them salvation through his Son.

> ⁶ If by **grace**, then it is no longer by works; if it were, grace would no longer be grace.
> (Romans 11:6)

God intended his ***gracious*** offer of salvation to be for the whole world of ***Jews and Gentiles***. The Lord's intension is that the Church be composed of Jews and Gentiles. In the aftermath of Stevens' martyrdom and ensuing persecution of Christians they began to scatter far and wide sharing the Gospel of God's grace with everyone they met -Jew and Gentile! The first Gentile converts were Greeks living in Syrian Antioch to the north of Judea.

> ¹⁹ Those who had been scattered by the persecution in connection with Stephen traveled as far as...Antioch...
>
> ²⁰ and began to speak to **Greeks** also, telling them the good news about the Lord Jesus.
>
> ²¹ The Lord's hand was with them, and a great number of people believed and turned to the Lord.
>
> ²² News of this reached the ears of the church at Jerusalem, and they sent Barnabas to Antioch.
>
> ²³ When he arrived and saw the **evidence of the grace of God**, he was glad and encouraged them all to remain true to the Lord with all their hearts.
> (Acts 11:19-23)

Paul always shared with both Jews and Gentiles the *gracious Good News* that the long awaited Jewish Messiah (Christ) had come, and he was offering *saving grace* indiscriminately to the whole world and not just to the Jews. The first thing Paul and Barnabas told new believers to do, whether Jew or gentile, was to *'continue in the grace of God'.*

> [43] When the congregation was dismissed, many of the Jews and devout converts to Judaism [gentiles]followed Paul and Barnabas, who talked with them and urged them to **continue in the grace of God!** (Acts 13:43)

Paul never failed in any of his letters to remind his readers first of all about the Grace of God that has been extended to the Church.

> [7] **Grace and peace to** you from God our Father and from the Lord Jesus Christ.
> (Romans 1:7, see: 1 Corinthians 1:2-3, 2 Corinthians 1:2; Galatians 1:2-3; Ephesians 1:1-2; Philippians 1:1-2; Colossians 1:2; 1 Thessalonians 1:1; 2 Thessalonians 1:2:16; 1 Timothy 1:2; Titus 1:4; 3:7; Philemon 1:3)

You might be thinking this was just a common salutation put at the beginning of a letter: 'Grace and peace to you'. That may have been the case in Paul's day with Christians writing to one another, but what a beautiful greeting -and reminder of God's grace with every letter. Maybe we should ask ourselves when we have ever started or ended a letter or a tweet with the words: 'Grace and peace to you my friend.'

# Daily evidence of the Grace of God

What is the 'evidence of the grace of God'? No one has answered this question more plainly or more beautifully then John Newton when in 1779 he penned the immortal words of his hymn Amazing Grace which is sung around the world to this day!

Amazing grace how sweet the sound
That sav'd a wretch like me!
I once was lost, but now am found
Was blind, but now I see.
'Twas grace that taught my heart to fear,
And grace my fears reliev'd;
How precious did that grace appear
The hour I first believ'd!

If ever there was a song that has bound together the Church worldwide it is John Newton's hymn, 'Amazing Grace'! God's amazing grace is our common experience!

*Daily* (this present moment) is always where we are in need of God's grace the most. It's *daily* that we're 'in the trenches' toughing out life moment-by-moment! But it is also daily that God wants to graciously bless us!

> [7] To each one of us **grace has been** given as Christ apportioned it. (Ephesians 4:7)

Jesus assures us that if we take life 'a day at a time' it will not prove overwhelming for us.

> [34] Do not worry about tomorrow, for tomorrow will worry about itself. Each day has enough trouble of its own. (Matthew 6:34)

> God stores up goodness or **grace** for our times of adversity. We do not receive it before we need it, but we never receive it too late.
> (Jerry Bridges, 'Trusting God'. P. 153)

Lewis Smedes has written realistically,

> **Grace** does not make everything right...**grace** is rather an amazing power to look reality full in the face, see its sad and tragic edges, feel its cruel cuts, join in the chorus

against its outrageous unfairness, and yet feel in your deepest being that it is good and right for you to be alive on God's good earth.
(Focal Point -a Denver Seminary periodical).

[9] It is good for our hearts to be strengthened by **grace**. (Hebrews 13:9)

John Newton encourages us to sing God's amazing grace as a way of getting us through each and every day.

> Thro' many dangers, toils, and snares,
> I have already come;
> 'Tis grace hath brought me safe thus far,
> And grace will lead me home.

Augustine writes,

> **What grace is meant to do** is to help good people, not to escape their sufferings, but to bear them with a stout heart, with a fortitude that finds its strength in faith. ('City of God', XXII, 22-23)

There was no one who needed a daily dose of God's *grace* more than Paul in light of all the stress and suffering he endured as he boldly declared the Gospel farther and farther into the world that was resistant to his message.

> [8] Although I am less than the least of all God's people, this **grace** was given me: to preach to the Gentiles the unsearchable riches of Christ, (Ephesians 3:8)

And 'preach' he did in the strength the Lord *graciously* offered him daily. Let us also be aware that the grace of God is operative in whatever we may be called on by the Lord to face that may be difficult or even life threatening.

[16] Let **us** then approach the **throne of grace with confidence**, so that we may receive mercy and find **grace** to help us in **our time of need**. (Hebrews 4:16)

[4] Even in darkness **light dawns** for the upright, **for the gracious** and compassionate and righteous man. (Psalm 112:4)

When addressing his dear friends in Philippi Paul reminded everyone that he didn't have a corner on 'grace', but God's grace has freely been given to all the members of the Body of Christ.

[7] Whether I am in chains or defending and confirming the gospel, **all of you share in God's grace with me**. (Philippians 1:7; Ephesians 4:7)

**"The entire Christian life** can be seen to result from God's **continuous bestowal of grace."** (Wayne Grudem, 'Systematic Theology', p. 201)

The Lord has *graciously* dispensed spiritual gifts to us who are the members of his Body -the Church.

[6] We have **different gifts,** according to the **grace given us.** (Romans 12:6)

Putting these spiritual gifts into play is how we '*grow in grace*'. Here were Peter's last written words to the Church:

[18] **Grow in the grace** and knowledge of our Lord and Savior Jesus Christ. To him be glory both now and forever! Amen. (2 Peter 3:18)

# What God's Grace Motivates Us to Do

The joy of **extending God's grace** to others is a far better reward than anything money could buy.
(John Piper, Desiring God, pp. 96-97)

We can do nothing to *achieve* our salvation, and nothing to *retain* our salvation, but we can *express* the joy of our salvation by the things the Lord has graciously put in our hearts to do in his strength, and for his glory.

[8] God is able to make all **grace abound** to you, **so that** in all things at all times, having all that you need, you will **abound in every good work.**
(2 Corinthians 9:8)

Those who have received grace should henceforth feel indebted to lovingly give themselves to doing what is good! All who have become a 'new creation in Christ' (2 Corinthians 5:17) are to radiate Christ in all they say and do. This is the new person we've become in Christ by his spiritually transforming power.

Once I accompanied someone who went to a lawyer about a problem. The first thing the lawyer did as an act of grace was to ask if he could start the session with prayer. The session went well!

An elderly lady who was our neighbor hired a home health aide. Shortly afterwards that helper helped herself by stealing a large amount of money from her. She hired a new helper and what a difference. She was a true Christian who radiated the love of the Lord. She proved to be a trusted helper; a *gracious*, compassionate and loving helper. She fit Paul's description of humble and gracious Christians who say

[12] "No" to ungodliness and worldly passions, and…live self-controlled, upright and godly lives in this present age…

[14] **eager to do what is good.** (Titus 2:12, 14)

I like the way a friend of mine described how we as God's 'new creation' are perceived in the world. We are *'points of light; flashes of grace in an otherwise very dark world'*. It's as Paul has said,

> [15] Become blameless and pure, children of God without fault in a crooked and depraved generation, in which you **shine like stars in the universe.**
> (Philippians 2:15)

## God's Grace Motivates Us to Grow in Faith

> 'Tis so sweet to trust in Jesus,
> Just to take Him at His Word
> Just to rest upon His promise,
> Just to know, "Thus saith the Lord!"
>
> Jesus, Jesus, how I trust Him!
> How I've proved Him o'er and o'er
> Jesus, Jesus, precious Jesus!
> **Oh, for grace to trust Him more!**
> -William Kirkpatrick (1838-1921)

Peter has informed us that faith is just the beginning of what it is to live a *gracious life*. He lists several 'add-ons' to faith.

> [5] Make every effort to **add to your faith** goodness; and to goodness, knowledge;
>
> [6] and to knowledge, self-control; and to self-control, perseverance; and to perseverance, godliness;
>
> [7] and to godliness, brotherly kindness; and to brotherly kindness, love.

⁸ For if you possess these qualities in increasing measure, they will keep you from being ineffective and unproductive in your knowledge of our Lord Jesus Christ. (2 Peter 1:4-8)

# God's Grace Inspires Generosity

Paul encouraged his friends in Corinth to ***graciously excel in generosity***.

> ⁷ Just as you excel in everything—in faith, in speech, in knowledge, in complete earnestness and in your love for us—see that you also excel in this **grace of giving**. (2 Corinthians 8:7)

He went on to offer a 'rule of thumb' regarding the matter of giving.

> ⁷ Each man should give what he has decided in his heart to give, not reluctantly or under compulsion, for **God loves a cheerful giver.**
>
> ⁸ And God is able to make all **grace abound** to you, so that in all things at all times, having all that you need, you will abound in every good work. (2 Corinthians 9:7-8)

Jesus pointed out that in the matter of gracious giving God sets the pace. The grace of God cascades over us in terms of his generosity toward us.

> ³⁸ Give, and it will be given to you. **A good measure, pressed down, shaken together and running over,** will be poured into your lap. For with the measure you use, it will be measured to you." (Luke 6:38)

The Lord always more than matches our gracious generosity. This is true, for example, when it comes to the matter of 'tithing'.

[10] Bring the whole tithe into the storehouse, that there may be food in my house. Test me in this," says the LORD Almighty, "and see if I will not throw open the floodgates of heaven and pour out so much blessing that **you will not have room enough for it**. (Malachi 3:10)

Paul didn't let the opportunity slip for him to praise the Corinthian Christians for a sacrificial gift of money they had collected to send to Christians living almost a thousand miles away in Judah whom they didn't know by name, but had learned were suffering from a famine.

[13] Because of the service by which you have proved yourselves, men will praise God for the obedience that accompanies your confession of the gospel of Christ, and for **your generosity** in sharing with them and with everyone else.

[14] And in their prayers for you their hearts will go out to you, because of **the surpassing grace** God has given you. (2 Corinthians 9:13-14)

Sometimes during a fund raiser a philanthropic donor will match dollar-for-dollar any contribution to a charity so every dollar given doubles or triples in value. Likewise, when we graciously give to meet a need there is *a double blessing*. The need is met -that is a blessing- but it also solicits thanksgiving and praise to God from the recipients of charitable gifts. This is a second blessing in that God himself is blessed.☺

[12] This service that you perform is [1] not only supplying the needs of God's people but is also [2] overflowing in many **expressions of thanks to God.** (2 Corinthians 9:12)

The most gracious donor of all time is our *gracious God*, and my-oh-my what he has given us ☺

²³ **The gift of God** is eternal life in Christ Jesus our Lord. (Romans 6:23)

¹⁵ Thanks be to God for **his indescribable gift!** (2 Corinthians 9)

# Witness God's grace to the World

From the start God has wanted us who believe in him to live graciously before everyone, everywhere, all the time. When this happens God makes his face shine upon us for all to see! ☺

¹ May God be **gracious** to us and bless us and make his face shine upon us,

² that **your ways** may be known on earth, **your salvation** among all nations. (Psalm 67:1-2)

Once I struck up a conversation with a young man I had just met in a city park. I attempted to share the Gospel with him, but the more he expressed resistance to receiving Christ as his Savior my words became less gracious and more confrontational. Unfortunately, this man was not seeing the grace of God shining on me. Since then I've prayed for him that he encountered someone who showed him the grace of God by speaking the truth in love rather than in a harsh manner. I learned from this experience to engage in 'friendship evangelism' rather than 'confrontational evangelism'. I regret that to the stranger in the park I was not the man Solomon praises.

¹² Words from a **wise man**'s mouth are **gracious**. (Ecclesiastes 10:12)

A key scripture regarding 'friendship evangelism' is 1 Peter 3:15.

[15] Always be prepared to **give an answer to everyone who asks you** to give the reason for the hope that you have. But do this **with gentleness and respect**. (1 Peter 3:15)

Solomon's words are wise!

[15] **A gentle tongue can break a bone.**
(Proverbs 25:15)

# The Power of God's Grace

Before anyone is willing to listen to our gospel witness they need to sense the ***grace of God*** flowing through us to them. *'Grace'* was the secret as to how the Apostles had the ***power*** to effectively bear witness to the Gospel.

[33] **With great power** the apostles **continued to testify** to the resurrection of the Lord Jesus, and **much grace** was upon them all. (Acts 4:33)

Paul reminded his 'spiritual son' Timothy regarding the significance of the two words *'grace'* and *'power'* in a Christian's life.

[1] You then, my son, **be strong** in the **grace** that is in Christ Jesus. (2 Timothy 2:1)

Luke melded together *'grace'* and *'power'* when describing Stephen -the first Christian martyr.

[8] Stephen, a man **full of God's grace and power**, did great wonders and miraculous signs among the people. (Acts 6:8)

Paul was more than willing to own up to the fact that the Lord's ***grace*** was the secret of his ***power***.

⁹ The Lord said to me, "**My grace** is sufficient for you, for **my power** is made perfect in weakness." Therefore I will boast all the more gladly about my weaknesses, so that **Christ's power** may rest on me.

¹⁰ That is why, for Christ's sake, I delight in weaknesses, in insults, in hardships, in persecutions, in difficulties. For **when I am weak, then I am strong**.
(2 Corinthians 12:9-10)

The Author of Hebrews writes:

⁹ It is good for our hearts to be **strengthened** by **grace**.
(Hebrews 13:9)

Paul's whole life and missionary ministry was a testimony of the Lord's *gracious power* at work in him. This great Apostle of the Faith revealed his determination to graciously share his Gospel witness to the world by pointing out on a map the full extent of his plans to travel 'to the very ends of the earth'!

¹⁹ From Jerusalem all the way around to **Illyricum**, I have fully proclaimed the gospel of Christ...

²³ Now that there is **no more place for me to work in these regions**, and since I have been longing for many years to see you,

²⁴ I plan to do so when I go to **Spain**. I hope to visit you [in Rome] while passing through and to have you assist me on my journey there, after I have enjoyed your company for a while.
(Romans 15:19, 23-24)

Illyricum was approximately 1500 miles northwest of Jerusalem (his starting point), situated across the Adriatic Sea from Italy, but he had his eyes on far off Spain another 1000 miles to the west to the very edge of the known world of that day.

Paul was more than willing to trust God for the power to suffer for Christ if that's what it took to get *the gospel of God's grace in Jesus Christ* out to the ends of the earth.

> [24] I consider my life worth nothing to me, if only I may finish the race and complete the task the Lord Jesus has given me—the task of testifying to the gospel of God's **grace**. (Acts 20:24; Phil 3:10)

Paul knew that any form of persecution he suffered as a result of sharing the Gospel of Grace would not be wasted because of what was certain to be the result.

> [15] **Grace…is reaching more and more people** [causing] thanksgiving to overflow to the glory of God. (2 Corinthians 4:15)

Paul sensed the *grace of God* from start to finish. It's interesting to note that in Paul's last letter, in the last sentence the word '**grace**' appears.

> [22] The Lord be with your spirit. **GRACE be with you**. (2 Timothy 4:22)

Peter has reminded us of the real possibility that when we share the *gospel of God's grace* not everyone will respond positively to our witness even if we 'speak the truth in love'. Persecution may occur to the point of martyrdom ('witness' and 'martyr' come from the same Greek word). But Peter added this encouraging word:

> [10] The God of all **grace**, who called you to his eternal glory in Christ, after you have suffered a little while, will himself restore you and make you strong, firm and steadfast.

> [11] To him be the **power** for ever and ever. Amen. (1 Peter 5:9-11)

Note that Peter, like Paul, was still placing '*grace*' and '*power*' side-by-side!

## Pray for God's Grace

People for a long time have been praying for God to be gracious to them. When in need we lift our eyes to heaven to pray, we are lifting our eyes to '*the throne of grace*'.

> <sup>16</sup> Let us then approach **the throne of grace** with confidence, so that we may receive mercy and find **grace** to help us in our time of need.
> (Hebrews 4:16)

When we find ourselves in great need know that the Lord is more than willing to 'graciously' meet the need in his time, in his way, and for his glory. In the Psalms David prayed for God's *grace to prevail* in his time of need.

> <sup>16</sup> Turn to me and **be gracious to me**, for I am lonely and afflicted. (Psalm 25:16)

It is always appropriate to *pray for God's grace* to be manifested, especially when difficult situations arise.

> <sup>18</sup> **The LORD longs to be gracious to you**; he rises to show you compassion…Blessed are all who wait for him…
>
> <sup>19</sup> **How gracious he will be** when you cry for help! **As soon as he hears, he will answer you.**
> (Isaiah 30:18-19)

The prophet Malachi exhorted the people to whom he ministered to *pray for God's grace* in their time of need.

> <sup>9</sup> "Implore God to be **gracious** to us. (Malachi 1:9)

Here was how God's grace fit into Paul's life when he found himself in a seemingly helpless and hopeless situation.

> [8] We do not want you to be uninformed, brothers, about the hardships we suffered in the province of Asia. We were under great pressure, far beyond our ability to endure, so that we despaired even of life.
>
> [9] Indeed, in our hearts we felt the sentence of death. But this happened that we might not rely on ourselves but on God, who raises the dead.
>
> [10] He has delivered us from such a deadly peril, and he will deliver us. On him we have set our hope that he will continue to deliver us,
>
> [11] Many will give thanks on our behalf for **the gracious favor** granted u**s in answer to the prayers of many**.
> (2 Corinthians 1:8-11)

Here is an ancient prayer of blessing that calls upon God's grace.

> [24] The LORD bless you and keep you;
>
> [25] the LORD make his face shine upon you and **be gracious to you;**
>
> [26] the LORD turn his face toward you and give you peace.
> (Numbers 6:24-26)

Whenever God manifests his grace in our lives in response to *prayer* it becomes a powerful witness to onlookers. Whenever my wife and I tell anyone about times the Lord has helped meet a need in our lives, they have concluded that God indeed is loving, kind, good and **gracious**!

# God's Grace is Ongoing

God's amazing grace will never end. Peter has noted that in the end when Christ returns from heaven to reign on earth 'grace' will still be the order of the day!

> [13] Set your hope fully on the **grace to be given you when Jesus Christ is revealed**. (1 Peter 1:13)

Of all the scriptural subjects John could have used to close out the New Testament scriptures focusing on the end of human history he chose to highlight the **grace** of our Lord Jesus Christ!

> [21] The **grace of the Lord Jesus** be with God's people. Amen. (Revelation 22:21)

**By his grace** I am redeemed
By His blood I am made clean;
And I now can know him face-to-face.
By his pow'r I have been raised,
Hidden now in Christ by faith;
**I will praise the glory of His grace.'**
    -Steve Fry

**To God be the Glory That His Way is Grace**☺

CHAPTER 9

# God's Way is Mercy

# The Way of God is Mercy

I have loved good music ever since I was a young child. I learned to play the trumpet when I was in 2$^{nd}$ grade. I had wanted to play the trombone but my father said that my arm was too short to work the slide. When I was in 5$^{th}$ grade I started piano lessons. In both cases one of the first pieces I learned to play was the hymn, 'At Calvary'. The reason, probably was because my teachers thought it was an easy piece to play. It was written in the key of C which meant no flats or sharps. I played the hymn again and again until I had it down, but in the process of time I also got the words of the hymn down. The older I have become the more meaningful the words have become focusing on God's great *mercy* demonstrated in Jesus Christ.

> Years I spent in vanity and pride,
> Caring not my Lord was crucified,
> Knowing not it was for me He died
> On Calvary.
>
> *Mercy* there was great, and grace was free;
> Pardon there was multiplied to me;
> There my burdened soul found liberty
> At Calvary.
> -William Newell (1868-1956)

# God is Merciful

A.W. Tozar in his book 'The Knowledge of the Holy' juxtaposes God's '*justice*' with his '*mercy*'.

> As judgment is **God's justice** confronting moral inequity, so **mercy** is the goodness of God confronting human suffering and guilt. (p.97)

If God's *grace* is all about God giving us *what we don't deserve*, namely, salvation, God's *mercy* is all about withholding from us *what we do deserve*, namely, condemnation, judgment and damnation. For the record, *God is merciful*.

> [31] The LORD your **God is a merciful God**; he will not abandon or destroy you or forget the covenant with your forefathers, which he confirmed to them by oath. (Deuteronomy 4:31)

Once when under God's discipline David had to choose one of three punishments: live through 3 years of a severe drought; fall into the hands of his enemies for 3 months, or be at the *mercy* of God for 3 days. Which one did he choose?

> [13] David said, "I am in deep distress. Let me fall into the hands of the LORD, for *his* mercy *is very great*; but do not let me fall into the hands of men." (1 Chronicles 21:13)

A wise choice, David; a very wise choice!☺

It was Daniel's conviction from having lived through the Babylonian conquest and exile that

> [9] The Lord our **God is merciful** and forgiving, even though we have rebelled against him; (Daniel 9:9)

> [18] Give ear, O God, and hear; open your eyes and see the desolation of the city that bears your Name. We do not make requests of you because we are righteous, but because of **your great mercy**.

> [19] O Lord, listen! O Lord, forgive! O Lord, hear and act! For your sake, O my God, do not delay, because your city and your people bear your Name." (Daniel 9:18-19)

Nehemiah writing a few years after Daniel reflected on this great truth as the Babylonian exile came to an end, and the Jews were free to the return to the Promised Land.

³¹ In your great **mercy** you did not put an end to them or abandon them, for you are a gracious and **merciful God**. (Nehemiah 9:31)

Lest there is any doubt, God himself goes on record that *his way is the way of mercy*! God has it down to three words:

¹² **I am merciful**,' declares the LORD. (Jeremiah 3:12)

Isaiah has left us with this word of instruction:

⁷ Let the wicked forsake his way and the evil man his thoughts. Let him turn to the LORD, and he will have **mercy** on him, and to our God, for he will freely pardon. (Isaiah 55:7)

## God Expresses Mercy with Compassion

We might want to consider *compassion* and *mercy* as *synonyms*.

¹¹ The Lord is full of **compassion** and **mercy**. (James 5:11)

Although our Heavenly Father may feel compelled to discipline us when we sin, he never ceases to *show us mercy by way of compassion*.

¹⁴ Zion said, "The LORD has forsaken me, the Lord has forgotten me."

¹⁵ "Can a mother forget the baby at her breast and have no *compassion* on the child she has borne? Though she may forget, *I will not forget you*!

¹⁶ See, *I have engraved you on the palms of my hands*; your walls are ever before me. (Isaiah 49:14-16)

When God does discipline us it is not to the degree our sins merit.

*Douglas Nelson*

⁸ The LORD is **compassionate** and gracious, slow to anger, abounding in love.

⁹ He will not always accuse, nor will he harbor his anger forever;

¹⁰ **he does not treat us as our sins deserve** or repay us according to our iniquities.
(Psalm 103:8-10)

# God Expresses Mercy with Comfort

We might also want to consider *comfort* and *mercy* as *synonyms*.

¹ **Comfort, comfort** my people, says your God.

² **Speak tenderly** to Jerusalem, and proclaim to her that her hard service has been completed, that her sin has been paid for, that she has received from the LORD's hand double for all her sins. (Isaiah 40:1-2)

¹³ Shout for joy, O heavens; rejoice, O earth; burst into song, O mountains! For the LORD **comforts his people** and will have compassion on his afflicted ones. (Isaiah 49:13)

'Comfort' is also a New Testament word.

⁴ God **comforts** us in all our troubles, so that we can **comfort** those in any trouble with the comfort we ourselves have received from God.

⁵ For just as the sufferings of Christ flow over into our lives, so also through Christ our **comfort** overflows.
(2 Corinthians 1:4-5)

¹ If you have any encouragement from being united with Christ, if any **comfort** from his love, if any fellowship with the Spirit, if any tenderness and compassion,

² then make my joy complete by being like-minded, having the same love, being one in spirit and purpose. (Philippians 2:1-2)

# God Expresses Mercy with Forgiveness

*Forgiveness* is also *a way God shows us his mercy*.

³⁸ He was **merciful**; he **forgave** their iniquities and did not destroy them. Time after time he restrained his anger and did not stir up his full wrath.
(Psalm 78:38)

⁹ The Lord our God is **merciful** and **forgiving**, even though we have rebelled against him;
(Daniel 9:9

⁸ Who is a God like you, who pardons sin and **forgives** the transgression of the remnant of his inheritance? You do not stay angry forever but **delight to show mercy**.
(Micah 7:18)

# God the Father is Merciful

Jesus instructs us to be *merciful* in keeping with the fact that *God our Father is merciful*.

³⁶ Be **merciful**, just as your **Father is merciful**.
(Luke 6:36)

James confirms that the wisdom the Father sends down to us from heaven is full of mercy.

> [17] The wisdom that comes from Heaven is first of all pure;
> then peace-loving, considerate, submissive, *full of* mercy
> and good fruit, impartial and sincere. (James 3:17)

## God the Son is Merciful

The Son of God who mirrors his Heavenly Father is *merciful*. Jesus showing *mercy* is a repeated story in the Gospels. Stepping out from the crowd two blind men called upon Jesus for *mercy*.

> [30] "Lord, Son of David, have **mercy** on us!"
> (Matthew 20:30)

He showed *mercy* by restoring their eyesight!

> [22] A Canaanite woman from that vicinity came to him,
> crying out, "Lord, Son of David, **have mercy on me**! My
> daughter is suffering terribly from demon-possession."
> (Matthew 15:22)

He showed *mercy* by driving the demon out of her tormented daughter and setting her free!

Right after Jesus descended from a 'mountain top experience' with Peter, James and John, he was approached by a distraught father.

> [15] "Lord, have **mercy** on my son," he said. "He has seizures
> and is suffering greatly. He often falls into the fire or into
> the water. (Matthew 17:15)

The Lord showed *mercy* and healed his epileptic son!

> [18] Jesus rebuked the demon, and it came out of the boy,
> and he was healed from that moment. (Matthew 17:18)

One day Jesus came across a man that haunted the tombs. He admitted to being overrun with a legion of demons which if taken literally numbered 6,000. The Lord freed the man of all of them and gave him a simple assignment.

> [19] "Go home to your family and tell them how much the Lord has done for you, and **how he has had mercy on you.**" (Mark 5:19)

The Lord is our *merciful 'High Priest'* to represent us before the Father in Heaven.

> [17] He had to be made like his brothers in every way, in order that he might become a **merciful** and faithful high priest in service to God, and that he might make atonement for the sins of the people. (Hebrews 2:17)

> [16] Let us then approach the throne of grace with confidence, so that we may receive **mercy** and find grace to help us in our time of need. (Hebrews 4:16)

> Recall the worship song,

> Lord have *mercy*; Christ have *mercy*; Lord have *mercy* on me.

> Lord have *mercy*; Christ have *mercy*; Lord have *mercy* on me.

# The Spirit is Merciful

> [5] He saved us, not because of righteous things we had done, but because of his **mercy**. He saved us through the washing of rebirth and renewal by the **Holy Spirit**. (Titus 3:5)

The *merciful* Holy Spirit is our *'Comforter'*

> [26] The **Comforter**, *which is* the Holy Ghost, whom the Father will send in my name, he shall teach you all things, and bring all things to your remembrance, whatsoever I have said unto you.
> (John 14:26 (**KJV**))

I have known from childhood the Holy Spirit to be a *merciful Comforter.* One of the hymns I grew up singing in church highlighted the comfort of the Holy Spirit.

> Oh, spread the tidings 'round, wherever man is found,
> Wherever human hearts and human woes abound;
> Let every Christian tongue proclaim the joyful sound:
> The **Comforter** has come!

> *Refrain:*
> The **Comforter** has come, the **Comforter** has come!
> The Holy Ghost from Heav'n, the Father's promise giv'n;
> Oh, spread the tidings 'round, wherever man is found—
> The **Comforter** has come! -John Bottome (1823-1894)

# God willingly Extends Mercy

From ancient times God has been in the business of extending mercy. The Lord said to Moses on the Mount,

> [19] I will cause all my goodness to pass in front of you, and I will proclaim my name, the LORD, in your presence. **I will have mercy on whom I will have mercy**, and I will have compassion on whom I will have compassion.
> (Exodus 33:19)

One of the greatest examples of God extending *mercy* to undeserving people was during the days of Israel's wandering in the desert for forty years with Moses.

> [37] Their hearts were **not loyal to God**, they were **not faithful to his covenant**.

> [38] **Yet he was merciful**; he forgave their iniquities and did not destroy them. Time after time he restrained his anger and did not stir up his full wrath.

> [39] He remembered that they were but flesh, a passing breeze that does not return.
> (Psalm 78:37-39)

They were unfaithful to the Lord generation after generation when they lived in the Promised Land, yet the Lord remained *'merciful'*. The prophet Micah made note of the fact that God had *mercy* on them!

> [18] Who is a God like you, who pardons sin and forgives the transgression of the remnant of his inheritance? You do not stay angry forever but **delight to show mercy**.
> (Micah 7:18)

In the beginning of the New Testament Mary remembered the multiple times God had shown *mercy* to Israel over the generations, and she incorporated this memory into her prayer the day of her conception of the Son of God.

> [50] His **mercy** extends to those who fear him, **from generation to generation…**

> [54] He has helped his servant Israel, remembering to be **merciful** (Luke 1:50,54)

Paul was profoundly grateful that *the Lord showed mercy* to him ending his out-of-control years when he was 'Saul of Tarsus' and mercilessly mistreated Christians.

> [13] Even though I was once a blasphemer and a persecutor and a violent man, I was shown **mercy** because I acted in ignorance and unbelief...

> [16] I was shown **mercy** so that in me, the worst of sinners, Christ Jesus might display his unlimited patience as an example for those who would believe on him and receive eternal life.
> (1 Timothy 1:13, 16)

Paul knew that it was God's great *love* that fueled his tender *mercy*.

> [3] All of us also lived among them at one time, gratifying the cravings of our sinful nature and following its desires and thoughts. Like the rest, we were by nature objects of wrath.

> [4] But because of his **great love for us**, God, who is rich in **mercy**,

> [5] made us alive with Christ even when we were dead in transgressions—it is by grace you have been saved.
> (Ephesians 2:3-5)

Peter contrasted the way it was before we were Christians, and the way it is now that we are Christians.

> [10] Once you were not a people, but now you are the people of God; once you *had not received* mercy, but now you *have received* mercy. (1 Peter 2:10)

# God Hears the Prayer for Mercy

David and all the Psalmists repeatedly *prayed for mercy*.

> [1] Answer me when I call to you, O my righteous God.
> Give me relief from my distress; **be merciful to me** and
> **hear my prayer.** (Psalm 4:1)

> [6] Remember, O LORD, your great **mercy** and love.
> (Psalm 25:6)

> [7] Hear my voice when I call, O LORD; **be merciful to
> me** and answer me.
> (Psalm 27:7; 26:11; 28:2; 30:8; 31:9; 40:11; 41:4; 69:16;
> 119:132; 140:6; 142:1-3, 5-6)

David was horrified at the very thought that God might *withhold his
mercy*. Here was *David's 'cave man' prayer* when he hid in the back of a
cave from the jealous King Saul who was searching for him to take his life.

> [1] Have **mercy** on me, O God, have **mercy** on me, for in
> you my soul takes refuge. I will take refuge in the shadow
> of your wings until the disaster has passed. (Psalm 57:1)

On another occasion David prayed:

> [3] **Have mercy on me, O Lord**, for I call to you all day
> long.

> [4] Bring joy to your servant, for to you, O Lord, I lift up
> my soul..

> [6] Hear my prayer, O LORD; listen to my **cry for mercy.**

> [7] In the day of my trouble I will call to you, for you will
> answer me...

<sup>16</sup> Turn to me and **have mercy on me**; grant your strength to your servant and save the son of your maidservant. (Psalm 86:3-4, 6-7, 16)

After his adulterous affair, David *prayed for mercy,*

<sup>1</sup> **Have mercy on me**, O God, according to your unfailing love; according to your great compassion blot out my transgressions. (Psalm 51:1)

Does *praying* to God for *mercy* have any effect? The Psalmists say it does!

<sup>9</sup> The LORD has **heard my cry for mercy**; the LORD accepts my prayer. (Psalm 6:9)

<sup>6</sup> Praise be to the LORD, for he has **heard my cry for mercy.** (Psalm 28:6; 31:22; 116:1; 130:3)

If there is no justice, what hope is there for the world? But if there is a judge, what hope is there for us? O Lord, **"if you kept a record of sins, who would be left standing?"** But here is a wonder: Jesus Christ is the judge of all the earth, who came the first time not with a sword in his hands but with nails through his hands —not to bring judgment but to bear judgment for us. (Tim Keller, Preaching, pp. 74-75)

<sup>17</sup> God did not send his Son into the world to condemn the world, but to save the world through him. (John 3:17)

*Desperate times* may call for desperate measures, but also for *desperate prayers for God to show mercy.* The prophet Habakkuk observed that Judah as a nation was overwhelmed facing the invading Babylonian army. But he was not overwhelmed because he was convinced that God almighty was greater in power than all the might of the invading army of numberless soldiers! So he held out for *God's mercy* to intervene.

² LORD, I have heard of your fame; I stand in awe of your deeds, O LORD. Renew them in our day, in our time make them known; in wrath remember **mercy**. (Habakkuk 3:2)

God not only *hears* prayers for *mercy* but *answers* them -*mercifully*!

# In His Mercy God Saves

Paul has informed us of the extensiveness of our disobedience, but also of the extensiveness of God's *mercy* -even though we have been disobedient.

³² God has bound **all** men over to **disobedience** so that he may have **mercy** on them **all.**
(Romans 11:32)

Yes, James says it all!

¹³ **Mercy triumphs** over **judgment!** (James 2:13)

God's tender *mercy* is what has made possible salvation from the guilt and consequences of our sins!

⁵ He **saved** us, not because of righteous things we had done, but **because of his mercy**. He saved us through the washing of rebirth and renewal by the Holy Spirit, (Titus 3:5)

³ Praise be to the God and Father of our Lord Jesus Christ! In his **great mercy** he has **given us new birth** into a living hope through the resurrection of Jesus Christ from the dead. (1 Peter 1:3)

# God Wants Us to Extend Mercy

Jesus indicates that our **showing mercy** is a big thing with God -a very big thing!

> <sup>23</sup> The kingdom of heaven is like a king who wanted to settle accounts with his servants.

> <sup>24</sup> As he began the settlement, a man who owed him ten thousand talents was brought to him.

> <sup>25</sup> Since he was not able to pay, the master ordered that he and his wife and his children and all that he had be sold to repay the debt.

> <sup>26</sup> "The servant fell on his knees before him. 'Be patient with me,' he begged, 'and I will pay back everything.'

> <sup>27</sup> The servant's master **took pity on him**, canceled the debt and let him go.

> <sup>28</sup> "But when that servant went out, he found one of his fellow servants who owed him a hundred denarii. He grabbed him and began to choke him. 'Pay back what you owe me!' he demanded.

> <sup>29</sup> "His fellow servant fell to his knees and begged him, 'Be patient with me, and I will pay you back.'

> <sup>30</sup> "But he refused. Instead, he went off and had the man thrown into prison until he could pay the debt.

> <sup>31</sup> When the other servants saw what had happened, they were greatly distressed and went and told their master everything that had happened.

<sup>32</sup> "Then the master called the servant in. 'You wicked servant,' he said, 'I canceled all that debt of yours because you begged me to.

<sup>33</sup> **Shouldn't you have had mercy** on your fellow servant just as I had on you?'

<sup>34</sup> In anger his master turned him over to the jailers to be tortured, until he should pay back all he owed.

<sup>35</sup> "This is how my heavenly Father will treat each of you unless you **forgive your brother from your heart.** (Matthew 18:23-35)

This is what we're consenting to every time we pray the 'Lord's Prayer'.

<sup>12</sup> Forgive us our debts, as we also have forgiven our debtors…

<sup>14</sup> For if you forgive men when they sin against you, your heavenly Father will also forgive you.

<sup>15</sup> But if you do not **forgive men their sins**, your Father will **not forgive your sins**.
(Matthew 6:12,14-15)

We who have been *shown mercy by God* ought to be more than willing, in turn, to *show mercy* to anyone in need of our forgiveness.

God does not demand of us what he himself is unwilling to do, namely, **show mercy**. Remember the humble sinner praying in the Temple Plaza in Jerusalem,

<sup>13</sup> He would not even look up to heaven, but beat his breast and said, **'God, have mercy on me, a sinner.'**

<sup>14</sup> "I tell you that this man…went home justified before God.." (Luke 18:13-14)

God not only desires for us to show *mercy*, he enables us to be *merciful* by granting us the *spiritual gift* of *mercy*.

> ⁶ If a man's **gift** is... showing **mercy**, let him do it cheerfully. (Romans 12:6, 8)

What does God's *mercy* fleshed out in our lives look like in our daily lives? The Lord's intention is that we show *mercy* even when it's painful to do so -which is whenever we think we would be justified to withhold *mercy*. The Lord desires that we look for *reasons to show mercy* rather than *reasons to withhold mercy*.

One evening Jesus was the guest of honor at the home of Matthew the Tax Collector -his newest disciple. It wasn't long, however, before Jesus' critics were on his case criticizing him for eating with 'tax collectors and 'sinners'.

> ¹² On hearing this, Jesus said, "It is not the healthy who need a doctor, but the sick.

> ¹³ But go and learn what this means: **'I desire mercy, not sacrifice.'** For I have not come to call the righteous, but sinners." (Matthew 9:12-13)

The time came when the Lord handed down an indictment to *unmerciful self-righteous people.*

> ²³ "You hypocrites! You give a tenth of your spices—mint, dill and cummin. But you have neglected the more important matters of the law—justice, **mercy** and faithfulness. You should have practiced the latter, without neglecting the former. (Matthew 23:23)

The Lord doesn't allow any excuse for withholding *mercy* even to those whom we determine are not worthy of mercy. He made this point in his parable of the 'Good Samaritan'. A priest and then a Levite came across a man lying on the path before them who had been robbed and beaten.

They looked the other way and passed him by. Then a third man came across the fallen man, and helped him at his own expense. Jesus asked:

> ³⁶ "Which of these three do you think was a neighbor to the man who fell into the hands of robbers?"

> ³⁷ The expert in the law replied, "The one who had **mercy** on him." Jesus told him, **"Go and do likewise."**
> (Luke 10:36-37)

We need to be willing to show *mercy* toward those who need to be rescued out of their helpless situations. God has gone on record with regard to how he wants us to respond whenever we come across an opportunity to be a 'Good Samaritan'.

> ⁸ He has showed you, O man, what is good. And what does the LORD require of you? To act justly and to love **mercy** and to walk humbly with your God. (Micah 6:8)

The Lord wants us to love mercy, because he desires mercy!

> ⁷ If you had known what these words mean, '**I desire mercy**, not sacrifice,' you would not have condemned the innocent.
> (Matthew 12:7; Hosea 6:6)

At the very beginning of Jesus' public ministry one of the first topics he addressed in his Sermon on the Mount was showing '*mercy*'.

> ⁷ **Blessed** are the **merciful**, for they will be shown **mercy**.
> (Matthew 5:7)

*VDP* stands for '*Very Draining People*'. They are the people who try our patience by their inordinate demands for our attention. But they are the very people who need to be the recipients of *our mercy.* Why? Because their baggage out of the past has incapacitated them from being able to function normally -maybe not able to function at all. Can we hear what the Lord is whispering (or shouting) into our hearts? 'Show him mercy; show her mercy!'

[22] **Be merciful** to those who doubt;

[23] snatch others from the fire and save them; to others **show mercy**, mixed with fear—hating even the clothing stained by corrupted flesh.
(Jude 1:22-23)

*Mercy is the way God expresses himself* to us. *Mercy is the way God wants us to show love* to the *VDP* in our world who lie helpless at our feet. We have our work cut out for us. It is often messy work, but it is good work! "Mercy me …it's good work!"

**Glory be to God that His Way is the Way of Mercy** ☺

CHAPTER 10

# The Way of God is Goodness

337

## God's Creation was Good.

One of the first words in the Bible is the word *'good'* –repeated six times in the first chapter with reference to God's great act of creation, and 560 times in the whole Bible.

> [4] God saw that the light was **good,** and he separated the light from the darkness. (Genesis 1:4)

Each day of creation was the same... 'It was good...it was good...it was good... Then at the end of the 6th day -the last day of creation- God stepped back and made the observation that *all* he had made, including Man, was *'very good'* (1:31)

In the New Testament Paul attaches the word *'good'* to God and his creation.

> [4] Everything God created is **good**, and nothing is to be rejected if it is received with thanksgiving,
> (1 Timothy 4:4)

> Everything God made was **good -including his 'children'**...**Goodness** lies deeper in the heart of man's nature than the sin which came later and entered from the outside. **Goodness** lies deeper in man because God put himself there...**Goodness** is intrinsic to man's nature; sin is not...**Goodness** lies deep in the bedrock of the universe, not merely because what God created was **good**, but because **goodness is intrinsic to God's nature itself**. (Michael Phillips, 'A God to Call Father' pp. 119-121)

## God is Good

If we want to know why God created everything *good*, John Calvin has suggested an answer in his 'Institutes of the Christian Religion' (1:5).

"If it be asked what cause induced God to create all things at first, and now inclines him to preserve them we shall find that there could be no other cause than **his own goodness.**"

The most important thing we can learn about God is that **God is good!**"
(Michael Phillips, 'A God to Call Father' p. 199)

C.S. Lewis notes in his book 'The Problem of Pain'
God is **goodness.** He can give **good,** but cannot need or get it...He eternally has and is all **goodness.** God wills **our good,** and **our good** is to love him.
(pp. 50-51, 53)

Theologian Grudem notes in his 'Systematic Theology' (p. 197-198):

The **goodness of God** means that **God is the final standard of good...** There is no higher standard of goodness than **God's own character....**God is the source of all good in the world....God is the ultimate good that we seek.

Wayne is merely following in the footsteps of the Authors of Scripture. But is God's goodness too good to be true? According to Scripture it is true. David, for example, affirmed God's *goodness* throughout his Psalms.

⁷**You are good**, O LORD.

⁸**Good** and upright is the LORD **therefore he instructs sinners in his ways.** (Psalm 25:7-8)

⁹The LORD is **good to all**; he has compassion on all he has made. (Psalm 145:9; 27:13; 86:5)

Later Psalmists echo David's conviction that *God is good.*

[5] **The LORD is good** and his love endures forever; his faithfulness continues through all generations. (Psalm 100:5; 106:1)

[68] **You are good, and what you do is good**; teach me your decrees. (Psalm 119:68)

A.W.Tozar defines God's goodness this way:

The **goodness of God** is that which disposes him to be kind, cordial, benevolent, and full of good will toward men...By his nature he is inclined to bestow blessedness and he takes holy pleasure in the happiness of his people. (The Knowledge of the Holy, p. 88)

Early on in history God made known that *his way* is to *express goodness.* He said to Moses,

[19] I will cause **all my goodness** to pass in front of you, and I will proclaim my name, the LORD, in your presence. I will have mercy on whom I will have mercy, and I will have compassion on whom I will have compassion. (Exodus 33:19)

Augustine (354-430) writing over 1600 years ago had this to say about *God's goodness*:

I want you to know how you may perceive the beauty of God...We normally think of perceiving beauty with our eyes but the beauty of God is in his complete **goodness** -consisting of virtues or high truths that are all of his nature.
(On Seeing God' (David Hazard, 'Early Will I Seek You', p. 77)

On the day Solomon dedicated the newly built Temple God manifested his glorious *goodness* in such an awesome way that everyone fell to their knees, and worshiped him for his *goodness* and his love!

> When all the Israelites saw the fire coming down and the glory of the LORD above the temple, they knelt on the pavement with their faces to the ground, and they worshiped and gave thanks to the LORD, saying, "**He is good; his love endures forever.**"
> (2 Chronicles 7:3; Ps 107:1; 136:1)

Now it's our turn to taste and see that the Lord is good!

> ⁸ Taste and see that the LORD is **good**.
> (Psalm 34:8)

We have nothing to lose by 'tasting'. Taste and you'll be pleasantly surprised like a little child who is sure he doesn't like the food that is set before him, but once he tastes it he likes it and wants more! When atheist C. S. Lewis became a Christian he reportedly said, "What I thought I didn't want was what I wanted my entire life."

We would do well to give the Lord a wide girth for expressing all his goodness to us. We need to *praise God for his goodness* when everything is going well, as well as praise him when things have the potential of not going well. At least this was the way Joab the Commander of David's Army lived. Listen to Joab's 'pep talk' to his troops as they prepared to go out to battle:

> ¹³ Be strong and let us fight bravely for our people and the cities of our God. The LORD will do what is **good** in his sight." (1 Chronicles 19:13)

If ever you want to experience the goodness of God it's when you're going into battle!

> ⁷ **The LORD is good**, a refuge in times of trouble. He cares for those who **trust in him.**(Nahum 1:7)

## -God the Father is Good

God our Father never asks of us his children to do what he himself is unwilling to do. Jesus said of his Heavenly Father,

> [11] If you, then, though you are evil, know how to give **good gifts** to your children, **how much more** will **your Father in heaven** give **good gifts** to those who ask him! (Matthew 7:11)

Could there ever have been a greater expression of his goodness than the gift of his Son?

> [16] God so loved the world that **he gave his one and only Son**, that whoever believes in him shall not perish but have eternal life. (John 3:16)

## -God the Son is Good

Some doubted that Jesus could be 'good' in light of where he had come from: Nazareth! Recall Nathaniel's derogatory comment upon learning of Jesus' home town,

> [46] "Nazareth! Can anything **good** come from there?" Nathanael asked. "Come and see," said Philip. (John 1:46)

You may have your doubts, but come and see and you will not be disappointed! When John the Baptist had his moment of doubt regarding Jesus, Jesus challenged him to *review all the good* things he was doing.

> [21] At that very time Jesus cured many who had diseases, sicknesses and evil spirits, and gave sight to many who were blind.

> [22] So he replied to the messengers, "Go back and report to John what you have seen and heard: The blind receive

sight, the lame walk, those who have leprosy are cured, the deaf hear, the dead are raised, and the **good** news is preached to the poor.

<sup>23</sup> Blessed is the man who does not fall away on account of me." (Luke 7:21-23)

Jesus stated categorically that *only God is good* in comparison to everyone else and everything else.

<sup>18</sup> A certain ruler asked him, "**Good teacher**, what must I do to inherit eternal life?"

<sup>19</sup> "Why do you call me good?" Jesus answered. "No one is **good**—except God alone.
(Luke 18:18-19)

Was Jesus contrasting himself with God and therefore saying he himself was not 'good'? The point Jesus was making was that he himself is truly 'goodness' itself, because he is indeed God in flesh. The question is whether or not this young man fully realized that he was staring 'Goodness' in the face when he was talking to the very Son of God come down from heaven; the One who said:

<sup>9</sup> Anyone who has seen me has seen the Father. (John 14:9)

Yes, Jesus was and is of the very essence of God's *goodness* in that he is the eternal Son of God. Jesus' very birth was announced as *good news* by an angel hovering in Bethlehem's night sky.

<sup>10</sup> The angel said, "I bring you **good news** of great joy that will be for all the people." (Luke 2:10)

Jesus identified himself as the *Good Shepherd* of his sheep who know his voice.

<sup>11</sup> I am the **good** shepherd. The **good** shepherd lays down his life for the sheep. (John 10:11)

Early on in his public ministry Jesus preached in the synagogue in his home town of Nazareth, and declared that he himself was the very person whom God had ordained to fulfill Isaiah's prophecy.

<sup>1</sup> The Spirit of the Sovereign LORD is on me, because the LORD has anointed me to preach **good news** to the poor. He has sent me to bind up the brokenhearted, to proclaim freedom for the captives and release from darkness for the prisoners.
(Isaiah 61:1)

<sup>20</sup> He rolled up the scroll, gave it back to the attendant and sat down. The eyes of everyone in the synagogue were fastened on him,

<sup>21</sup> and he began by saying to them, "Today this scripture is fulfilled in your hearing."
(Luke 4:20-21)

In the Gospels Jesus was noted for going around and ***doing good*** even as Isaiah prophesied he would do. Peter in sharing the Gospel with Cornelius summed everything up this way:

<sup>38</sup> God anointed Jesus of Nazareth with the Holy Spirit and power, and ...**he went around doing good** and healing all who were under the power of the devil, because God was with him. (Acts 10:38)

In C.S. Lewis' 'The Lion, the Witch and the Wardrobe' Mr. Beaver emphasized to Lucy, Susan and Peter that Aslan (the Christ figure) above all things was **good**!

"It says in an old rhyme in these parts:
-Wrong will be right, when Aslan comes in sight,

344

At the sound of his roar, sorrows will be no more,
When he bears his teeth, winter meets its death
And when he shakes his mane, we shall have spring again.
You'll understand when you see him."

"But shall we see him?" asked Susan...
"Is -is he a man?"
"Aslan is a lion -*the* Lion, the great Lion."
"Ooh!" said Susan, "I'd thought he was a man. Is he -quite safe?"...
"If there is anyone who can appear before Aslan without their knees knocking, they're either braver than most or else just silly."
"Then he isn't safe?" said Lucy.
"Safe?" said Mr. Beaver..."who said anything about safe? Course he isn't safe. But he's **good**! He's the King, I tell you."
"I'm longing to see him," said Peter, "even if I do feel frightened." (pp 74-76)

Our Lord and Savior, the Son of God is all powerful, but *he is also good*, and this has made all the difference. The Lord's goodness puts our hearts at peace!

# -The Holy Spirit is Good

Nehemiah reviewed Israel's past history recalling when they had survived forty years in the wilderness after having left Egyptian slavery behind. Their slavery had been wretched, but at least they had had food and water, whereas, in the wilderness they complained that they had nothing. Not quite. Nehemiah noted that they had God's Holy Spirit -his 'good' Spirit.

> [20] You gave your **good Spirit** to instruct them. You did not withhold your manna from their mouths, and you gave them water for their thirst.
> (Nehemiah 9:20)

This '***good Spirit***' instructed Moses to have everyone to put their faith in God that he would provide for them. He did provide for them -manna and water for forty years!

David wanted to be led by this same 'good Spirit'.

> [10] May your **good Spirit** lead me on level ground.
> (Psalm 143:10)

The Lord has sent us his same *good* Spirit to fill our lives with his presence, his power, his protection and his goodness!

> [22] The fruit of the Spirit is love, joy, peace, patience, kindness, **goodness**, faithfulness,
>
> [23] gentleness and self-control. Against such things there is no law. (Galatians 5:22-23)

## God Satisfies Us With Good Things

When the Israelites were prepared to cross over into the Promised Land Moses disclosed all the good things God had waiting for them.

> [10] When the LORD your God brings you into the land he swore to your fathers, to Abraham, Isaac and Jacob, to give you—a land with large, flourishing cities you did not build,
>
> [11] houses filled with **all kinds of good things** you did not provide, wells you did not dig, and vineyards and olive groves you did not plant. (Deuteronomy 6:10-11; 8:7-9)

Moses said they had just cause to rejoice.

> [11] **Rejoice** in all the **good things the LORD your God has given to you** and your household.
> (Deuteronomy 26:11)

Because ***God is good all the time***, it follows that ***all he does for us is good***. Surely we can say with David,

> [19] **How great is your goodness**, which you have stored up for those who fear you. (Psalm 31:19)

> [2] You are my Lord; **apart from you I have no good thing**. (Psalm 16:2)

It is as the Psalmist has said,

> [9] He satisfies the thirsty and fills the hungry with **good things**. (Psalm 107:9)

> [4] We are filled with the **good things** of your house, of your holy temple. (Psalm 65:4)

> [28] As for me, **it is good to be near God**. I have made the Sovereign LORD my refuge; I will tell of all your deeds. (Psalm 73:28)

Twenty-five hundred years later at the time of the Protestant Reformation Martin Luther found himself as overwhelmed as David was by the unchanging ***goodness of God.***

> God is not moved to make his promises by our worthiness, merits or good works, but he promises purely on the basis of his inexhaustible and **eternal goodness** and mercy. (Luther, Galatians 1:288)

Now, how about us, coming 500 years after Luther? Isn't it true that God expresses his goodness to us, also? Are you ready now for some 'soul talk' about the 'goodness' of God?

> [7] **Be at rest once more, O my soul**, for the LORD has been **good to you**.

[8] For you, O LORD, have delivered my soul from death, my eyes from tears, my feet from stumbling…

[12] How can I repay the LORD for all his **goodness** to me?

[13] I will lift up the cup of salvation and call on the name of the LORD.

[14] I will fulfill my vows to the LORD in the presence of all his people. (Psalm 116:7-8, 12-14)

## No One Does Good

*No one is good* when compared with *God's perfect goodness*!

"The **goodness** of God means God is the final standard of **good**." (Wayne Grudem, Systematic theology, p. 197)

Reflecting on David's words in the Psalms Paul has written,

[12] There is **no one** who **does good**, not even one. (Romans 3:1; Psalm 14:1-3, 53:1-3)

Sin syphons goodness out of our lives.

[25] Your sins have **deprived you of good**. (Jeremiah 5:25)

As 'sinners' our *'good works'* (tainted as they are with sin) cannot begin to compare with *God's perfect goodness*. We all fall short of *God's goodness*. David spells this out Psalm 36.

[1] An oracle is within my heart concerning the **sinfulness** of the wicked:

³ The words of his mouth are wicked and deceitful; he has ceased to be wise and to do **good**. (Psalm 36:1, 3)

# Turn From Evil and Do Good

David pleads with everyone as a father would with his own dear children.

> ¹¹ Come, my children, listen to me; I will teach you the fear of the LORD.

> ¹² Whoever of you loves life and desires to **see many good days**,

> ¹³ keep your tongue from evil and your lips from speaking lies.

> ¹⁴ **Turn from evil and do good**; seek peace and pursue it. (Psalm 34:11-14)

God's intention for us is always that we might do what is good.

> ⁸ He has showed you, O man, what is **good**. And what does the LORD require of you? To act justly and to love mercy and to walk humbly with your God. (Micah 6:8)

Doing 'good' is what the Law of God is all about. The Law of God defines 'good' for us in black and white.

> ³⁹ Your *laws are* **good**. (Psalm 119:39)

> ¹² The law is holy, and the commandment is holy, righteous and **good**. (Romans 7:12)

To do what is good, then, is to do whatever the Law of God says we should do. Paul was very honest, however, in saying there is a great gulf fixed between knowing the good God wants us to do and actually doing good.

> [18] I know that **nothing good lives in me**, that is, in my sinful nature. For I have the **desire to do what is good**, but I cannot carry it out.
>
> [19] For **what I do is not the good I want to do**; no, the evil I do not want to do—this I keep on doing.
>
> [20] Now if I do what I do not want to do, it is no longer I who do it, but it is sin living in me that does it. (Romans 7:18-20)

Yes, we as sinful, fallen creatures can never do enough **good** to **merit** salvation, nor to **retain** our salvation, but, rather, we find that God by his indwelling Holy Spirit gives us the desire and ability to do **good** to **express** our salvation which is the gift of God. As such, being spiritually transformed Christians **we can do good** as an expression of our gratefulness for our salvation, but even then only in the Lord's strength through his indwelling Holy Spirit -for his glory alone! It's as Paul has stated so plainly,

> [10] **We are God's workmanship**, created in Christ Jesus to **do good works**, which God prepared in advance for us to do. (Ephesians 2:10)
>
> [13] **It is God** who works in you **to will** and **to act** according to his **good** purpose. (Philippians 2:13)

## Trust in the Lord and Do Good

Moses instructed the Israelites when they were about to enter the Promised Land,

[18] **Do what is right and good** in the LORD's sight, so that it may go well with you and you may go in and take over the **good land** that the LORD promised on oath to your forefathers.
(Deuteronomy 6:18)

Moses also told them what **not** to do when they experienced prosperity.

[10] When you have eaten and are satisfied, praise the LORD your God for the good land he has given you.

[11] Be careful that you do not forget the LORD your God, failing to observe his commands, his laws and his decrees that I am giving you this day.

[12] Otherwise, when you eat and are satisfied, when you build fine houses and settle down,

[13] and when your herds and flocks grow large and your silver and gold increase and all you have is multiplied,

[14] then your heart will become proud and you will forget the LORD your God, who brought you out of Egypt, out of the land of slavery.
(Deuteronomy 8:10-14)

David's desire for his friends was that they trust in the Lord and *do good*.

[3] **Trust in the LORD** and **do good**…

[4] Delight yourself in the LORD and he will give you the desires of your heart…

[12] Whoever of you loves life and desires to see many **good days**,

Douglas Nelson

> ¹³ keep your tongue from evil and your lips from speaking lies.

> ¹⁴ Turn from evil and do good; seek peace and pursue it…

> ²⁷ **Turn from evil and do good**; then you will dwell in the land forever. (Psalm 37:3-4, 12-14, 27)

God was forced to render this sad commentary upon Judah in the days of Jeremiah..

> ²² They are skilled in doing evil; *they know not how to do good*. (Jeremiah 4:22)

Jeremiah taught his people, however, that having *the desire to do good* could begin to turn things around.

> ¹⁶ This is what the LORD says: "Stand at the crossroads and look; ask for the ancient paths, **ask where the good way** is, and walk in it, and you will find rest for your souls."(Jeremiah 6:16)

Our transformation into a new creation (2 Corinthians 5:17) puts us on the '*good way*'. It is all about having a new desire to *be good* and the ability now to *do good*, because of the Spirit of God dwelling within us. We can even take on Jesus' hard assignment.

> ²⁷ Love your enemies, **do good to those who hate you**. (Luke 6:27)

To *love what is good* became part of the 'job description' for anyone seeking to become an elder in the Church.

> ⁸ He must be hospitable, **one who loves what is good**, who is self-controlled, upright, holy and disciplined. (Titus 1:8).

Actually *living for the good of others* was the mark of all the early Christians, and not just the Church elders. Paul stressed to the Corinthian Christians,

> [24] Nobody should **seek** his own good, but **the good of others**. (1 Corinthians 10:24)

Dorcas was an example in the early Church of a godly woman who *did good* to everyone.

> [36] In Joppa there was a disciple named Tabitha...who was **always doing good** and helping the poor. (Acts 9:36)

Paul instructed Pastor Titus to encourage the members of his church who have been spiritually transformed by Christ to be

> [14] **eager to do what is good**. (Titus 2:13-14)

John has stated that this is proof that

> [11] Anyone who does what is **good** is from God. (3 John 1:11)

There are no laws against doing what is good. It is always lawful to do **good** -even on the Sabbath!

> [12] **It is lawful to do good** on the Sabbath." (Matthew 12:12)

No one goes to jail for having done too much good! I recall reading years ago an interesting true story in The Reader's Digest about a husband and wife who helped a friend in need by giving him gift of $10. To their surprise after a few days seemingly out of the blue someone gave them $10 (That was a time when $10 was worth a lot more than it is today.). They said to each other, "This is interesting; let's give our $10 away again." And they did so again, and again, and again. It kept coming back to them in one way or another. When they stopped counting they had given away over a million dollars!

God allows us to put him to *one 'test'*.

> <sup>10</sup> Bring the whole tithe into the storehouse, that there may be food in my house. **Test me** in this," says the LORD Almighty, "and see if I will not throw open the floodgates of heaven and pour out so much blessing that you will not have room enough for it. (Malachi 3:10)

The truth is this: we cannot out give *our good God*.

> <sup>38</sup> Give, and it will be given to you. A **good measure**, pressed down, shaken together and running over, will be poured into your lap. For with the measure you use, it will be measured to you." (Luke 6:38)

The 'Lord of the harvest' returns to us much more than we plant.

> <sup>8</sup> Seed fell on **good soil**, where it produced a crop—a hundred, sixty or thirty times what was sown. (Matthew 13:8; Ps 85:12)

We are all left with this challenge:

> <sup>24</sup> Let us consider how we may spur one another on toward love and **good deeds**. (Hebrews 10:24)

> <sup>16</sup> **Do not forget to do good** and to share with others, for with such sacrifices
> God is pleased. (Hebrews 13:16)

## God Does Not Withhold What is Good

Early in the Psalms David noted,

> <sup>6</sup> Many are asking, "**Who** can show us any **good**?" (Psalm 4:6)

David, writing in a later Psalm, answered the question by listing *a litany of good things* that come from the Lord. God shows us good!

> ³ God forgives all your sins and heals all your diseases,
>
> ⁴ who redeems your life from the pit and crowns you with love and compassion,
>
> ⁵ who **satisfies your desires with good things** so that your youth is renewed like the eagle's.
> (Psalm 103:3-5)

The Psalmist Korah also gave a positive response to the question David posed.

> ¹¹ The LORD God is a sun and shield; the LORD bestows favor and honor; **no good thing does he withhold** from those whose walk is blameless. (Psalm 84:11)

The Law of God is a good thing.

> ³⁹ Take away the disgrace I dread, for **your laws are good**.
> (Psalm 119:39)

God does *not withhold his goodness* from those who are generous.

> ⁵ **Good will come** to him who is **generous** and **lends freely**, who conducts his affairs with **justice**.
> (Psalm 112:5)

Jeremiah, writing in the midst of the rubble that was Jerusalem after its conquest, did not give up on his belief in the *goodness of God* -not after hearing these words from God.

> ³⁹ I'll make them of one mind and heart, always honoring me, so that they can **live good** and whole lives, they and their children after them.

⁴⁰ What's more, I'll make a covenant with them that will last forever, a covenant to stick with them no matter what, and **work for their good**. I'll fill their hearts with a deep respect for me so they'll not even think of turning away from me.

⁴¹ " 'Oh how I'll rejoice in them! Oh how **I'll delight in doing good things for them**! Heart and soul, I'll plant them in this country and keep them here!'
(Jeremiah 32:39-41 (MSG))

God does *not withhold his goodness from those who put their hope in him*. He simply waits for the time when giving his goodness will do the most good!

²⁵ **The LORD is good to those whose hope is in him**, to the one who seeks him;

²⁶ it is good to **wait** quietly for the salvation of the LORD.
(Lamentations 3:25-26; Jere 26:14)

God does *not withhold goodness* from *those who are suffering*. The Lord assures us that his goodness and mercy will follow us all the days of our lives.

⁴ Though I walk through the valley of the shadow of death, I will fear no evil, for you are with me; your rod and your staff, they comfort me...

⁶ Surely **goodness** and love **will follow me all the days of my life**.
(Psalm 23:4, 6)

I have been made aware of a young wife and mother who recently had her life unexpectedly rearranged by being confronted with the 'C' word -*cancer*. She has blogged her feelings that the Lord will transform this 'storm' in such a way that it will prove to be his goodness deepening the love that is between them.

> Lord may I always be peaceful…regardless of what is going on around me. It's easy to be peaceful when the sun is glowing radiant and the water is calm. Give me a heart that is steady as I gaze at Your radiance that transforms any storms that may rage into tools that drive me deeper into your love for me.

Shortly after writing these words she started feeling intense pain and at 2 AM was rushed to the Emergency Room of a hospital. Although the trial continues, so does her trust -even the dogged trust of a Job who wrote in the midst of his life threatening ordeal,

> [10] Shall we accept **good from God**, and not trouble?"
> (Job 2:10; 13:15)

Even when there is *no* 'sign' of relief at the moment from a severe trial it's possible to remain convinced of the ***goodness of God*** by the way he accompanies us in and through the trial. Paul ***witnessed the Lord's goodness countering every difficulty*** in life he was called upon to endure. In light of what was happening he also noted what was not happening.

> [8] We are hard pressed on every side, but **not crushed**; perplexed, but **not in despair**;
>
> [9] persecuted, but **not abandoned**; struck down, but **not destroyed**. (2 Corinthians 4:8-9)

No sign of relief was what Paul experienced on a regular basis.

> [4] As servants of God we commend ourselves in every way: in great endurance; in troubles, hardships and distresses;
>
> [5] in beatings, imprisonments and riots; in hard work, sleepless nights and hunger;

⁶ in purity, understanding, patience and kindness; in the Holy Spirit and in sincere love;

⁷ in truthful speech and in the power of God; with weapons of righteousness in the right hand and in the left;

⁸ through glory and dishonor, bad report and good report; genuine, yet regarded as impostors;

⁹ known, yet regarded as unknown; dying, and yet we live on; beaten, and yet not killed;

¹⁰ sorrowful, yet always rejoicing; poor, yet making many rich; having nothing, and yet possessing everything.
(2 Corinthians 6:4-10)

Andrew Murray has offered insight on *waiting* for the *goodness of God* to be revealed in a situation.

We must learn …how to wait upon Him to reveal His **goodness** in due time…Do you want to fully know the **goodness of God**? Then give yourself more than ever to a life of **waiting on Him**, of resting all your hope in Him…It is often for this reason that He withholds the gifts we are asking for…(It is) only as we rest in God himself, who is **goodness**, (that our) soul can even begin to find its satisfaction.
('Believer's Secret of Waiting on God', David Hazard, 'Mighty Is Your Hand', p. 48)

When staring suffering and death in the face the temptation is to doubt the goodness of God. This is nowhere more the case than when the world is caught up in the vortex of war. Henry Longfellow (1807-1882) is famous in part for a poem he wrote on Christmas Day 1861 when the American Civil War was raging on. Although the temptation was to despair the possibility of the goodness of God through the din of war and destruction, he distinctly heard church bells ringing out the Christian hope in the ongoing goodness of God.

I heard the bells on Christmas Day
Their old, familiar carols play,
and wild and sweet
The words repeat
Of peace on earth, **good-will to men!**

And thought how, as the day had come,
The belfries of all Christendom
Had rolled along
The unbroken song
Of peace on earth, **good-will to men!**

Till ringing, singing on its way,
The world revolved from night to day,
A voice, a chime,
A chant sublime
Of peace on earth, **good-will to men!**

Then from each black, accursed mouth
The cannon thundered in the South,
And with the sound
The carols drowned
Of peace on earth, **good-will to men!**

It was as if an earthquake rent
The hearth-stones of a continent,
And made forlorn
The households born
Of peace on earth, **good-will to men!**

And in despair I bowed my head;
"There is no peace on earth," I said;
"For hate is strong,
And mocks the song
Of peace on earth, **good-will to men!**"

Then pealed the bells more loud and deep:
"God is not dead, nor doth He sleep;
The Wrong shall fail,
The Right prevail,
With peace on earth, **good-will to men.**"

It would be good right here to repeat the first lines of Longfellow's prayer.

I heard the bells on Christmas Day
Their old, familiar carols play,
and wild and sweet
The words repeat
Of peace on earth, **good-will to men!**

# Hate Evil; Love Good

Amos the prophet from Judah travelled north to wicked Israel and pled with the people.

> [14] **Seek good, not evil**, that you may live. Then the LORD God Almighty will be with you, just as you say he is.
>
> [15] **Hate evil, love good**; maintain justice in the courts. Perhaps the LORD God Almighty will have mercy on the remnant of Joseph. (Amos 5:14-15)

As Christians we need to embrace the Lord's instruction to:

> [27] Love your enemies, do **good** to those who hate you. (Luke 6:27)

How can we do this? The Lord has called us out of darkness to become the 'light of the world'.

> [14] "You are the light of the world. (Matthew 5:14)

<sup>8</sup> You were once darkness, but now you are light in the Lord. Live as children of light

<sup>9</sup> (for **the fruit of the light consists in all goodness**, righteousness and truth)
(Ephesians 5:8-9)

We are no longer to be a part of the problem but a part of the solution. Paul has described our God-given assignment in these words:

<sup>21</sup> Do not be overcome by evil, but **overcome evil with good**. (Romans 12:21; 12:9; 1 Pe 3:11)

*It is good to hate evil*, but it is *not good to hate evil people*. We are to hate what sin and wickedness do to people, but not hate sinful and wicked people. Paul reminds us that we live in a fallen world that is a *stranger to goodness*.

<sup>9</sup> I have written you in my letter not to associate with sexually immoral people—

<sup>10</sup> not at all meaning the people of this world who are immoral, or the greedy and swindlers, or idolaters. In that case you would have to leave this world.
(1 Corinthians 5:9-10)

# Abound in Doing Good

Augustine reminds us to *define 'goodness'* not as the world defines goodness, but as God defines goodness.

I mean to remind you that God has promised us ineffable sweetness and **goodness**…but so often we allow ourselves to be sidetracked from following him because we focus our attention on temporal affairs. We let the world tempt us with what is 'good' according to its evil standards.

*Douglas Nelson*

(Homilies on the 1ˢᵗ Epistle of John, David Hazard, Early
Will I Seek You, p. 90)

Recall that the Serpent's skewed definition of 'goodness' led to Eve's
downfall in the Garden of Eden.

> ⁶ When the woman saw that the fruit of the tree was **good**
> for food and pleasing to the eye, and also desirable for
> gaining wisdom, she took some and ate it. She also gave
> some to her husband, who was with her, and he ate it.
> (Genesis 3:6)

Isaiah has alerted us not to be deceived by

> ²⁰ those who call evil **good** and **good** evil. (Isaiah 5:20)

People who call evil 'good' and good 'evil' are people who

> ³ love evil rather than good, falsehood rather than speaking
> the truth. (Psalm 52:3)

> ¹ They are corrupt, their deeds are vile; there **is no one
> who does good**. (Psalm 14:1)

They conclude falsely that if there is no 'God' they are not morally
accountable for anything and are, therefore, free to be morally lawless,
and give in to unbridled lusts more and more by forsaking every form of
goodness -crushing everything and everyone who stands in their way.

Peter, by contrast, counsels us not to give in to sinful desires that are
fueled by our fallen sinful nature. Rather, focus on doing ***good!***

> ¹¹ Dear friends, I urge you, as aliens and strangers in the
> world, to **abstain from sinful desires**, which war against
> your soul.

[12] Live such **good lives** among the pagans that, though they accuse you of doing wrong, they may see **your good deeds** and glorify God on the day he visits us. (1 Peter 2:11-12)

Paul noted for Timothy that this is especially to be the case for church leaders such as an elder.

[7] He must also have a **good reputation** with outsiders, so that he will not fall into disgrace and into the devil's trap. (1 Timothy 3:7)

God is able to give us the ability to ***know what is good***, and ***do good*** to as many people as possible, as often as possible, and for as long as possible! The Lord wants us to be a ***'good'*** tree bearing ***'good*** fruit'!

[43] "No good tree bears bad fruit, nor does a bad tree bear good fruit.

[44] Each tree is recognized by its own fruit. People do not pick figs from thorn bushes, or grapes from briers.

[45] The **good man** brings **good things** out of the **good stored up in his heart**, and the evil man brings evil things out of the evil stored up in his heart. For out of the overflow of his heart his mouth speaks. (Luke 6:43-45)

Doing good is a recurring theme of Paul in his inspired writings.

[10] As we have opportunity, **let us do good to all people**, especially to those who belong to the family of believers. (Galatians 6:10; 2 Cor 9:8; Eph 2:10; 5:8-9)

Paul emphasized that it's familiarization with Scripture that equips us to engage in good works.

[16] All Scripture is God-breathed and is useful for teaching, rebuking, correcting and training in righteousness,

[17] so that the man of God may be thoroughly equipped for **every good work**.
(2 Timothy 3:16-17)

Paul challenged Timothy to teach the members of his church

[18] to **do good**, to be rich in **good deeds**, and to be generous and willing to share. (1 Timothy 6:18)

Lest there was any doubt what genuine good deeds looked like he gave Timothy some examples.

[9] No widow may be put on the list of widows unless she is over sixty, has been faithful to her husband,

[10] and is well known for her **good deeds, such as** bringing up children, showing hospitality, washing the feet of the saints, helping those in trouble and devoting herself to **all kinds of good deeds**.
(1 Timothy 5:9-10)

Paul reminded Pastor Titus why Jesus came into the world to save us.

[13] Our great God and Savior, Jesus Christ...

[14] gave himself for us to redeem us from all wickedness and to purify for himself a people that are his very own, **eager to do what is good**.
(Titus 2:13-14)

Titus as a pastor was to teach his people by word and example.

[7] Set them **an example** by **doing** what is **good**. (Titus 2:7)

Only then would Pastor Titus be in a position to

¹ Remind the people…to be ready to **do whatever is good**…

⁸ I want you to stress these things, so that those who have trusted in God may be careful to **devote themselves to doing what is good**. These things are excellent and profitable for everyone….

¹⁴ Our people must learn to devote themselves to **doing what is good**, in order that they may provide for daily necessities and not live unproductive lives.
(Titus 3:1, 8 14)

A godly life can be defined very simply.

³ Trust in the LORD and do **good**. (Psalm 37:3)

The Author of Hebrews reminds us

¹⁶ Do not forget to **do good.** (Hebrews 13:16)

# Hold on to the Good

There are many things we can let go of in life and be the better for it, but one thing we must never let go of is 'doing good'.

²¹ Hold on to the **good.** (1 Thessalonians 5:21)

The command to 'hold on' is all about spiritual battle -fighting for the good; fighting against all that is not good.

¹² Fight the **good fight** of the faith.
(1 Timothy 6:12)

Stephen Curtis Chapman and his wife *held on* desperately to belief in *God's goodness* in the face of their young daughter's death.

> **'All things good and beautiful'** became very important for me....A Psalm that became a prayer of hope and encouragement to me and my family was Psalm 34:8 'Taste and see that **the LORD is good**'. I also discovered Psalm 27, which says, 'I remain confident of this: I will see **the goodness of the LORD** in the land of the living'... 'God, these are Your promises; I am going to declare that these things are true. I can't imagine right now how my family will ever again taste **goodness**...but I believe we will.'
> (Between Heaven and the Real World, pp. 344-345)

Whenever we're tempted by stressful circumstances to doubt the *goodness of God*, the Psalmist says we should think twice about doing so because God has only good intentions for us.

> [68] You are **good**, and what you do is **good**.

God even has *good intentions* for allowing us to be afflicted.

> [71] It was **good** for me to be afflicted so that I might learn your decrees. (Psalm 119:68, 71)

God goes so far as to *discipline us for our own good*.

> [10] Our fathers disciplined us for a little while as they thought best; but **God disciplines us for our good**, that we may share in his holiness.
> (Hebrews 12:10)

When we are afflicted we're tempted to become weary in well-doing. Paul says, 'Don't!'

⁹ Let us not become weary in doing **good**, for at the proper time we will reap a harvest if we do not give up. (Galatians 6:9)

Let's also encourage one another to hold on and not give up in the face of any crisis.

²⁴ Let us consider how we may **spur one another on** toward love and **good deeds**. (Hebrews 10:24)

## Be Willing to Suffer for Doing Good

Jesus has given us fair warning.

³³ "I have told you these things, so that in me you may have peace. In this world you will have trouble. But take heart! I have overcome the world." (John 16:33; Matt 5:11-12; Jn 15:18)

Jesus has laid before us this unprecedented challenge,

²⁷ I tell you who hear me: Love your enemies, **do good to those who hate you,**

²⁸ bless those who curse you, pray for those who mistreat you...

³¹ Do to others as you would have them do to you. (Luke 6:27-28, 31)

Peter reflected on these words he had heard from the Lord's lips.

²⁰ **If you suffer for doing good** and you endure it, this is commendable before God. (1 Peter 2:12, 15, 20)

The disciples early on considered it a privilege if called upon to *suffer for sharing the good news* about Jesus their Savior.

> [40] They called the apostles in and had them flogged. Then they ordered them not to speak in the name of Jesus, and let them go.

> [41] The apostles left the Sanhedrin, **rejoicing because they had been counted worthy of suffering disgrace for the Name.**

> [42] Day after day, in the temple courts and from house to house, they never stopped teaching and proclaiming the **good news** that Jesus is the Christ.
> (Acts 5:40-42)

This marked the beginning of almost 200 years of Christian persecution, until the Roman Emperor **Constantine** put a stop to it throughout the Roman Empire.

> Pagan Rome's last major attack fell upon Cyprian and other Church leaders in A.D. 249…The persecutions… were swift and bloody: Christians were scourged to death, burned with irons –and if you think they died begging for their lives, think again. Read Cyprian's accounts of the martyrs, and you'll witness them at the moment they leap across the border from death to Life with a shout – 'Christ is the Victor!' In A.D. 258 Cyprian would leave this life, also a martyr, with those same exultant words on his lips.
> (David Hazard, You Give Me New Life, p. 20)

Shortly before his own martyrdom Cyprian wrote

> Christ goes before us preparing the **good works** He has for each of us to do. We know that some of you are sad that you were not called by the Lord to give your lives, like the martyrs. You think that perhaps you were not worthy

to be His spokesmen to the world, or to enter into His presence by the high road. The Lord knows your **good hearts**. He searches your hearts and knows how motivated you are to serve Him, in whatever way He asks…You need not worry that you have not put on the scarlet robes of the martyrs…Humbly receive whatever crown has been fashioned for you…Accept whatever task the Lord gives you, and whatever honor, as a **good soldier** in this spiritual contest between the powers of the world and Christ. (Ibid., p130-132, Cyprian, Eighth Epistle)

1800 years later I'm reading articles in a *Voice of the Martyrs* magazine recounting unspeakable suffering of Christians right now in several countries around the world. Here is one 'voice' out of many crying out to us, *"Please tell the…church to pray for us. And also, don't forget us."*

(We will pray; we won't forget! -let's keep that promise! Let's pray right now!!! [I did; did you?]) (VOM, 7/17, p.7)

Accepting undeserved suffering does disclose depth of character and commitment to the Lord. The Lord himself takes notice when anyone suffers for doing good. It is precious in his sight.

> [17] It is better, if it is God's will, to **suffer for doing good** than for doing evil. (1 Peter 3:17)

Nik Ripken is the author of 'The Insanity of God' which is the fruit of his extensive research on the persecuted church in approximately 60 countries. In his companion book, 'The Insanity of Obedience' he challenges Christians not to 'rest comfortably in the status quo', but rather be willing to be a good and faithful witness to the truth of the Gospel in even the toughest places to live on this planet. Ripken gives this reminder,

> Followers of Jesus…are called to embrace a lifestyle that includes suffering, persecution and martyrdom…We have the high privilege of answering Jesus' call to go, but let us be clear about this: we go on his terms, not ours. If we go at all, we go as 'sheep among wolves'. Remember that the

last place a sheep wants to be is in the middle of a pack of ravenous wolves…
(Nik Ripkin, The Insanity of Obedience, p. 299)

³ Go! I am sending you out like lambs among wolves. (Luke 10:3)

We need not fear, having the assurance that

⁴ the one who is in you is greater than the one who is in the world. (1 John 4:4)

Christ in us is greater than the Evil One who is in the world! Because this is true, being in the midst of a pack of 'wolves' is the safest place to be! Or, as Jesus has put it,

²⁷ My sheep listen to my voice; I know them, and they follow me.

²⁸ I give them eternal life, and they shall never perish; **no one can snatch them out of my hand.**

²⁹ My Father, who has given them to me, is greater than all; **no one can snatch them out of my Father's hand.** (John 10:27-29)

Paul says that there's one thing we can know for sure as Christians:

²⁸ We know that in all things **God works for the good** of those who love him, who have been called according to his purpose. (Romans 8:28)

# Well Done Good and Faithful Servant

² A **good** man obtains favor from the LORD. (Proverbs 12:2)

In the end, when we first set foot on the streets of Heaven no sweeter words will ever be said to us then these words coming from the lips of our Savior,

> [21] 'Well done, **good** and faithful servant! You have been faithful with a few things; I will put you in charge of many things. Come and share your master's happiness!' (Matthew 25:21, 23)

May we be able to say along with Paul when we 'finish our race in life':

> [7] I have fought **the good fight**, I have **finished the race**, I have kept the faith.

> [8] Now there is in store for me the crown of righteousness, which the Lord, the righteous Judge, will award to me on that day—and not only to me, but also to all who have longed for his appearing. (2 Timothy 4:7-8)

> [8] The Lord will **reward** everyone for whatever **good** he does. (Ephesians 6:8)

# Sing God's Goodness

King David has been known throughout history as the 'Sweet Singer of Israel' (2 Sam 23:1). He often wrote and sang songs *in praise of God's goodness*.

> [6] I will sing to the LORD, for **he has been good to me**. (Psalm 13:6)

He sang *praises for God's goodness*, even when he was on the run from his enemies.

> [6] **I will praise your name, O LORD, for it is good.**

⁷ For he has delivered me from all my troubles, and my
eyes have looked in triumph on my foes.
(Psalm 54:6-7)

The Psalmist has exhorted us to praise the Lord, but not without good reason. The reason being that *God is Good*!

³ Praise the LORD, for **the LORD is good**; sing praise to
his name, for that is pleasant.
(Psalm 135:3)

Fanny Crosby (1829-1915) was a blind 19ᵗʰ century composer of hymns. In spite of her blindness she was able to focus the eyes of her heart and see with clarity the **goodness** of God. *Blessed Assurance* was a hymn she wrote praising the Lord's goodness.

Perfect submission, all is at rest,
I in my Savior am happy and blest,
Watching and waiting, **looking above**,
Filled with **His goodness**, lost in His love.

This is my story, this is my song,
Praising my Savior all the day long;
This is my story, this is my song,
Praising my Savior all the day long.

Say to any Christian anywhere in the world, '*God is GOOD*☺' and the inevitable response is '*All the time*!'☺

On the day David and all Israel brought the Ark of the Covenant to Jerusalem and set it in its final resting place, David wrote a Psalm for the occasion to *praise God's goodness.*

³¹ Let the heavens rejoice, let the earth be glad; let them
say among the nations, "The LORD reigns!"

³⁴ **Give thanks to the LORD, for he is good**; his love
endures forever. (1 Chronicles 16:31, 34)

David was optimistic that he would *see God's goodness* as long as he lived.

> [13] I am still confident of this: **I will see the goodness of the LORD** in the land of the living. (Psalm 27:13)

At the conclusion of Solomon's prayer of dedication for the newly constructed Temple the focus of the celebration was on the *goodness* of God.

> [12] All the Levites who were musicians…stood on the east side of the altar, dressed in fine linen and playing cymbals, harps and lyres. They were accompanied by 120 priests sounding trumpets.
>
> [13] The trumpeters and singers joined in unison, as with one voice, to give praise and thanks to the LORD. Accompanied by trumpets, cymbals and other instruments, they raised their voices in praise to the LORD and sang:
>
> **"He is good; his love endures forever."**
>
> Then the temple of the LORD was filled with a cloud,
>
> [14] and the priests could not perform their service because of the cloud, for the glory of the LORD filled the temple of God. (2 Chronicles 5:12-14)

Solomon then ended this festive occasion with this blessing:

> [41] "Now arise, O LORD God, and come to your resting place, you and the ark of your might. May your priests, O LORD God, be clothed with salvation, **may your saints rejoice in your goodness.** (2 Chronicles 6:41)

The early Christian saint Tertullian reminded his readers,

*Douglas Nelson*

We should speak well of God at all times in every circumstance. We should not be like the unbeliever **doubting his goodness.** Instead, we should fix in our thoughts all that he has done for our benefit, and by speaking well of God we build ourselves up in the faith. (David Hazard, You Give Me New Life, p. 6)

## Pray We Become Recipients of God's Goodness

David pleaded with the Lord in prayer (and I've pled the same prayer):

⁷ Remember not the sins of my youth and my rebellious ways; according to your love **remember me**, for **you are good**, O LORD. (Psalm 25:7)

¹⁶ Answer me, O LORD, out of the **goodness** of your love; in your great mercy turn to me
(Psalm 69:16; 86:5, 17; 109:21; 142:7)

Oher Psalmists also prayed for God's *goodness.*

¹⁷ Do **good** to your servant, and I will live; I will obey your word (Psalm 119:17, 65; 125:4)

When God does the *good* we have prayed for we must not forget to thank him!

³⁴ **Give thanks** to the LORD, for **he is good**; his love endures forever. (1 Chronicles 16:34)

An ancient letter has come down to us from the early days of the Church. It was a letter written to a man named Diogenetus. The focus of the letter was on the **goodness of God.**

God always was, and always is, and always will be the outpouring of **goodness.** For as Jesus revealed, 'The Father

374

is **goodness** itself'. Open the eyes of your soul, then, and in faith behold Him: He is **goodness**. Then you will know Him as He is…He wants us to live in spirit by believing fully in His **goodness**…He wants his **goodness** to fill and form our every thought and to light our way through this crooked and dark world that is anything but good. As you meditate on His **goodness**, it indeed will fill you…it will become your honor, your glory, your strength. **Goodness** will become life to your soul…Our faith is not based on the speculations of men. It is based on the **goodness** of God revealed in Christ Jesus. And it is the kind of faith you can have -making you strong against all the onslaught of the world.
(Letter to Diognetus (256 AD) Written to the Tutor of a Roman Emperor, David Hazard, 'You Give Me New Life'; 'We Have Seen Him', pp. 34-35)

Can you answer this question the Psalmist has raised?

¹² How can I repay the LORD for all **his goodness to me**?

He went on to suggest an answer.

¹³ I will lift up the cup of salvation and call on the name of the LORD.

¹⁴ I will fulfill my vows to the LORD in the presence of all his people.
(Psalm 116:12-14)

Yes, may we find ourselves living out David's words,

⁴ One generation will commend your works to another; they will tell of your mighty acts…

⁷ They will **celebrate your abundant goodness** and joyfully sing of your righteousness…

⁹ **The LORD is good to all**; he has compassion on all he
has made.
(Psalm 145:4, 7, 9)

Peter suggests we *add 'goodness' to our 'bucket list'* of characteristics
that define us.

⁵ Make every effort to **add** to your faith **goodness.**
(2 Peter 1:5)

May we *reflect God's goodness* as evidence that the Holy Spirit dwells
within us.

²² The fruit of the Spirit [who lives in us]is love, joy, peace,
patience, kindness, **goodness**, faithfulness,

²³ gentleness and self-control. Against such things there is
no law. (Galatians 5:22-23)

If Paul were writing to us, could he write the same words he wrote to
his fellow Christians in Rome?

¹⁴ I myself am convinced, my brothers, that **you yourselves
are full of goodness,**. (Romans 15:14)

Let's rise to the challenge David has set before us:

⁸ Taste and see that **the LORD is good.**
(Psalm 34:8)

**To God be the Glory that His Way is Goodness!** ☺

# CHAPTER 11

# Doxology of Praise to God for His Ways

*Douglas Nelson*

# 'Doxology' is All About Singing God's Praises

When I attended an Urbana Intervarsity Fellowship Missions Conference the first time, I was one of over 17,000 registrants -all missionaries and students from around the world. In the first session when we started singing God's praises the melodious sound that filled the arena was so overwhelming and so joyful I thought I had died and gone to heaven. The sounds of worship and praise started my heart pulsating with joy!

> [5] **Sing to the LORD, for he has done glorious things**;
> let this be known to all the world.
>
> [6] **Shout aloud and sing for joy**. (Isaiah 12:5-6)

Ever since the 1700's Isaac Watts's hymns have been joyfully praising in song the wonderful ways of God. Here are a few lines from one of his uplifting hymns:

> When I have learned my Father's will, I'll teach the world
> **his ways**. My thankful lips, inspir'd with zeal, Shall loud
> pronounce his praise.

This was the story of the Psalmist in Psalm 71. His life of song and joyful praise is an inspiration for us to do the same!

> [22] I will praise you with the harp for your faithfulness, O
> my God;
> **I will sing praise to you with the lyre**,
> O Holy One of Israel.
>
> [23] **My lips will shout for joy**
> **when I sing praise to you—**
> I, whom you have redeemed.
> (Psalm 71:22-23; 147:1, 7)

This music of praise we sing to the Lord for who he is and for what he has done is certainly a preview of the day we will join all the saints and angels gathered together from the beginning of time, and from the ends of the earth, surrounding Heaven's throne singing praises nonstop to God the Father and to the Lamb!

> ¹¹ I looked and heard the voice of many angels, numbering thousands upon thousands, and ten thousand times ten thousand. They encircled the throne and the living creatures and the elders.
>
> ¹² **In a loud voice they sang**: "Worthy is the Lamb, who was slain, to receive power and wealth and wisdom and strength and honor and glory and praise!"
>
> ¹³ Then I heard every creature in heaven and on earth and under the earth and on the sea, and all that is in them, **singing**: "To him who sits on the throne and to the Lamb be praise and honor and glory and power, for ever and ever!"
>
> ¹⁴ The four living creatures said, "Amen," and the elders fell down and worshiped.
> (Revelation 5:11-14)

It's good news we don't have to wait till heaven to *sing of the ways of the Lord*. We can begin now!

> ¹ I will praise you, O LORD, with all my heart; before the "gods" **I will sing your praise...**
>
> ⁴ May all the kings of the earth praise you, O LORD, when they hear the words of your mouth.
>
> ⁵ May they **sing of the ways of the LORD**, for the glory of the LORD is great. (Psalm 138:1, 4-5)

Jesus joined in harmony with his disciples on the evening of the Last Supper to sing a hymn.

> [26] When they had **sung a hymn**, they went out to the Mount of Olives. (Mark 14:26)

For all we know they may have sung the last of the 'Psalms of Ascent' (134) which the pilgrims sang every year as they made their way from their homes to the Temple Mount to celebrate Passover. This Psalm contained these words of praise:

> [1] Praise the LORD, all you servants of the LORD who minister by night in the house of the LORD.
>
> [2] Lift up your hands in the sanctuary and praise the LORD.
>
> [3] May the LORD, the Maker of heaven and earth, bless you from Zion. (Psalm 134:1-3)

Many hymns of the church through the centuries, as well as contemporary praise songs contain joyful words praising God's ways -his holiness, righteousness, truth, justice, love, grace, mercy, goodness, and more!

> [19] Speak to one another with psalms, **hymns and spiritual songs**. Sing and make music in your heart to the Lord,
>
> [20] always giving thanks to God the Father for everything, in the name of our Lord Jesus Christ. (Ephesians 5:19-20)

Yes, there is even room for '**noise**' when praising the Lord for the wonderful ways he has disclosed himself in Scripture.

> [1] Sing **aloud** unto God our strength: **make a joyful noise** unto the God of Jacob. (Psalm 81:1 KJV)

<sup>2</sup> Let us come before his presence with thanksgiving, and **make a joyful noise** unto him with psalms.
(Psalm 95:2 KJV)

There was a young lady who 'made a joyful noise' (unbeknown to her) every Sunday. She was tone deaf, and sang in the church choir just a little off tune! Everyone in the choir was spurred on to sing loud enough so that her 'joyful noise' was only heard by God!

We can also praise the Lord with '*instrumental' noise*! Many contemporary musicians take this mandate seriously playing loudly their electronic instruments and drums! I know of at least one church that provides ear plugs to soften the incredibly loud 'noise' resounding from the instruments being played on the platform!

<sup>3</sup> Play skillfuly with a <u>loud noise</u>.
(Psalm 33:3 KJV)

<sup>5</sup> Make music to the LORD with the harp, with the harp and the sound of singing,

<sup>6</sup> with **trumpets** and the **blast of the ram's horn— shout for joy** before the LORD, the King.
(Psalm 98:4-6)

<sup>5</sup> Praise him with the **clash of cymbals**, praise him with **resounding cymbals**. (Psalm 150:5)

When the Ark of the Covenant was paraded into Jerusalem,

<sup>5</sup> David and the whole house of Israel were celebrating with all their might before the LORD, with songs and with harps, lyres, tambourines…and cymbals. (2 Samuel 6:5)

It would be an understatement to say David loved music -a lot of music. Think of all the songs he wrote which we call 'Psalms'. He didn't live to see the construction of the Temple, but he prescribed the ***number*** *of musicians* who were to provide sacred music in the Temple when it was built. It was no small number!

> [1] David...set apart some...for the ministry of prophesying, accompanied by **harps, lyres and cymbals**. ...

> [6] All these men were under the supervision of their fathers for the music of the temple of the LORD, with **cymbals, lyres and harps**, for the ministry at the house of God. — all of them trained and skilled in music for the LORD— **they numbered 288.**
> (1 Chronicles 25:1, 6)

Consider the scene in Solomon's day during the dedication of the newly constructed Temple when the Ark of the Covenant was brought into the Temple to be placed in its permanent position in the Holy of Holies. The music of praise reverberated throughout the Temple plaza from the large assembly of singers and musicians that performed that day. Try to envision this sight and the sound of a large number of voices accompanied by brass, woodwinds, strings and percussion.

> [2] All the Levites who were musicians...stood on the east side of the altar, dressed in fine linen and were playing **cymbals, harps and lyres**. They were accompanied by **120 priests sounding trumpets.**

> [13] The trumpeters and singers joined in unison, as with one voice, to give praise and thanks to the LORD. **Accompanied by trumpets, cymbals and other instruments, they raised their voices in praise to the LORD and sang**: "He is good; his love endures forever." Then the temple of the LORD was filled with a cloud,

> [14] and the priests could not perform their service because of the cloud, for the glory of the LORD filled the temple of God! (2 Chronicles 5:12-14)

Hundreds of years later after the end of the 70 year Babylonian exile and the rebuilding of the walls surrounding Jerusalem, Nehemiah and Ezra held a gigantic dedication celebration! Nehemiah recorded the details in his journal.

> ²⁷ At the dedication of the wall of Jerusalem, the Levites were sought out from where they lived and were brought to Jerusalem to **celebrate joyfully** the dedication with **songs of thanksgiving** and with **the music of cymbals, harps and lyres…**
>
> ³¹ I also assigned **two large choirs** to give thanks.
>
> ⁴⁰ The two choirs that gave thanks then took their places in the house of God; so did I, together with half the officials…
>
> ⁴³ And on that day they offered great sacrifices, rejoicing because God had given them great joy. The women and children also rejoiced. **The sound of rejoicing** in Jerusalem **could be heard far away.**
> (Nehemiah 12:27, 31, 40, 43)

Job's young friend had some good advice.

> ²⁴ Remember to extol his work, which men have **praised in song**. (Job 36:24)

Will you join your voice with mine in church this coming Lord's day, and help augment 'the sound of rejoicing' -whether on tune or off tune? God doesn't care as long as he knows it's coming from the heart! Let's *praise him in song for all his glorious ways*! Praise the Lord!

# We Know Only the Fringes of God's Ways

At one point Job reviewed with his four friends *God's ways* in nature and was forced to come up with a surprising conclusion -the conclusion that he still knew so little about God.

> [4] His wisdom is profound, his power is vast...

> [10] He performs wonders that cannot be fathomed, miracles that cannot be counted. (Job 9:4, 10)

> [14] **These are but the outer fringe of his works [ways];** how faint the whisper we hear of him! Who then can understand the thunder of his power?"
> (Job 26:14)

At least, Job's friends Zophar and Elihu agreed with him on this.

> [7] "Can you fathom the mysteries of God? Can you probe the limits of the Almighty? (Job 11:7)

> [23] Who has prescribed **his ways** for him?...

> [26] How great is God—**beyond our understanding**! The number of his years is past finding out.
> (Job 36:23, 26)

> [23] The Almighty is **beyond our reach** and exalted in power. (Job 37:23)

David, too, was in agreement about the *unfathomable greatness* of *God's way* in creation.

> [10] **You are great and do marvelous deeds**; you alone are God. (Psalm 86:10)

⁵ Many, O LORD my God, are the wonders you have done. **The things you planned for us no one can recount to you**; were I to speak and tell of them, they would be too many to declare.
(Psalm 40:5)

¹⁷ How precious to me are **your thoughts**, O God! How vast is the sum of them!

¹⁸ Were I to count them, they would **outnumber the grains of sand**. When I awake, I am still with you.
(Psalm 139:17-18)

³ Great is the LORD and most worthy of praise; **his greatness no one can fathom**. (Psalm 145:3)

Isaiah pondered the profundity of God's knowledge and understanding.

²⁸ Do you not know? Have you not heard? The LORD is the everlasting God, the Creator of the ends of the earth. He will not grow tired or weary, and **his understanding no one can fathom**.
(Isaiah 40:28)

# Praise God for Revealing His Ways in Scripture

It is true that *God's ways are beyond tracing out* in that they stretch out in every direction to infinity.

³³ Oh, the depth of the riches of the wisdom and knowledge of God! How unsearchable his judgments, and **his paths beyond tracing out**! (Romans 11:33)

However, God has not left us totally in the dark regarding his existence, his character, or his ways.

²⁹ The secret things belong to the LORD our God, but **the things revealed belong to us and to our children forever.** (Deuteronomy 29:29)

If we do what James instructs us to do, **God's ways** will not be 'beyond tracing out'. He asks us to come near to him in prayer!

⁸ Come near to God and he will come near to you. (James 4:8; Deut 4:7; Ps 143:1, 6; 145:18)

The nearer we approach an object the clearer are the details of what we're observing. The nearer we draw to God by faith the clearer and more knowable his ways will become.

God has revealed at least an inkling of his many *unchanging ways* -enough so that we might believe in him, know him, love him, serve him and rest all our hopes in him for time and eternity. By observing God's ways revealed to us in the Scriptures we know the one true God is not only the Creator of the heavens and earth, but that he is also *holy, righteous, true, just, loving, gracious, merciful, and good.*

Yes, *Holy* is his name in that he is sinless forever. God always does what is *right*. He is the Author of unchanging *truth*. His decisions are always unbiased, fair and *just*, his *love* is unconditional, unfailing and unlimited. His *grace* is abounding and amazing, his tender *mercy* triumphs over judgment. He is *good* all the time.

What Christian authors of long ago were writing about I find interesting. Once when browsing in a rare books store, I came across a book that was published in 1801. (I enjoyed knowing that the same book I was holding in my hands was once literally held in the hands of someone who lived over 200 years ago.) As I began reading, the subject being addressed caught my attention. It was titled '*The Gospel a Doctrine According to Godliness*'. I was amazed that in just one paragraph the author summarized just about everything I've written here on the ways of God. It's almost like he was reading over my shoulder. What is actually the case is that we were both reading from the same book -the Bible. Here is what this 19ᵗʰ century author **wrote about the ways of God** as he understood them.

God, according to the doctrine of Christ and his apostles as exhibited in the Scriptures, is an eternal being, existing from everlasting to everlasting -independent and self-existent, almighty, omnipresent and omniscient, the searcher of hearts, infinitely pure and **holy** -the only wise- impartially and infinitely **just** and **righteous**, and inviolably faithful and **true**, and infinitely **good, gracious** and **merciful** -creator and preserver, and supreme Lord and rightful sovereign of the universe- the fountain, and source, and comprehension of being and of all good. (The Connecticut Evangelical Magazine, Vol 1 January 1801, No. 7, p.253)

The question remains: how much of what we now know regarding the *ways of God* are we willing to take to heart?

Are we singing his praises? This is gives a clue

The Lord speaks to the Church through his Holy Spirit in his inspired Word,

> [7] He who has an ear, **let him hear** what the Spirit says to the churches.
> (Revelation 2:7; 2:11; 2:17; 2:29; 3:6; 3:13; 3:22)

Do you treasure the Scriptures?

We will *take seriously God's Word regarding his ways* to the degree we recognize his Word for being the treasure that it is.

> [72] The law from your mouth is more precious to me than thousands of pieces of silver and gold.
> (Psalm 119:72)

## Offer a Doxology of Praise to God Whom We've Come to Know Through His Ways

Let's join heart and voice with the saints of old in their *doxologies of praise* to *our great God* who has shown by *his 'ways'* that he alone is our

**rock and salvation,** and is thus worthy of all honor, and praise, and glory pouring forth from our hearts and our lips forever! In our bedroom hangs a framed cross-stitched scripture verse that reads:

*My soul finds rest in God alone;*

*my salvation comes from him.*

*Psalm 62:1*

We can confidently **rest our souls in God alone,** because of what we know to be true from Scripture about his **unchanging promise of offering us eternal salvation** in response to our faith in him.

Recently my wife and I had the privilege of speaking at a Christian conference in a Southeast Asian country. The Sunday before the conference started we attended an English-speaking interdenominational church service along with 5000 worshipers. (There were four more worship services to follow that day -each with 5000 worshipers!) We soon found ourselves joyfully singing praise for God's wonderful ways!

The next morning we were moved in spirit by the singing of praise by one person –a little girl. While riding to the conference site this 6 year old got us all singing 'Bless the Lord, O my Soul Worship His Holy Name.' All of us in the car were moved in our spirits by this little girl singing with all her heart this 'doxology of praise' to the Lord! (We would do well to listen to the praises of little children for of such is the Kingdom of God! ☺)

[16] From the lips of children and infants you have ordained praise. (Matthew 21:16)

It's a new day dawning
It's time to sing Your song again
Whatever may pass and whatever lies before me
Let me be singing when the evening comes
**Bless the Lord, O my soul, O my soul**
**Worship His Holy name**
**Sing like never before, O my soul**
**I'll worship Your Holy name**
　　　　-Matt Redman

The Psalmist has thrown out to us this challenge:

> ¹ **It is fitting** for the upright **to praise him**☺
> (Psalm 33:1)

> ⁶ Sing praises to God, sing praises; sing praises to our King, sing praises. (Psalm 47:6)

David heeded his own advice!

> ⁹ **I will praise you forever for what you have done**; in your name I will hope, for your name is good.
> (Psalm 52:9)

Oh that we could be as faithful as David in singing *doxologies of praise* to the Lord in appreciation for all he has done in our world and in our lives. *Doxology after doxology was the order of the day* for David and all the Psalmists.

To this day their doxologies help put adequate words into our hearts and onto our lips when it comes to voicing full-throated praise to our great God and Savior whom *we have come to know personally through his ways*.

> ¹ Ascribe to the LORD, O mighty ones, ascribe to the LORD glory and strength.

> ² Ascribe to the LORD the glory due his name; worship the LORD in the splendor of his holiness. (Psalm 29:1-2)

> ¹ I will extol the LORD at all times; his praise will always be on my lips.

> ² My soul will boast in the LORD; let the afflicted hear and rejoice.

> ³ Glorify the LORD with me; let us exalt his name together. (Psalm 34:1-3)

[11] Yours, O LORD, is the greatness and the power and the glory and the majesty and the splendor, for everything in heaven and earth is yours.

Yours, O LORD, is the kingdom; you are exalted as head over all.

[12] Wealth and honor come from you; you are the ruler of all things. In your hands are strength and power to exalt and give strength to all.

[13] Now, our God, we give you thanks, and praise your glorious name. (1 Chronicles 29:11-13)

[1] Shout with joy to God, all the earth!

[2] Sing the glory of his name; make his praise glorious!

[3] Say to God, "How awesome are your deeds! So great is your power that your enemies cringe before you.

[4] All the earth bows down to you; they sing praise to you, they sing praise to your name."

[5] Come and see what God has done, how awesome his works in man's behalf! (Psalm 66:1-5)

All nature joins in a doxology of praise to its Creator.

[22] Praise the LORD, **all his works everywhere** in his dominion. Praise the LORD, O my soul.
(Psalm 103:22)

[10] **All you have made** will **praise you, O LORD.**
(Psalm 145:10)

In the spirit of Psalm 150 may we now and for all eternity never stop praising God with all creation for *his wonderful ways*! To God be the glory!

> ¹ **Praise the LORD. Praise God** in his sanctuary; **praise him** in his mighty heavens.
>
> ² **Praise him** for his acts of power; **praise him** for his surpassing greatness.
>
> ³ **Praise him** with the sounding of the trumpet, **praise him** with the harp and lyre,
>
> ⁴ **praise him** with tambourine and dancing, **praise him** with the strings and flute,
>
> ⁵ **praise him** with the clash of cymbals, praise him with resounding cymbals.
>
> ⁶ Let everything that has breath **praise the LORD. Praise the LORD.** (Psalm 150:1-6)

Who isn't familiar Thomas Ken's 'Old Hundreth' Doxology which he composed in 1647?

> Praise God, from Whom all blessings flow;
> Praise Him, **all creatures** here below;
> Praise Him **above, ye heav'nly host**;
> Praise Father, Son, and Holy Ghost.

In the New Testament *doxologies* also flow from the lips of the Lord's inspired servants. In spite of all his hardships and persecutions over a period of many years, Paul never ceased singing doxologies of praise to God! His doxology in Romans harmonized with prophet Isaiah's doxology.

<sup>36</sup> From him and through him and to him are all things.
To him be the glory forever! Amen.
(Romans 11:36; Isaiah 40:13; Philippians 4:20)

Paul encouraged Timothy to join his voice with him in singing praise to God!

<sup>17</sup> Now to the King eternal, immortal, invisible, the only God, be honor and glory for ever and ever. Amen. (1 Timothy 1:17)

<sup>15</sup> God, the blessed and only Ruler, the King of kings and Lord of lords,

<sup>16</sup> who alone is immortal and who lives in unapproachable light, whom no one has seen or can see. To him be honor and might forever. Amen.
(1 Timothy 6:15-16)

The author of Hebrews chimes in!

<sup>15</sup> Through Jesus, therefore, let us continually offer to God a sacrifice of praise—the fruit of lips that confess his name. (Hebrews 13:15)

Paul and Silas found that even though Roughhoused, thrown in Jail, and unable to sleep they could still sing hymns of praise to the Lord at midnight.

<sup>25</sup> About midnight Paul and Silas were praying and **singing hymns to God**, and the other prisoners were listening to them. (Acts 16:25)

Everything in the vast heavens that is beyond our world is committed to praising God!

¹ The **heavens declare the glory of God**; the skies proclaim the work of his hands. (Psalm 19:1)

²¹ My mouth will speak in praise of the LORD. Let every creature praise his holy name for ever and ever. (Psalm 145:21)

¹ Praise the LORD. **Praise the LORD from the heavens**, praise him in the heights above.

² Praise him, **all his angels**, praise him, all his **heavenly hosts**.

³ Praise him, **sun** and **moon**, praise him, all you shining stars.

⁴ Praise him, you **highest heavens** and you waters above the skies. (Psalm 148:1-4)

Heaven is where there is heard unending doxologies of praise from all its citizens!

In the early 1800s Swedish hymnist Samuel Johan Hedborn (1783-1849) composed this lovely doxology of praise.

"Glorious Majesty, before Thee
We bow to worship and adore Thee;
With grateful hearts to Thee we sing.
Earth and heaven tell the story
Of Thine eternal might and glory,
And all Thy works their incense bring.
Lo, hosts of Cherubim
And countless Seraphim
Sing, Hosanna,
Holy is God, almighty God,
All-merciful and all-wise God!"

[11] All the angels were standing around the throne and around the elders and the four living creatures. They fell down on their faces before the throne and worshiped God,

[12] saying: "**Amen! Praise and glory and wisdom and thanks and honor and power and strength be to our God for ever and ever.** Amen!"
(Revelation 7:11-12)

[3] "Great and marvelous are your deeds, Lord God Almighty. Just and true are **your ways,** King of the ages.

[4] Who will not fear you, O Lord, and bring glory to your name? For you alone are holy. All nations will come and worship before you, for your righteous acts have been revealed." (Revelation 15:3-4)

May we be willing to offer up to the one and only living and eternal *Triune God the Father, Son and Holy Spirit* a doxology of praise for all *his ways* he has willingly disclosed to us in the Holy Scriptures!

Dear *God,*

All praise and honor and glory to you our great *God -our Father who is the Almighty Creator* and the sustainer of our lives. We praise you for *your ways,* that you are forever *holy* and *righteous,* as well as *true* and *just.* We are humbled that you have extended to us your *love, grace* and *mercy* and *goodness..*

We praise you *Lord Jesus Christ* -Son of God; Son of Man- for laying down your life for us on the cross as an expression of divine *love.* The result for us who believe you did this for us is that you have forgiven all our sins, and saved us from guilt and condemnation. Your way was to ransom, redeem, reconcile, and justify us by imputing to us your *righteousness,* and you have now seated us permanently in heavenly realms to rule and reign with you forever in your presence at your right hand where there is fullness of joy and pleasures forevermore. We affirm our love for you Lord Jesus Christ in granting us saving faith to believe in you, the desire and ability to serve you with joy, and entrust our eternal destiny to you.

By your **Holy Spirit** indwelling our lives you enable us to reflect **your ways** O God in all we think, and say and do. In Jesus' Name, Amen!

This is my prayer of doxology to the God who has let me **know him** by the **ways** he has made himself known to me through his Word -the Holy Scriptures!

²⁵ Whom have I in heaven but you? And earth has nothing I desire besides you. (Psalm 73:25)

'Through all eternity to Thee a joyful song I'll raise
But, oh eternity's too short to utter all Thy praise!'
-Joseph Addison (1672-1719)

***TO GOD BE THE GLORY FOR DISPLAYING
HIS WAYS IN HIS HOLY WORD
WHERE
GOD SPEAKS FOR HIMSELF!***

***Show me your ways, O LORD!
Psalm 25:4***

***Have you discovered the ways of our
glorious God in the Word of God?
I pray you have!***

Printed in the United States
By Bookmasters